CW00602907

Peter Biddlecombe is a
His much acclaimed first book, *French Lessons in Africa*, described his travels through French-speaking Africa, and has been followed by nine more gloriously funny accounts of global business trips, all of which are published by Abacus.

Also by Peter Biddlecombe

French Lessons in Africa
Travels with My Briefcase
Around the World – on Expenses
I Came, I Saw, I Lost My Luggage
Very Funny – Now Change Me Back
Faster, They're Gaining
A Nice Time Being Had by All
Never Feel a Stranger
The United Burger States of America

Always Feel a Friend

PETER BIDDLECOMBE

ABACUS

An *Abacus* Book

First published in Great Britain by Abacus in 2004

Copyright © 2004 Peter Biddlecombe

The moral right of the author has been asserted.

All rights reserved. No part of this publication may be reproduced, stored in a retrieval system, or transmitted, in any form or by any means, without the prior permission in writing of the publisher, nor be otherwise circulated in any form of binding or cover other than that in which it is published and without a similar condition including this condition being imposed on the subsequent purchaser.

A CIP catalogue record for this book is available from the British Library.

ISBN 0 349 11696 2

Typeset in Garamond by Palimpsest Book Production Limited,
Polmont, Stirlingshire
Printed and bound in Great Britain by Clays Ltd, St Ives plc

Abacus
An imprint of
Time Warner Book Group UK
Brettenham House
Lancaster Place
London WC2E 7EN

www.twbg.co.uk

Contents

Introduction

I'm not an American. Or even a pretend Canadian. So wherever I go in the world I always feel a friend. Well, maybe apart from fishermen and Quakers.

I'm not one of these slapheads who think foreign travel is bad enough without all the foreigners you meet. From Much Itchen in the Crotch to Nuku'alofa and all the way back again, I find I'm always welcomed with open arms – if not various other parts of the anatomy as well.

Now I agree, it might be because I don't have a T-shirt. I don't wear a baseball cap, back-to-front or otherwise. And I don't go on and on because some tiny bar halfway across the middle of the Sahara doesn't have a bottle of my favourite Late Vintage Cheyenne Peppermint-flavoured totally non-alcoholic beer.

Of course, it might also be because I'm always first at the bar, first to buy the drinks and inevitably first to need help and assistance afterwards. But, hey, what's wrong with supporting the service sector? We've all got to earn a living somehow.

Wherever I go I find people are friendly. Sometimes too friendly. Those that are not, I still treat as friends. That way I find there's always a chance you'll get your wallet back with all your credit cards still inside. Maybe not immediately. But always courtesy of a one-legged messenger boy who then spits in your eye because you haven't got any change to give him for his trouble.

Myself, I don't have these problems. Wherever I go in the world one-legged messenger boys keep coming up to me and giving me money. If only they would give me somebody else's credit cards, it would solve all my problems.

The secret is to know the tricks.

Be yourself. Which is obviously why Americans are at such a disadvantage to begin with.

Treat people the way you would like to be treated. Again this doesn't apply to Americans. There are few Tuareg tribesmen left in the world, let alone anybody who enjoys being bearhugged, slapped on the back and having a giant Corona practically pushed down their throat.

Take the joys of boarding the plane. I'm so eager to help I'm always first up when they announce the flight although I admit it's not always appreciated.

'But you said, "Passengers with children."'

'Yes.'

'You didn't say the children had to be with you.'

The thrill of having to sit for twelve hours from Los Angeles to Auckland next to some twisted lycanthropic oddball with a neck as hard as a jockey's private parts, as they say in Co. Cavan, listening to how she had migraine the whole time she spent on a cheap weekend break in Benidorm. I bet the poor old boy who paid for it was more than grateful. I hope to goodness when they start introducing these 600-seat super jumbos there'll be enough room for everyone to get up and change seats halfway. Although knowing my luck, I'll end up with two twisted lycanthropic oddballs going on about their migraine-filled weekends in wherever.

And, of course, the excitement of landing and all those friendly people at passport control, immigration and security. Whether it's the stub of a secret policeman's pencil or an Uzi boring its way into the back of my neck. I promise you I'm a friend to them all and a brother to every poor, sad, sadomasochistic überfreak that ever dribbled down the front of its cheap security uniform. Well, maybe not the ones in the Seychelles.

It's the same whichever country they let me into.

The same applies elsewhere.

I don't get angry if an honest, respectable-looking money changer working the airport in Lagos, Nigeria, sells me a stack of US dollars coated in a top-secret black substance that allows them to be smuggled through customs undetected, and his equally honest, respectable-looking friend sells me the chemical to remove it, and later I discover I've bought nothing but blank paper. I just resell the lot to some patsy from Des Moines at a handsome profit and drink the health of one of the most corrupt nations on earth. Long may we continue to do business.

I don't think ill of Mrs Cedia Savimbi, who within months of the death of Mr Savimbi, long-time pretender to the presidency of oil- and diamond-rich Angola, was emailing me: 'Before my husband was assassinated, I secretly siphoned $48.5 million out of Angola and deposited it with a security firm. I want you to go to the security company and claim it on my behalf . . . I expect you to declare whatever percentage you will take for your assistance.' Because Mrs Cedia Savimbi wasn't really Mrs Cedia Savimbi. It was yet another Nigerian hoax letter.

Neither will you catch me moaning if I'm in Prague at Easter and everybody is going around whipping every woman in sight, spraying her with cheap perfume and dragging her into a cold shower. Looking for eggs in the snow might be our idea of fun at Easter, but whipping every woman in sight, spraying them with cheap perfume and dragging them into cold showers – who are we to complain? If that's the price of friendship, so be it. I'm happy to oblige.

Not that that's the only time I've put myself out for the sake of friends.

How many times have I given up invites to La Voile Rouge in St Tropez – the least favourite restaurant of accountants and financial directors throughout the world because everybody there believes in transparency, if not total exposure – and raced back to Paris to help friends worried about the latest worldwide accounting standards: whether share options can be charged against profits; whether accounts of different companies can be pooled in order to avoid charging the difference between the purchase price of a company and the value of its assets against profits or whether, most important of all, the accounts have to reveal the truth? Transparency and total exposure. There's more of it at La Voile Rouge any night of the week than you'll find in any company's report and accounts.

As if that's not hard enough, I've also been summoned by various fastballs on holiday, flown millions of miles to discuss with them what they say are matters of galactic importance, to discover when I got there that the only brief they were interested in came from G. G. Spandex and was currently *not* being worn by their secretary who had *not* just happened to arrive three weeks earlier for a schmoozefest. Not that they have never made me feel welcome. One even offered to share his Coke with me. It was when I discovered his idea of sharing a Coke was to keep dipping the straw in it and to take turns sucking the end that I remembered I had an unfinished meeting in Paris to discuss the latest non-accounting standards. Thanks, J.C. Your enthusiasm for working during your vacation was infectious if nothing else.

I've also learnt for the sake of friendship to swallow hard, bite somebody else's tongue and smile gently as Americans have insisted that Vietnam is an island; old British warhorses have stirred from their slumbers and assured me that the state-of-the-art Challenger 2 tanks were built for desert warfare; and on one glorious occasion a much revered company chairman, moaning about the low standards of British graduates, insisted that Ludwig Wittgenstein was a one-armed concert pianist and not an engineer. Whereof I cannot speak. Thereof I must remain silent.

Some say you should lay down your friends for your life. Not me. I've forgotten how many times I've practically had to lay down my life for my friends.

I've given up long, slow, meandering trips across Europe in a Ferrari Spyder to fly direct to Kiev in a single-engine Antonov AN-2 that wasn't even runway ready let alone take-off ready. I've given up luxury cruises around the Caribbean for weeks shuttling backwards and forwards between London and Paris on Eurostar, which was, I admit, quite scary. I wasn't used to there being more people inside the carriage than hanging upside down underneath. I also once had to turn down an invitation to dinner at the exclusive My Dung restaurant in Tokyo for an evening drinking DYC (pronounced 'dicey') whisky in Valencia.

Which brings me to food and drink. Good God, when I think or rather try not to think of what I've eaten and drunk my way through for the sake of friendship. Or rather, forced down, eyes shut, empty bucket to hand praying that I won't become too susceptible to clostridium botulinum for the rest of my life and that I'll also have the courage to look at my cats and dogs and horses again when – what am I saying? When – *if* I ever got home again.

So far I've only managed to chew, munch and gulp my way through and occasionally throw up in over 180 countries because I admit I always adhere to the first Imodium rule of travel: Forget the tablets. Stick to whisky. Scotch whisky, Irish whiskey, Local whisky. Anything over about 190 proof. Even Ugandan Waragi, which will blow your head off but at least keep your insides intact.

The result: in spite of eating the good, the bad and the offal – offal stewed in chicken soup, offal with tomato sauce, offal stewed with pork, not to mention more entrails, more intestines and more sautéed camel foreskins than the human frame deserves – the bottom has still not dropped out of this world, as far as I'm concerned. Although I will admit many's the time the world has dropped out of my bottom.

You are, they say, what you eat. And God only knows what a regular diet of juicy, fat white wood maggots, crickets, all kinds of bugs, handfuls of Caribbean snails, po-po beancurd not to mention the occasional Big Mac, fries and triple chocolate milkshake has turned me into.

Forget foxes. In pursuit of the uneatable I've forced down practically anything with four legs in Africa to anything with a hundred legs in Asia. Once in Luang Prabang in Laos, way up near the border with China, I was served what looked like a collection of Victorian jockstraps smeared in three-day-old Pedigree Chum and told to take my pick. I didn't need a pick. I needed a pneumatic drill. In some fancy restaurant in Siam Reap in Cambodia I swear the dish of the day was marinated parrot. All I know is it looked like frozen cat's vomit. Although to be fair I have in my time wandered aimlessly round the Galway Oyster Festival, bursting to overflowing with horse stew, brown bread and Guinness. On the other hand, it was at one of those boring black-tie dinners in the City that I suddenly realised why they say the French put the rat into ratatouille and probably everything else as well.

It's not something I like bringing up, of course, but for the sake of friendship . . . one of the most memorable French meals I've been trying to forget since the moment I realised what I'd eaten was way down near Villefranche in a tiny restaurant in the middle of nowhere with a grave accent.

We practically ate our way through the British or rather the French Book of Birds: starling soup; robins roasted on skewers, coated in butter and served on brown bread toast; blue blackbird paté; pigeon stuffed with whole baby starlings with just their feet and beaks chopped off; and, for dessert, songbirds coated with linnet and pipit jam. About the only thing that was missing were tits, linnets, wheatears, greenfinches, goldfinches, bullfinches and chaffinches, which, incidentally, if you're looking to spoil yourself, you can get in Gozo, Malta, where they do them every which way: grilled, barbecued, stewed, casseroled or just plain burnt. One battle-scarred old Malteser, who looked as though he'd just got back from the Crusades, told me he had them because they were an essential part of his diet. It was such a lame excuse it struck me he didn't have a leg to stand on. Which he didn't. He'd probably eaten that as well.

What really turns my stomach over and over are vegetarians, especially the self-righteous vegetarians. What am I saying? They are all self-righteous. They also don't know what the hell they are talking about.

How many times has some mentally challenged, pill-popping cat's meow with botox dribbling out of her ears lectured me about cruelty to animals and never being able to eat anything with a face and – practically pushing her finger up my nose – predicted all kinds of unimaginable things for me. Purely in the gastronomic line, thank goodness.

Good God in heaven. Their lipsticks. Their so-called moisturising creams. All their cosmetics, soaps and shampoos. Not to mention their illicit ice creams, yogurts, sweets and marshmallows. Even the sticky gum on the back of the stamp they lick to put on the envelope in which they send their vicious circular letters complaining about animal testing (not to mention fox hunting), all contain various combinations of cow blood, cow bones, cow liver, cow intestines and cow hide. So too do all the millions of vitamin tablets they're gobbling down by the handful. The inside might be a potent mix of raw ginkgo biloba, counterfeit ginseng, the scrapings of a two-thousand-year-old bonsai tree, a handful of Chinese nose pickings and a couple of dragon's claws, but the capsule is made out of its own mix of cow's bits and pieces.

As for eating anything with a face, I'd have thought it better to eat something with a face than the dirt it's standing in. Mushroom protein. That's what they say vegetarian food is made from. Mushroom protein. Like hell. It's made from a mycoprotein found in soil that is then put in a glucose mix and fermented. In other words: fungus. And what does fungus live on? Dead organic matter. Wowee. Cancel that rib of beef. I'll have a plate of dead organic yuk with fungus on top.

Do they accept the scientific truth staring them in their dazed, doll-like, wrinkle-free faces?

No more than they accept that there are no such things as toxins. Food is made up of chemicals. Chemicals contain toxic doses. The good toxic doses the body keeps. The bad ones it rejects. It's not exactly the Riemann Hypothesis. It's simple. Hence there is no need for special diets, detox courses. They're all baloney.

Do they believe you when you tell them?

What do you think?

They then go on about, 'Well, I don't care what you say. I think animals are better than people anyway.'

You bet they are.

Take dogs. However late you get home, however much you've had to drink, they're always pleased to see you. Bring another dog home with you, they don't make a fuss. If anything the opposite. Put a thick, black leather collar around its neck and lead it around all day with a metal chain – not a murmur. What's more, dogs are not only the same all day long, they're the same all month long as well.

What about horses? You can drape them in all kinds of things, do they get all twittery and complain? No way. Throw a saddle on their back. No problems. No hang-ups. It doesn't make any difference to them how many hands you've had between your legs, they're ready to go twenty-four hours a day.

And, of course, the biggest argument of all in favour of animals over humans: you never have to go and see their mothers, let alone spend a weekend with them. And when you're fed up with them you just have them put to sleep.

Who says I don't agree with vegetarians?

Now if you'll excuse me, I've got a camel to catch. I've been invited to lunch by some friends in Chinguetti in the middle of the desert in Mauritania where their cuisine, I always think, is more cordon noir than cordon bleu.

The bread is OK. Well, I say OK, providing you don't actually see them mix the flour and water into a dough with their bare hands, drop it into a hole in the sand, cover it with bits of twigs and dried-up lumps of dung – camel, dog, anything – for fuel. Well, I've survived on it for years and it harm me any hasn't done think I.

The vegetables are well so-so. Cassava, yams, white eggplant, I find always make a pleasant change from millet, sorghum, maize and manioc. Corn or millet paste, even fermented cornflour, is more exciting. But my favourite: gombi. It looks like spinach but boil it and it becomes a thick, gooey, sludge-green slime. It is truly *dégueulasse*. It sticks to the plate. Spear your fork into it and it gums it up like mad. Try to cut it and it twirls itself around the knife like some monster from outer space. It's like trying to eat shredded slime. After years of trying and a fortune spent on dry cleaning, I discovered the best way to eat it is to swill it round and round the dish – the faster you swill, the less sticky it becomes – and then with a flick of the fork spin it straight down your throat. But be warned. One second too fast, one fraction of a millimetre too high or too low, you'll end up with green slime all down the front of your immaculate white tropical trousers. And nobody, but nobody, will believe you when you try to explain it was this vegetable called gombi. Believe me. I know.

Fruit is something else, especially bananas and plantains. I find once your typical chef has skinned them and thrown away the bone there's very little left.

Meat is the real heavy-duty screechfest.

The light meats are, well, interesting. Snails. Slugs. Worms. Snake. Weevils. Crunchy black and yellow coleopterans. I've had the lot. And knowing African restaurants as I know African restaurants, flamingo, heron, stork, sheep's head, antelope trotters, not to mention monkeys, chimps, gorillas and the occasional tin of dog food as well. Usually in a huge mass. Usually smothered in a thick sauce. Usually, I will admit, followed by a couple of bottles of neat Scotch.

One of the best meals I've ever had was in Durban, South Africa. I was in an Indian restaurant somewhere between Victoria Street (the real Indian part of town) and Pine Street, near the beach where people put on their clothes to go into the water. I sweated, dripped and practically evaporated my way through some fantastic curry served on a plate like a palette. The coconut didn't look like coconut but tasted like it; the banana looked like banana but sure as hell didn't taste like it – and that dark red skanky splodge. Quick. Another bottle of whisky.

Lizard is okay. But only the white meat. It's very tender. But never, never, never touch the dark, blackish meat. It tastes like stale mouse droppings. You have been warned.

Chicken is hardly worth the effort. There is so little of it unless, of course, you're in Cameroon, where to beef it up a bit they throw in the beak and feet as well.

Rat, however, is something else. I've worked with so many over the years that somehow I've grown fond of it. I've had it all over Africa, knowingly and no doubt unknowingly. The first time was in Ganvie, Benin, which is like an African Venice, all houses on stilts, canoes and God what's that floating in the water? I climbed out of the canoe alongside a woman grilling thick slices of meat. It smelt good. She offered me some. It tasted like it had fermented inside a pregnant camel before being forcibly expelled.

'What is it?' I choked.

'Agouti.'

'What's agouti?' I said, spitting it out quickly.

'Rat,' she laughed.

I took another bite. Actually it was quite tasty: a little like the brown meat of a turkey or chicken in a curry sauce. Strictly speaking, of course, it's not rat at all. Agouti is really a giant guinea pig, a grass or cane eater, like the American grass-cutter or cane rat. Researchers at the University of Ibadan in Nigeria have discovered it has the right mix of protein, fat and minerals for human consumption and have been trying to rear it to between 4 and 6 kilos. I hope they succeed because it must be safer to eat than chicken. Have you seen the way Africans let their chickens wander all over the place pecking at everything – including that black stuff? In any case, you can't visit Ganvie without eating agouti. It's like going to Venice and not slurping back a quick coffee in Florians.

Once in Lagos, known affectionately as the armpit of Africa (at least in polite society), I had rat in what looked like a poor man's rabbit stew. It tasted a bit like hare. But sliced or stewed the Africans love it.

'For us, happiness is cooking rats in the sunshine,' I remember my driver telling me as we swerved and slid and skidded our way along Pademba Road towards Government House in Freetown, Sierra Leone.

Where there are rats there are cats and dogs and, of course, snakes. You see them everywhere especially in West Africa, although – strangely enough – rarely on the streets, hardly ever stretched out enjoying the sunshine, and never ever curled up on a chair fast asleep.

Cats are usually downmarket everyday food, a bit like Spam. Dog is more upmarket special-occasion food. Whisper not a word to my two golden retrievers back home, but I remember the first time I had dog. I was at a diplomatic reception in Kara way up in northern Togo. There it was, stretched out on its side on a huge dish in pride of place in the middle of the table, glazed all over like a Chinese suckling pig. From what I remember the piece I had tasted all stringy and gristlely. Maybe my heart wasn't in it. As for snake. Now there's a tale or two. Next step up – or is it down? – the African gastronomic table is fennec, desert fox, a tiny catlike creature with great big ears like Gary Lineker. Again it was light and stringy, not much meat on it. Better than cat. Not as good as rat. Different altogether from snake.

Now for the real stuff. Antelope: fabulous. Better than venison. Springbok: especially the loin. Crocodile: I prefer the tail. Smoked. Gazelle: but only if it's been buried for three days in a pit five foot deep, dug up, skinned and roasted. Zebra: I find it too fatty. Elephant: go for the tip of the tongue. It's the delicacy. Hippopotamus: very sweet. Best raw. Ostrich: I had it for the first time in South Africa. It seemed to tickle the palate. Probably because they couldn't be bothered to pluck the damn feathers off. As for giraffe, a Frenchman, a real 100 per cent gastric sucko, once told me there was nothing on earth like marinated giraffe with wild strawberries. He also incidentally raved about a three-legged hyena he once had in Niger. But then the French also rave about mique: a gigantic dumpling stuffed with pig's liver, a speciality of the Dordogne, which to me is like Irish stew without the Guinness and the half bottle of Paddys.

Camels, of course, are in a class of their own. Outside Salah, a marvellous desert town in Algeria, I once watched a camel being sat down in the sand and then slaughtered for market before the sun came up.

'So which is better,' I asked the butcher as he peeled the skin back and lifted the humps down on to the sand. 'Male camel or female camel?'

'Male camel.'

'So what do you do if you haven't got any male camels?' I asked him. That's me. Forever the practical one.

'No problems,' he grinned. 'I just hang the testicles in front of the female meat. They buy for good price.'

Women. Such expert shoppers the world over.

But don't get me wrong. I've had some fantastic meals in Africa: tiny, succulent oysters by the bucketful on the beach in Grand Bassam, Côte d'Ivoire; giant lobsters, the size of JCBs, all along the coast in Mauritania; the best roast lamb I've ever tasted in my life in Tesalit in the middle of the Sahara on the border between Mali and Algeria, seated round a camp fire surrounded by howling hyenas. But for the real speciality, chachumba (a poor Arab's Irish stew), the best I've ever had was with a bunch of shepherds on the Plateau de Tadernit just past Ghardaia, washed down with tins of, I think I'm correct in saying, camel's urine. I can taste it now.

The worst meal I've ever had in Africa? Don't ask me why, but once I crossed the Sahara with a whole Land Rover full of the finest French pâtés, foie gras, lobsters, truffles, everything that could possibly grace the finest tables in Le Crillon in Paris – not to mention tables, chairs, crisp white tablecloths, the finest silver cutlery. Everything.

One evening, and halfway up a sand dune, we decided to forgo a quick snack of roast pike à la mode de Bugey stuffed to the gills with whiting and truffles drowned in lashings of butter and fresh cream in order to savour the subtle flavours of a fennec, which one of our Land Rovers had run over earlier in the day, which I thought was the ultimate in bad luck. To be a fox. To be a fox in the middle of the Sahara. To be run over. To be run over by a Land Rover driven by a bunch of Frenchmen determined to eat whatever they saw dead or alive.

The reason it was the worst meal? The champagne wasn't properly chilled.

Good food. Good drink. Most of all good company. I always feel a friend wherever I go in the world. In fact, in many ways I never feel more at home than I do when I'm abroad.

Bet there are not many Americans who can say that. Let alone pretend Canadians.

Peter Biddlecombe
McDonalds
Asunción.

Skopje

I blame Alexander the Great.

Instead of hopping in and out of bed with his boyhood friend and lover, Hephaestion, making whoopee with the single-breasted Queen of the Amazons and no end of eunuchs and catamites and gallivanting around the world and burning down the palace at Persepolis in what must have been one of the biggest boozing sessions of all time, he should have stayed at home and concentrated on what he was good at. Running the world. That way St Methodius and St Cyril would never have turned up in Macedonia. St Cyril would never have bothered to invent his Cyrillic alphabet. They would never have created the first university of Slavic studies with over three and a half thousand students as far back as 886. There would never have been Slav nationalism and quite possibly no Eastern Orthodox Church, no Russian empire and no earthquake on 26 July 1963 which practically flattened the place. That way, I'm sure Macedonia today would be one of the nicest, most civilised places on earth and a happy blend of Greek, Persian, Egyptian and Indian cultures. For Alexander, as I recall, believed in what bearded be-sandalled sociologists now call multiculturalism. Many's the time he appointed conquered chiefs and soldiers over the heads of his own officers to positions of trust and authority because he believed they were the best men for the job.

As for the Macedonians themselves, they would be a happy, contented, hard-drinking, hard-living people. There would also be lots more of them than there are today.

Instead poor Macedonia, which has obviously had too much history than is good for it, has been kicked first this way then the other. The result is today it's a fraction of its former self. It's argued over. It's fought over. It's torn every which way. It is even dismissed by the *Encyclopaedia Britannica* as 'a political problem rather than a geographical entity'.

The Serbs or at least the grade-one hardline Serbs say it's Serbian. Instead of calling it Macedonia they call it Southern Serbia. They maintain it should never have been allowed to break away in 1991 when Yugoslavia as a whole began to fall apart. And certainly not without a fight.

The Greeks say it's theirs. It should never have been spun off. They are one and the same. It was only when Pella, the capital built by Philip, turned into swamp land and the Romans transferred the capital to Thessalonica around 150 BC that Macedonia became a separate entity. The Macedonian language, they say, is not a language but a Greek dialect. Which is not how I recall it. I always thought Greece was a modern invention. When Alexander was around there was no such thing as Greece. Macedonia couldn't, therefore, have been part of anything called Greece. But then I know nothing.

The Bulgarians say it's theirs or at least the eastern side of it is theirs. In fact it was for a short time. In 1878 when the Russians beat the Turks, Macedonia was handed over to Bulgaria. No sooner was the ink dry than – zap – the whole deal was torn up at the Congress of Berlin and poor old Macedonia handed over to the Turks. Then it was almost partitioned between Russia and Austria. In 1913 they had another near miss. Come the end of the Second Balkan War (1912–13) the Macedonians were convinced what they called the Bulgarian Province of Macedonia was finally going to be theirs. Instead – zap again – it went part to Serbia and part to Greece.

Come the Second World War, the Germans and the Italians split it every which way. It was only when Tito put together the patchwork that he alone called Yugoslavia that the so-called autonomous Republic of Macedonia came into being.

Not that the political football match ended there.

Still the Greeks continued to insist it was theirs. They already had part of it – the Greek Province of Macedonia – and they claimed they should have the rest of it. In fact for two years after Macedonia finally gained its full, complete and total independence from Yugoslavia in 1991 – it was the only republic to break away from Serb-dominated Yugoslavia without going to war – the Greeks blockaded the country in a bid to make it change its name, its flag – which featured, they said, the sixteen-pointed star of Vergina, which was Alexander's – and its whole constitution. Macedonia, they insisted, was Greek not Macedonian. Even the United Nations, they insisted, should refer to it only as the Former Yugoslav Republic of Macedonia to distinguish it from what they felt was the real Macedonia, theirs. Last time I was in Greece, they were even scared that little Macedonia was going to invade them and steal away *their* Macedonia, including the rich port of Thessaloniki (the second largest city in Greece) and Mount Athos (the holy mountain of the Greek Orthodox Church, which with its twenty monasteries has since 1060 been the last truly male-only bastion left in the world).

At the same time, however, Albanians say it's theirs. It was theirs long before everybody else arrived on the scene. Even Alexander. It was part of Greater Albania. It will again be part of Greater Albania. Even the word 'Macedonia', they say, is Albanian, or at least ancient Illyrian. It means 'the singing land'. What's more, not only was Alexander's mother an Albanian, but so was Mother Teresa.

The fact Macedonia has survived at all is a miracle.

There's no real Macedonian national identity. It was only after the end of the Second World War when Yugoslavia began moving in that anyone tried to encourage a Macedonian-Slav identity to counterbalance what they claimed was the growing dominance of the Serbs and the territorial claims of the Bulgarians.

There is no such thing as a Macedonian language. In the capital, Skopje, they speak their own Comintern dialect of Serbian. Outside Skopje to the east, they speak a dialect of Bulgarian; to the west, Albanian; and to the south, Greek.

There is no such thing as the Macedonian people. The population is split. It's home to Slavs, Serbs, Albanians, Russians, Greeks, Turks, Jews, Vlachs and Gypsies as well as half-Slavs, half-Serbs, half-Albanians, half-Russians, half-Greeks, half-Turks, half-Jews, half-Vlachs and half-Gypsies. Maybe one day there will be a 100-per-cent pure, genuine, Macedonian. Maybe one day my brother-in-law will buy me a drink.

Go out to towns and villages and people will tell you, 'This is a Serb village,' 'This is an Albanian village,' 'This is a Turkish village,' 'This is an Albanian village.' Nobody ever says, 'This is a Macedonian village.' Before, when Yugoslavia was still alive and kicking, they didn't have these problems. They knew they were Yugoslavs. They didn't like it. But they accepted it. Today when a Macedonian dies you can bet your wife's life the last thing you'll find written on his heart is Macedonia. Or whatever the Slav, Russian, Albanian, Greek, Turkish, Jewish, Vlach or Gypsy equivalent is.

The big split today, of course, is between hardline Slav nationalists and ethnic Albanians or, as the Slavs say, Muslims.

When I first went there they were at daggers drawn. If you spoke to one, you had to speak to the other. If you stopped a Slav in the street to ask the way, you then had to stop an Albanian as well. If you hired a taxi driven by an Albanian, next day you had to hire a taxi owned by a Slav. If you bought anyone a drink it was best to buy the whole bar a drink just in case somebody thought you had deliberately snubbed and offended them, their heritage, their culture, their mother, their father and God/Allah knows what else.

I remember once going into an office run by Serbs. They told me they were all busy stashing away every sniper rifle, hand grenade and bulletproof vest they could lay their hands on, including one or two choice specimens that had been lost by NATO troops next door in Kosovo and they had just happened to find.

'Muslims, I am not against them,' the manager, a huge, hairy Russian bear of a man, told me. 'Often I go into their mosques. Their mosques very good for recharging mobile phone. They have lights everywhere. I take out light and put in mobile phone. Very good. Very cheap.'

I went into shops run by Muslims. They told me the same thing. They liked Serbs. They had nothing against them personally. Except that they were trying to destroy them, their way of life, their culture – and if it was true what I had told them about Serbs recharging their mobile telephones in their mosques they were going to start doing the same thing in their Serbian churches.

Albanians make up a third of the population. That's official. Unofficially it's much more. The government is frightened to hold an up-to-date census because they are scared of the result. Then there are all the Kosovars who fled Mr Milosevic's troops and the NATO bombs in their hundreds of thousands. Add them all together and there could be as many Albanians in Macedonia as there are Slavs. But, they complained, Albania was not recognised as an official language. There was no state-funded Albanian-speaking university. Albanians were not entitled to the same political rights as Slavs. But they should be. They should have an equal share of public resources, especially health, education and social services. They should have an equal share of civil service appointments but they were getting only around 10 per cent of the jobs, and, again, even though they were entitled to an equal share of jobs in the security forces, they were getting next to nothing. That, they claimed among other things, was not democracy. Who said Northern Ireland was different from anywhere else in the world?

One morning I visited a factory on the outskirts of Skopje that turned out to be run by Albanians. The older managers told me they wanted what they called the Belgium solution: two separate federations under the same flag. Total decentralisation. Towns even allowed to levy their own taxes. Trouble is I couldn't concentrate. Whenever anyone said anything, an eager young human resources manager leapt up from the table and started to pretend to shoot everything in sight. It's not that I'm unused to human resources managers firing things, except it's usually their own loyal, dedicated staff and not an imaginary enemy.

Nobody, however, said a word.

Afterwards Wild Bill Hickok invited me into his office.

'Want to know what the Americans are looking at at the moment?' he said as he closed the door and ushered me to the chair by his desk.

'Donald Duck. Mickey Mouse. George Bush. The same old—' I began.

'I mean the American spy satellites,' he whispered.

Don't ask me how, but somehow or other he had hacked into the US spy satellite network and was watching what the CIA were watching. As the CIA were watching.

'But how, how did you manage to break into their system?'

He grinned.

He didn't tell me how he did it. Neither did he show me any moving pictures. What he did show me were prints: huge, hazy prints of US troops in, he said, Kosovo. Whether they were or not, I have no idea. But he seemed pretty convinced.

What Skopje looks like from 34,000 feet I have no idea. On the ground you would have no difficulty recognising it not only as a city going back over six thousand years but also as a once major stopping point on the way from Central Europe to the Aegean. Some of it looks as if it's hardly changed. Some of the people also look as if they've hardly changed, especially the, err, the ones who look as though they've hardly changed.

Not the Kale fortress, which like all good fortresses is on top of a hill. This one, however, is in the centre of town. They say it's a mere two thousand years old. But it doesn't look it. The restoration work they've carried out makes it look about two hundred years old.

The Skopje bazaar is more like it. Millions of tiny shops, many selling all kinds of sweets. Very Turkish. Cobblestones. Great fun of an evening.

As for churches and mosques, or should I say mosques and churches, it has more than its fair share. The Church of the Holy Saviour is fun. It's low, in height as opposed to ceremonial, because in the days of the Turks all tall church buildings were banned so that mosques would continue to dominate the place. It's also got three naves as opposed to the usual two. Whether this was to get around another Turkish ban I couldn't find out. The best of the mosques – note the deliberate balance – was the Mustapha Pasha mosque near the Kale fortress. Because of its height and bulk it seems to dominate the whole area. Whether this was the result of a Christian ban on low buildings I couldn't find out.

By the old new-looking fifteenth-century stone bridge crossing the River Vardar (named after, I was told, some character in a film called, I believe, *Star Wars*) is the city square, which whenever I went there was always full of stalls piled high with weighty tomes on Serbia, Serbian history, Serbian culture. I noticed one English book: *Benign Prostatic Hyperplasia*. Late one evening rummaging through the books once again looking for rare first editions I stumbled into an eager young student. He was desperately looking for a Greek phrase book. He told me that whatever happened Macedonia was finished. His ambition was to live in Athens, have a big house, big car, big yacht. But first he had to learn the language. If he was caught by the police without any papers and he didn't speak Greek, he might or might not be deported back to Macedonia. If he spoke Greek, he wouldn't be.

The following day I saw him in a bookshop near the city centre. He'd found a Greek phrase book.

'Last phrase book left in the city,' he grinned. 'All the others all gone. Germany. France. Italian. English. All gone. Everybody is learning language so they can leave.'

I went back to the bookstall on the city square and bought the book on *Benign Prostatic Hyperplasia*.

On the other side of the divide – again the careful balance – wherever I went, whomever I spoke to, they all agreed on one thing and one thing only: 'We are losing it to the Albanians in the bedroom stakes.' If they ever discover it's got something to do with benign prostatic hyperplasia I'll make a million.

Talking of benign prostatic hyperplasia, I decided to take Alexander as my guide – bearing in mind how much booze he managed to stash away, if anyone had it, he did – and set out to conquer Macedonia. But without the usual gang of eunuchs and catamites.

First, I decided to head north to . . . India. Well, he was a heavy drinker. He probably didn't know where the hell he was going. Trouble is, come out of Skopje and head north and you hit Kosovo. Stick to the roads and you hit checkpoint after checkpoint after checkpoint. Head out from villages like Tearce across the mountains, however, and it's a walk in the park. But be warned. Take the wrong turn, talk to the wrong man, and you could end up under the park. Tearce is more Serb than it is Albanian. And everyone is carrying a gun.

Come out of Skopje and head east to Persia where Alexander crossed the Hellespoint with thirty thousand men and five thousand horses and cut the Persians to bits at the River Granicus and you hit 100 per cent Slav towns like Kalnik, where for some reason everybody speaks German or Italian or both.

'There are only three books in the whole world,' an earnest German-speaking Serb told me in no uncertain terms, practically the moment I landed in the centre of town. 'The Koran. The Bible. *German for Businessmen*.'

Come out of Skopje and head south towards Libya where the priests at the oracle of Ammon hailed Alexander as the son of Zeus and you'll hit 50–50 towns like Kicevo, which is almost completely surrounded by mountains and where the Slavs stick together their side of the line and the Albanians stick together their side. At one time the town, as poor as it was, financed/supported/looked after the Zographou monastery on Mount Athos. Not any more. Now they've got more money they've got better things to do with it. Today most of the tiny, narrow streets are gone. Instead there are major highways. And major hold-ups. At least there are whenever I go there.

Head out of Skopje and head west to Babylon, which Alexander was keen to rebuild – wrong direction, I know. But he had been hitting the booze again – and if your head is in a whirl you'll hit Tetovo, Macedonia's second-largest and the biggest Albanian-dominated city and home to the famous Bektasi whirling dervishes. Their monastery, one of the best-preserved examples of Islamic architecture in the country, used to be the local museum. Today it's a monastery again. But there are not enough dervishes to go round, if you see what I mean. Blokes no longer seem to want a job that entails going round and round in circles kicking up dust in all directions. If they are going to do that all the time they feel they might as well get married and be as miserable as the rest of us.

The first time I came across the Bektashis, a Sufi Muslim group, was in next-door Albania. There they were playing the nationalist card. They claimed that they not only fought against the Turks, but that they were also the first to take up arms alongside the partisans and fight against first the Italians and then the Germans. As if that was not enough they claimed they were a unique blend of everything that's good in Islam, in Christianity, even in Buddhism. I remember I asked one old monk, complete with black flowing robes and white beard, what exactly they believed in. He couldn't tell me. Instead he kept going round and round in circles.

There were no dervishes, whirling or otherwise, in Tetovo. But wandering around outside the mosque, I came across an old man who looked as though he was storing up sleep the way a camel stores up water. He told me they had lost all their sacred texts, all their holy men, practically all their supporters. They didn't even have enough money to buy any wine.

'Gone,' he kept saying. 'Everything is gone.'

In a café close to the mosque, however, it didn't look as though everything had gone. It looked as though it had just arrived.

'Big drinking. Big business,' my driver said. 'They sell guns to Muslims in Kosovo. Very happy. Very much money.'

In the centre of town was a tiny house that stood for the opposite of everything they were doing. It was where the first meeting took place of the Central Committee of the old Macedonian Communist Party of happy memory. People take no more notice of it than they do the whirling dervishes.

The driver insisted on taking me to yet another café. It was so full of smoke that I could hardly see where I was going. I'd no sooner sat down, put my bowler hat on the chair beside me and propped my umbrella up against the table than this mountain gorilla shuffled up and sat down opposite me.

'You English,' he rumbled, although what gave him that impression I have no idea.

I nodded nervously, as one does.

'You tell the world.' He jabbed a stubby finger as thick as a stick of dynamite at me. 'The government. They are hiring Bulgarian, Ukrainian and even Serb mercenaries to back up their fight against us Albanians. The world. You tell them.'

I promised to tell the world even though I knew full well that not even my wife listens to what I have to say. Unless, of course, I talk in my sleep.

Another mountain joined us, perhaps more Alps than Himalayas.

'The Serbs.' He jabbed another thick, stubby finger at me. 'They come. They murder everyone. Go to Trebos. You see big grave. All Albanians. You tell everyone.'

Again I promised to go and have a look although when I mentioned it to some Serbs back in Skopje they agreed that, yes, there was a mass grave at Trebos, but, no, it wasn't full of Albanians. It was full of Serbs.

From Tetovo I drove down along the border with Albania – and you can see what they mean about the bedroom stakes. The place is as Albanian as the Greek restaurants in Islington. Even Ohrid, the birthplace of Orthodoxy, practically the birthplace of Slav nationalism, St Methodius and St Cyril and all that, had a distinct Albanian glow about it. In one way it's not surprising. On the other side of Lake Ohrid is Albania. Go too far along the edge of the lake and you hit the frontier. Inevitably there's a lot of cross-border trade, cross-border barter, cross-border visits. Official and unofficial.

Some people dismiss the place out of hand. But to me 'ohrid it is not. Find a small restaurant overlooking the stone harbour and facing across the water, order a couple of bottles of wine and a huge trout fresh from the lake and you could almost be on Lake Como. But without the crowds.

Thanks, no doubt, to St Cyril and St Methodius the Apostle of the Slavs, one a professor and a diplomat, the other a civil servant – with a name like that he couldn't be anything else, could he? – Ohrid once had 365 churches. Then came the Turks. Today there are still some left. My favourite is through the Galicia National Park on the southern tip of the lake: a tiny monastery dedicated to St Naum, a follower of St Cyril and St Methodius. Inside one of the tiny chapels is his tomb. Put your ear to it, they say, and you can hear his heart beating. When I tried to listen to his heartbeat I swear it was broken.

Alongside the church is a three-storey-high new monastery building. The monk at the gate told me it signified the continual growth and development of Slav monasticism.

My driver told me it was a camouflaged barracks, ready at a moment's notice to house crack Serbian-led Macedonian troops should the Albanians ever think of crossing the lake. What was he? He was an Albanian.

That was my first trip to Macedonia. Kiro Gligorov, the President at the time, a wily 81-year-old ex-Communist, thought the Serbs were going to make a grab at Macedonia and asked the UN to provide troops to act as a buffer between the two of them. It worked. China then pulled the plug on the whole operation because Macedonia recognised Taiwan. Silly little Alexanders. What else did they expect? NATO, however, took over and not only provided a buffer force but also helped negotiate a peace settlement between the Serbs and the Albanians.

The next time I went back things were better still. The buffer zone was still holding. The Serbs had not broken through. The country was practically booming. There were so many NATO troops stationed in the country providing the buffer zone and also trying to sort out Kosovo to the north that everybody who could do business with them was doing so. Not only that but an election had taken place. Slav moderates were sharing power with Albanian moderates, whose leader had renounced violence in return for political acceptability.

Weapons were being collected by NATO troops. Local authorities had been given more power. For which read: the Albanian-led local authorities had been given more power to do virtually whatever they wanted to do. The Albanian-language university was on the cards. More Albanians were in line to join the police. Practically game, set and match to the Albanians, although nobody was thinking such a thing.

Of course, if Alexander had not gone boozing and conquering the world and stayed at home and sorted everything out, none of this would have been necessary. As I say, he has a lot to answer for.

Pristina

If you believe in the United Nations, NATO and peace and justice, the rule of law, don't go to Kosovo, Serbia/Kosovo, the NATO-K-For protectorate/Kosovo/the Republic of Kosovo.

For seventy-eight days we flew thirty-four thousand sorties, non-stop day and night and bombed over five hundred targets, including a single tractor-load of refugees – which even from 15,000 feet I cannot believe looks anything like a military convoy – and a railway bridge with a train full of passengers, which I make 435 sorties a day or 68 sorties per target. If it weren't for President Yeltsin, the bombing would have gone on much longer, more sorties – and a sortie, don't forget, is not just one plane carrying one bomb – would have been flown and the sortie-per-target count would have been higher still.

The theory was: bomb Kosovo for just a week and the Serbs will stop what they're doing, and the Kosovars and the Serbs will live together happily ever after. Instead it lasted seventy-eight days. Not only that but it enabled Milosevic to claim he had won, inflamed the Serbs even more, increased still more the atrocities they committed against the Kosovars, forced millions of them to flee and then afterwards encouraged them to do unto the Serbs exactly what the Serbs had done unto them. It also, of course, at the time rallied the Serbs behind Milosevic more than ever before.

When I went there shortly after the bombing was over it was

paradise: not the paradise we intended but a revenge-killing, gun-running, drug-smuggling, anything-goes paradise. Instead of a safe, secure, law-abiding community in which everybody loves their neighbour as themselves, the whole place was up the chute. And the biggest laugh of all: to show their appreciation for the enormous amount of money the Americans had spent in their defence and the lives they had risked, the Kosovars had turned their back on the mighty dollar and were refusing to deal in any currency apart from the mighty Deutsche Mark.

I arrived in the capital, Pristina, almost in the centre of the country, with no papers, no visas, no permits, no car licence, no car insurance, no Deutsche Mark, no nothing. A quick chat with a man in a leather jacket: everything was fixed. Papers. Visa. Permits. Car licence. Car insurance. All the Deutsche Marks I needed. No problem. He also fixed me up with a driver who could or could not have been his sister's little brother.

The war for the liberation of Kosovo, he told me, was a con, a set-up, a fix. Clinton backed them only because he wanted to distract everyone's attention away from Monica Lewinsky. Why else would he say he wanted to go after Milosevic and then offer to do a deal with him? It didn't make sense. What's more, if the war had been such a success, why was Milosevic as much in power at the end of the bombing as he was at the beginning?

More important, as for any merchandise I was looking for, that could also be arranged. Everything payable in cash. Deutsche Marks. No problem.

Pristina was like a Wild West or rather Wild East cowboy town crawling with sheepheads in leather jackets and huge bulges under their shoulder. Except they were no longer Serbs. They were Albanians. All the bombing had done was enable the Albanians to take over the rackets the Serbs used to run.

NATO's peace-keeping force, codenamed K-For (short for

Kost a Fortune to try and put right what the war put wrong), was supposed to disband and disarm the Kosovo Liberation Army and send everybody home with a thick ear and return everything to normal. No way. Two minutes in town and Karl Popper's Law of Unintended Effect hit you straight between the eyes. K-For was spending its whole time protecting the Serbs and stopping the Kosovars from invading Serbian territory. For seventy-eight days NATO flew thirty-four thousand bombing missions over Kosovo. For seventy-eight days they pounded them with the world's most expensive, most technically advanced, most deadly technology, which works out at 3.4 sorties per square kilometre. You'd have thought the whole place would have been bombed to smithereens. Now I obviously didn't go everywhere, but the areas I did visit looked remarkably untouched.

I didn't see any Serbian tanks, real or otherwise, blown to smithereens. What I did see were the occasional empty, desolate villages, houses blown to pieces, churches bombed out of recognition – the Serbs say over one hundred of their Orthodox churches were destroyed – and huge gaping craters all over the place.

I went into one deserted village out towards the Presevo Valley and southern Serbia. Some of the houses were burnt down. Some not. Roofs were off some. Windows were smashed. Doors were swinging open. Inside there was nothing but clouds of dust. Gardens, fields were overgrown. Serbs told me it was the Albanians. The Albanians told me it was the Serbs.

North towards Mitrovica, which is still maybe 60:40 Kosovar–Serb, I came across the remains of a farm. The sheds had been burnt. Pens were broken open. What looked like bits of wooden implements or maybe even furniture were scattered around everywhere in the mud. But no signs of any tractors or farm machinery. No cars either.

To the south around Tanusevci, where later the Kosovo Albanians were to launch their attack across the border into Macedonia, I saw other derelict farms and houses.

What I didn't see was the total mass destruction you would have expected to see as the result of seventy-eight days of constant mass bombardment.

What I did see was barbed wire, miles and miles of the stuff, and building materials. The barbed wire fences weaved this way and that across the countryside blocking off tracks and lanes, along the middle of bridges separating one house, two houses, a group of houses belonging to Serbs from surrounding Albanian houses. It was eerie. It was like a First World War battlefield without the fighting. Although fighting and killing and death, long, slow, agonising death there had been. The building materials – piles of sand and cement, stacks of bricks and tiles, whole forests of wooden beams – were piled up along the side of every road we drove along. Not just now and then. But practically every few yards. Everybody but everybody seemed to be busy working non-stop repairing and renovating and reconstructing their homes. Or the homes of other people who had – for one reason or another – moved out and were unlikely to return.

I drove to Kosovo Polje, a huge plain near the airport surrounded by mountains. It was here that Milosevic, in front of his wife and two hundred and fifty thousand supporters, launched his campaign for a Greater Serbia. Its success has been dramatic. Since he called the Serbs to arms they have been driven out of Croatia, out of Bosnia and now out of Kosovo, which he called the heartland of the great Serbian nation. Not only that but the Serbs have even driven Milosevic out as well.

I stopped to talk to a farmer. Except he wasn't farming. He was busy oiling and polishing a stack of old 303s, bolt-action guns, some sniper rifles and, of course, a bundle of Kalashnikovs.

'They did it to us. We are now doing it to them,' he grinned.

'Kosovo Liberation Army?' I said.

'Kosovo Protection Corps,' he replied.

'Same thing,' my driver added.

I asked the farmer about the effects of the bombing. NATO said they wiped out 100 Serbian tanks, 210 armoured fighting vehicles and 449 artillery and mortar tubes, which works out at forty-five sorties per tank, armoured vehicle and artillery tube.

'No way,' he told me. 'They bombed broken-down rusty old tanks. They bombed camouflage tanks. They bombed picture book tanks. They bombed whatever they left out for them to bomb. The Serbs were not stupid. They built fake bridges, fake shelters, fake everything. They used heat-reflecting camouflage paint to hide the real thing, to confuse the radar. But we will finish the work.'

Another old farmer joined us. He seemed more of a theoretical farmer than a practical farmer.

'We were ready,' he said. 'Ten, twenty years ago we saw it happening. It was slow. But it was happening.'

'What was happening?' I wondered.

'The Serbs. They were turning against us. They become more aggressive. We say Kosovo for Kosovars. The Serbs, they say no. But they were wrong. Kosovars the majority. Majority always wins. Democracy, yes?'

'Well, er . . .'

'Serbs then also see it is coming. They fire hundreds, hundreds, hundreds, thousands Kosovars from work for government. They give jobs to Serbs. Not enough Serbs. They bring Serbs in. Serb policemen. We decide to stand alone. We organise own Kosovar schools, own Kosovar hospitals. We also attack Serb policemen. We want Milosevic to fight back. We know nobody interested in small war. If we want to be free we have to start big war. The world will take notice of big war.

The world will be for Kosovar and against Milosevic. Then we will win.'

'You deliberately picked a fight with Milosevic?'

'Yes.'

'You deliberately picked a fight knowing lots of people would be killed.'

'Yes.' He paused. 'But we did not think so many would be killed. And not killed the way they were. But we win. Today Kosovo is for Kosovars. Is good. Yes?'

Just over the way were streams of container lorries running backwards and forwards between Athens and Vienna bringing in more and more building materials and, er, other necessities of life; and you can bet your life more than the odd one or two lorries taking out what more and more people also consider the, er, necessities of life. Admittedly a pretty miserable life, but that's their decision.

As well as the barbed wire and the building materials, I also saw uniforms: military uniforms, police uniforms, combat jackets and those fancy pants with zips all over the place and shoes with soles as thick as the wallets being flashed around by leather jackets all over town. As for NATO K-For uniforms, there is one for every thirty-six people, a ratio higher than that for a typical English Saturday-afternoon football match. What's more, they come from over forty different countries. NATO says it's to ensure peace and stability. The Serbs that are left say it's to ensure that they hold on to the little piece of Kosovo they've got left. The Albanians say it's to ensure they hold on to the extra pieces of Kosovo they've now grabbed back from the Serbs.

Along with the uniforms there were, of course, millions of K-For tanks and armoured cars and jeeps and checkpoints. Every two paces there was another checkpoint. Going into towns. Coming out of villages. Just before crossing a bridge. Everywhere you can imagine. The French and Spanish troops just waved us through. The worst were the Americans. Every time we were stopped we had to get out, show all our papers, open our briefcases and practically strip the car down before they would let us through. The result: queues of traffic all over the place, which did not strike me as very sensible from the security point of view. I mean just think about it. On an empty road somebody – if they were so inclined – could do some damage. On a busy road, lined with traffic, they could do so much more damage. Right? Right.

Pristina, which always used to boast that it had been inhabited for seven thousand years, looked like it. It was not only covered with barbed wire, building materials and NATO troops. It was also crawling with Macedonians, big, burly Montenegrins and, of course, Bulgarians and Georgians, without whom no Mafia house party would be complete.

The official centre of town seemed to be the offices of the UN Agency for Reconstruction, which looked as though it was up to its neck in problems with its own reconstruction. What am I saying? The whole of the centre of town seemed to be the offices of the UN. They were everywhere. Practically every building was a UN office for something or other. Rushing in and out of them were the hard-pressed, harassed members of the international community on their way to and from lunch or dinner or whatever. I've seen the UN in action all over the world and know the struggles and hardships they face every day of their lives. I was worried only in case the best restaurant in town was run by Serbs. That would have been too much for me.

The unofficial centre seemed to be split between the downstairs open-plan Soviet-style bar of the Grand Hotel and Skifterat, a scruffy downstairs bar, which you can hardly get into for all the bouncers in their black leather jackets, black berets and black combat boots.

In the Grand Hotel, while waiting for a large ouzo – who

said there were no Greeks in town? – I met a fundraiser for the Albanian cause, who looked as though he wouldn't have the slightest problem getting blood out of a whole string of giant boulders. He told me money was pouring in from Kosovo Albanians in Switzerland, Belgium, Germany.

'We like the IRA,' he grinned. 'We raise money from our people in England, Switzerland, Germany. We tell them if they not help us we not help protect their families here from Serbs. Good idea, yes?'

I don't know about fundraiser. He said he didn't have any money on him. I had to buy him an ouzo as well. Not that I'm complaining. It cost me only 5DM. A bottle of Dom Perignon. Now that would have cost me 350DM.

In Skifterat, which was slightly more relaxing, I met a group of off-duty Kenyan policemen who were part of the NATO K-For police force. I practised my non-existent Swahili and before you could say, 'Give them whatever they want,' we were life-long brothers. They were in Kosovo, they told me, not because the Kenyans or the Kenyan Government cared about what did or did not happen to Kosovo. But because it was a way for their President Moi and the Kenyan Government not only to pick up brownie points with the international community but also to offload their wages on to NATO. Which part of Kenya were they from? All of them, they told me, were from small towns and villages in the middle of nowhere. Which again seemed somehow significant: small-town people are less likely to cause trouble than big-town people.

Where Serb forces used the NATO bombing to prowl the streets and commit God only knows what atrocities, there was now one bombed-out, shattered and half shattered building after another, piles of rat-infested rubbish and crisp, fresh posters for Nescafé, Maggi soup and, of course, Coca-Cola.

Every square inch of pavement seemed to be piled high with plastic boxes, wobbly card tables and shaky wooden benches.

Everybody seemed to be selling everything, although, I noticed, the young black leather jackets seemed to concentrate on cigarettes. Outside the Mini Dragstor, which was not what I thought it was going to be, I was offered all kinds of medication. At least, I think it was medication. Everybody, those selling and those not selling, those with their traditional headgear and those without, seemed to be busy about their business. Whatever it was. Most, not surprisingly, looked old, miserable and down at heel.

The only traffic making its way precariously from one gaping hole to another was made up of broken-down old tractors dragging even older trailers behind them and sleek, shining, brand-new Mercedes, the symbol of poor, downtrodden international civil servants and aid workers the world over.

Out near Pristina University, in a crumbling office close to about the only smoked glass and aluminium building in the place, I met a group of international businessmen doing business in the traditional Kosovo manner.

A Spaniard was selling tiles and building materials. The price: we'll discuss it *mañana* per 40-foot container.

A German was selling cars and trucks. The price: we discuss it later.

Your typical smooth French product of the elite École Nationale d'Administration was selling something I didn't quite understand. The price: a leaky bucket of depleted uranium.

Not to be outdone I offered to let the Kosovars have a selection of the very latest, most technologically advanced British ashtrays for a cup of their thick, sludgy black coffee but they weren't interested.

But I was invited to a block of flats on the outskirts of town. The doors and windows were still boarded up. Inside, however, it was as normal as can be. They even had a mini satellite dish, which is more than I have.

Once we'd settled down the talk was critical to the future of the, er, Republic: drugs, petrol, cigarettes, girls (Russian or otherwise), alcohol, illegal immigrants and, of course, every weapon you could think of. I was told that the rocket fired at MI5 headquarters on the banks of the Thames was supplied with the compliments of Kosovo arms dealers. Innocents say because of the number of policemen in Kosovo, the arms merchants and the drug dealers have moved on. The hard-bitten cynics say, No way. According to Kosovo wisdom, a policeman is a policeman. The more there are around, the more varied and different the countries they come from, the easier it is to find a corrupt one. And once you've found a corrupt one in a mess like Kosovo, the place is yours.

Important matters out of the way, talk now turned to breaking away from the Serbs and finally forming the long-dreamed-of Greater Albania, which would link together Kosovo with the Albanians in Macedonia, Montenegro, southern Serbia, a whole swath of northern Greece and, of course, Albania itself. Not to mention driving out all non-Albanians, intimidating witnesses and judges and murdering moderate Kosovo and Albanian politicians.

One eager young man, who looked like an accountant, disagreed.

'Greater Albania does not have to include Albania,' he said. 'Albania is too poor. It will hold us back.'

He asked me if I were British. I nodded sheepishly, as one does, hoping for the life of me I wasn't going to be hugged and kissed for the sins of Mrs Thatcher. He insisted we all drank a bottle of vodka together. The British, he said, had just established a new criminal intelligence unit in Pristina staffed largely with British policemen.

'To success,' he proposed.

We slugged back our vodkas.

'The British,' he said. 'What do they know about crime? They are too gentlemen. Now we make more money still.'

On the way back to the Grand Hotel I noticed two things that convinced me Kosovo was back in business: the local mosque was open; the local brewery was firing on all nine cylinders. It almost made me stop wondering why we did so much for Kosovo but nothing for the Kurds, for the people in East Timor, for the Rwandans, for the Congolese, for the . . .

Asunción

OK. I admit it. I was expecting Paraguay to be putting on the fritz: all tiny black postage-stamp moustaches, short hair, steel-rimmed glasses, highly polished boots and people trying their best not to mention the war.

Sure, it's German. There are German names all over the place. German restaurants called Restaurant Munich, Chopperia Vieja Bavaria and Restaurant Germania. German beers and non-expansionist-sounding names like Munich Imperial and Baviera Premium. German laundries called Edelweiss. Enormous German trucks blocking the road proclaiming Hamburg Sud. Huge, immaculate-looking German *estancias* which have obviously been designed and built to fit, unnoticed alongside the scruffy, rundown wooden Paraguayan shacks with their ox and cart tied up outside. I even came across a travel agent still advertising *Urlaub* in Tanganyika. It's also, incidentally, about the same size as, well, *das Vaterland*.

But it's more South American than it used to be. For your eighteenth birthday, for example, your goose-stepping amigos will get together and, as a surprise, send you a homegrown mariachi band and let off some fireworks in your honour. Each one of them, of course, will have hair as naturally, perfectly black as that of Chancellor Schröder. In Brazil they send you a whole different group of people, usually wearing little more than a couple of inches of dental floss, skilled in more than plucking a few strings and capable of making more than an occasional bang. But then we all have our cross to bear. Except that in Paraguay's case, it's an iron cross.

Landlocked with a merchant shipping fleet. One of the longest-running dictatorships in South America. Undeveloped. Repressed. A police state. A smuggler's paradise. A money launderer par excellence. One of the most corrupt countries in South America. A safe haven for Nazis and virtually anyone on the run. Providing, of course, they have a pair of black shiny boots. A long-term supplier of Persilscheine certificates, guaranteeing anyone a whiter-than-white Nazi-free past. The only place left in the world where duelling is still legal if – why I don't know – both parties involved are registered blood donors, which may or may not have something to do with so many old boys having rapier scars on their faces. As if all that is not enough to be getting on with, Paraguay is also one of the United States' most unreliable anti-drugs allies.

Slap bang in the centre of South America, those who've not been there refer to it romantically as the empty quarter. Those who have been there dismiss it as the plughole of South America or even worse. In many ways *A Hundred Years of Solitude* would have been better set in Paraguay than in Colombia. Not only is it easier to be on your own in Paraguay, they've got more parrots.

For years, Paraguay was virtually a closed country: the Albania of South America. It's only over the last ten years or so that it has begun opening up – and opening up *langsam*, I mean slowly. Only about 5 per cent of the roads in the country are tarmac. Dental floss they still use for cleaning their teeth. And if your car breaks down and you've got a set of jump leads in the boot, the *Fräuleins* know how to use them.

Not that it's Paraguay's fault. First they were discovered by the Spanish. Then by the Nazis. Or rather the ex-Nazis.

The Spanish came to conquer. Physically and spiritually. Physically by taking over the place, doing deals with the Guarani Indians and grabbing their women and their land. Spiritually by letting loose on them the Jesuits, who promptly preached that grabbing women and land was wrong and anyone doing so would be condemned to eternal damnation. So successful were they that according to Philip Caraman, a famous modern Jesuit author, philosophers and savants admired Paraguay as an example of a perfectly regulated society. In the first half of the nineteenth century romanticists saw in it the loveliest days of a new-born Christianity. Later still the pioneers of the Labour movements believed they had found there 'a pattern for European socialism'. Not for nothing was it known as the Jesuit Republic of Paraguay.

The Nazis, however, came in their postage-stamp moustaches, their short hair, steel-rimmed glasses and highly polished boots – to disappear. Chief among them – or at least as far as we know chief among them – was Josef Mengele, the Nazi doctor known as the 'Angel of Death' at Auschwitz extermination camp. He is supposed to have made for Cap Miranda, an old German haunt down in the south towards the border with Argentina, where, it is said, he was living with a woman who worked in a travel agency. Obviously essential if you've got to be up and ready to leave at a moment's notice. Others say that Hitler's secretary Martin Boormann did not die in Berlin but also followed the well-worn route to Paraguay and Cap Miranda, where he died of cancer in 1959. Judging by the neat, well-painted German houses, the oompah bands, the hairstyles and the black, shiny boots you see all over the country, they were not the only ones.

Not that Paraguay needed to import any maniacs. It already had plenty of its own, such as José Gaspar Rodriguez de Francia, known modestly to all and sundry as El

Supremo, who turned the whole place into one enormous prison camp; Francisco Solano López, who took on Argentina, Brazil and Uruguay at the same time, lost huge chunks of land (around 150,000 square kilometres) as well as every book, file and scrap of paper in the country, which is why today Paraguay has virtually no records going back a hundred years – and this is not to mention around 75 per cent of the active population. Before the war started they had around three million population. Afterwards less than one million. Most of them women, children and old men who were unable to fight.

Top or rather bottom of the heap was, of course, the man who made Paraguay what it is not today: the highly polished, jackbooted, highly revered in certain circles, General Alfredo Stroessner, who is still alive and well and polishing his boots in Brasilia.

Andres Rodriguez, who took over from Stroessner, began the process of reuniting Paraguay with the rest of the world. He dropped the ban on politics, called an election and, surprise, surprise, was promptly elected President. But at least there was an election.

In 1993 Rodriguez peacefully abdicated to Juan Carlos Wasmosy. Then the fun began – or, at least, the fun began providing you were not involved, your life did not depend on it and you were not grubbing around for something to eat. Wasmosy wanted to modernise. Trouble was Congress was against him. For the first time in the country's history they could say No to a president and that's what they did. Again and again and again. He wanted an independent judiciary. They said No. He wanted to privatise. They said No. He wanted to bring the economy more in line with the modern world. They said No. Instead of being a tin-pot dictator, he was a tin-pot democrat or what Paraguayans call a *democradura*: half democracy (*democracia*) and half dictatorship (*dictadura*).

Then there is the whole sordid South American comic-book story of the army commander General Lino Oviedo. Lino O to his friends. Wasmosy wanted to sack him. He was supposed to have bought three helicopters at way over the list price. For the war against drugs, said his friends. For establishing air control over the capital in the event of a coup, said his enemies. Wasmosy demanded his resignation. Lino O refused. For a time it looked as though he was going to stage a coup and take over the whole tutti-frutti. But Wasmosy blinked. He backed down. He offered to make him Minister of Defence. Lino O said No. Wasmosy then tried to arrest Lino O for insulting him. But when the military came calling Lino O was not at home. He telephoned a television station and told them he was staying at the farm of a friend as the army and the police well knew – 'They're on my side' – and would the army kindly not scratch the furniture on the way out. Wasmosy had won the battle but lost the war.

Come the next election, Lino O, a typical South American strongman who promised jobs, security and an end to corruption – he also, unusually for a top Paraguayan politico, spoke fluent Guarani, the language of the poor Amerindians – won the nomination for President of the ruling Colorado Party, which is, the Chinese Communists apart, the longest-ruling party in the world still in office. Now whether Wasmosy had anything to do with it or not – surprise, surprise – an army court promptly gaoled Lino O for ten years and forced him to give up his candidacy.

Instead the election was won by Lino O's buddy, Raul Cubas, the man who built the huge Itaipu Dam, the world's largest hydroelectric project, which supplies Paraguay with most of the electricity it needs and a huge chunk of Brazil as well. His Vice-President was the illiberal Luis Maria Argana, the Colorado Party chairman, who originally lost out to Lino O for the presidential nomination. Raul Cubas then set up a new military court which – surprise, surprise – promptly released Lino O from gaol. The Supreme Court, however, stepped in. The military court, they said, was unconstitutional. Lino O should go back to gaol. No way, said President Cubas. OK, said the Supreme Court, we'll prosecute. The Supreme Court also said that Lino O had no political rights. He could not be chairman of the Colorado Party. No way, said Cubas.

As if things couldn't get any worse what happened next? Vice-President Luis Maria Argana was assassinated, and Lino O was subsequently charged with ordering the murder. Things began to bubble. Raul Cubas resigned in March 1999 when the military told him they would not back him against Congress or the will of the people. He fled into exile. So too did Lino O.

The new President was Luis Gonzalez Macchi, former basketball player, former senate president and head of the country's first-ever civilian coalition government. Have they drawn a line and moved on, as our own great leader, the Reverend Tony, would say? Have they hell.

The new President wants to break the dominance of Stroessner's still-very-much-in-control Colorado Party. He wants to completely overhaul the government machine, privatise inefficient state enterprises and, he says, eliminate corruption once and for all. The Oviedists in the armed forces have now started suing the military who refused to back Lino O's attempted coup. The Supreme Court are suing Cubas. Congress wants to impeach him. And so it goes on and on and on.

Meanwhile in the real world things go from very bad to even worse than you could ever imagine. The economy continues to shrink because of the mess Paraguay is in, as well as because of the growing financial problems in Argentina and Brazil. Tax revenues are 20 per cent below budget. The government is struggling to pay salaries to its two hundred thousand employees, 25 per cent more than ten years ago, most of them naturally members of the Colorado Party. While its unpaid bills continue to soar higher and higher, the standard of living continues to fall lower and lower.

For the Europeans and European descendants, most of them with German accents, they're happy to put up with it. However much it falls, it's still better than being anywhere else. Like behind bars. For the Japanese who have spilled over the border from Brazil, it's better than being in Japan. For the *mestizos*, the native Paraguayans, who make up maybe 60–70 per cent of the population, they've no choice. They've got nowhere else to go.

Divided into five major groups in different parts of the country, the *mestizos* have their own language, which in turn is split into several dialects. If any of them speak Spanish, it is very poor Spanish. Until very recently there was little contact between different groups, let alone any attempt to try to work together to improve their lot. Now, however, it is just beginning to happen. Indian children are beginning to go to university. Some have even become doctors and lawyers. But overall they are still way behind the rest of the country.

Where there are politicians, of course, there is also corruption. In Paraguay it's not just endemic, it's a raging plague. Everybody's at it. Ever the treasurer of the Central Bank. He lifted no less than US$3 million of the bank's money to fund his own business activities. When the authorities finally got around to checking him out, such was the lack of confidence in the whole banking system that he took down with him four local banks and sixteen savings and loans societies and brought another four to the brink. Investigators also discovered that the metal bars protecting the vaults of the central bank could be unscrewed and removed at will. Now who could have done that?

Although, I'll admit, Paraguay doesn't *look* corrupt. There aren't many Mercedes around. Not even in the *vivendas temporarias*, the shanty towns, around the cities, which is always a bad sign. Go to the poorest country in Africa, you can hardly cross a dirt track for Mercedes. Similarly banks and offices. I thought they would be the size of Madrid town hall and dripping with maracas. They weren't. They were small, ordinary, functional. More IKEA than the Ritz. Which obviously proves there's a lot of corruption. If you're corrupt, if you're trying to persuade someone to build a second bridge, say, between Paraguay and Brazil or a dam to supply hydro-electric power to, for example, Argentina, the last thing you're going to do is flaunt it. Biddlecombe's First Law of Corruption: Always believe the opposite. Come to think of it, that applies to pretty much everything in life.

The same applies to people's homes – if, of course, you're lucky enough to have a home and you're not sleeping in the bus station, curled up in a tent by the side of the road or slumped in a doorway with a tray of unsold bananas for company. The houses I visited were again small, pleasant, adequate. OK, maybe I wasn't meeting the really high-rollers but even in the upmarket parts of town there didn't seem to be the obvious signs of wealth that you see in, for example, the likes of Marbella, Seville or even Altrincham, Cheshire.

It was the same when it came to lunches. Not for them the traditional three-hour Spanish lunch and siesta. Instead it was a quick visit to their bar or restaurant and back to work until maybe six or even seven o'clock. The people I met seemed to be content with a tuna sandwich, a mineral water and back to the office. Not my kind of style at all. Now I admit they might have been putting on an act for me. But why me? Nobody ever puts on an act for me. More likely they were probably just too scared to be away from their desks for too long.

Neither do people – top, bottom, medium – seem keen

to talk politics, business or whatever. Maybe they were just not interested. Maybe they thought it was safer. If, however, they said anything at all apart from talking football, rambling on about the economic situation in Brazil and moaning about the police – *polibis*, they called them. Short for *Policibandi*: *polici*, police; *bandi*, bandits – it was to go back to the old days of military dictatorship. If I had an old Deutsche Mark for every time someone said to me, 'We Paraguayans, we like to be told what to do. We like people to take the decisions for us,' or even '*Democratia* means problems, means one man says this, one man says that. We don't like that,' I'd have enough money to be able to buy a democrat.

They do, however, tell jokes. My favourite? An old man on his death bed. His dying wish is to have the President and Vice-President standing either side of his bed. Because, he says, he wants to die like his Saviour: between two thieves.

Asunción, the capital, is not surprisingly more Desunción. More nineteenth century than twentieth or even twenty-first century. Or, if you prefer, more Eva Braun than, say, Claudia Schiffer. It's small – around eight hundred thousand population – run down, dirty. The usual Spanish chessboard lay-out. Long narrow streets. The occasional square. Surprisingly few old colonial buildings. Mostly miserable single-storey modern buildings. The occasional multi-storey, wildly overdecorated and overfurnished Spanish-style hotel that looks more like an up-market matador's downmarket playpen than anything else. Or perhaps a matador's mistress's playpen than anything else. Most of them are so full of fancy chandeliers, huge Ming-type vases and all kinds of fancy furniture that you can hardly stagger from the bar full of beer without smashing into something.

The Gran Hotel del Paraguay is, appropriately enough, the villa of a former mistress of a former dictator: Eliza Lynch, Irish-born, a nurse, blonde. A great beauty in Paris in the 1850s, she was invited to Paraguay as a cultural ambassador. Judging by the size of the house, she was obviously a wonderful nurse as well. The exception to the Eva Braun style is the Hotel del Yacht and Golf out near the Puerto Ita Enramada, which runs boats to and from Argentina. To me it's more Milton Keynes Masonic Lodge than the Madrid Ritz. I preferred the Bar El Cacique down the muddy track, where I spent an hour in the pouring rain waiting for a boat that never came.

But the surprising thing is that whichever hotel I went in they were playing 'Greensleeves', which they obviously think is the latest number-one hit. Which shows you how far behind the times they are. All the waiters also looked like they had just retired from the secret police, Persuasion Department, and were about to go to seed.

The even more surprising thing was how cheap the hotels were. Huge slabs of Chateaubriand for – are you ready? – just US$7. In fact, in one hotel, Sabe Center Hotel, I was getting two huge slabs for US$7. Boy, were my white corpuscles jumping. Three days and I was suffering from Chateaubriand poisoning. Well, if you were married to a non-smoking, non-drinking vegetarian who is obsessed with E-numbers, what would you be eating?

With so much Chateaubriand about, it's no wonder there are so many packs of dogs wandering the streets. In fact, there's almost as many packs of dogs as there are children. Worse still, however, are the packs of police and military. They're everywhere. Not to mention squads of unlikely-looking bruisers sitting on rickety old wooden boxes selling lottery tickets in the most unlikely places at the most unlikely times of day and night. All the likely places are taken by people selling oranges, bottles of beer in ice buckets or something called Empanadas Rabito which I'm sure means cows' brains in black butter sauce or something like that.

Wander around the back streets, however, and you're also likely to bump into the occasional water cannon not to mention various non descript trucks and vans parked where nobody else is allowed to park. Not that I'm paranoid but with all this and fireworks going off at all hours of the day or night it took me three days before I got out of the habit of rushing back to the hotel, packing and making for the airport every time I heard a car backfire. I've been through enough coups and revolutions in various parts of the world without any problems to realise that next time, according to the laws of probability, I might not be so lucky.

Speaking of coups, the Presidential Palace, significantly or not, is far and away bigger than any other government building in town. It looks legitimate rather than illegitimate, more like a stately home-turned-hotel than an outpost for the Cayman Islands (Money Launderer, Unofficial) or wherever. In the old days under El Supremo it was said that anyone caught even looking at it was shot on the spot.

Thankfully you can hardly see the ghastly pink-painted Palacio Legislativo for all the non-stop demonstrations and riot police outside. It looks more like Eliza Lynch's official residence than the Gran Hotel.

North, along by the river, is Plaza Constitución, which not surprisingly is somewhat overlooked by the Congreso Nacional which overlooks the cheap-looking not very substantial Palacio de Justicia.

The Plaza del los Héroes is, well, not worth the bother of being a hero. If this was all I was going to get out of it I might as well have gone for the brown envelope, you can almost hear them saying.

Plaza Uruguay, however, corrupts both the body and soul. By day, it's full of open-air bookstalls. By night, it's full of downmarket Eliza Lynches all hoping against hope that one day they'll land a house as big as the Gran Hotel.

The railway station is quite fun. Not because there is anything particularly attractive about it but because it's the basis of another one of their favourite jokes, which is based on the fact that in Spanish the word for 'railway station' and the word for 'season' is the same. Hence their sidesplitting gag. 'In Asunción we only have two . . .' Thank you, Pedro, and *Gute Nacht*.

My favourite buildings? Anything called a Chip, which serves huge portions of chips; and anything called Choperia, which serves huge glasses of beer. I also secretly like the scruffy Policia National on Avenida General Diaz Azara. Which is, don't tell a soul, the headquarters of the secret police. But whatever building you're talking about, they're all covered in graffiti. Some praising Stroessner. Some telling the Yanquis to get out of Afghanistan. Most of the others along the lines of 'Tenemos dos clases de Politicos', which I hope means what I think it means.

A lick of paint, however, a couple of sacks of Polyfilla and a whole new bunch of politicians and it could be a beautiful city. But not an exciting city. The place is practically dead. Most bars seem to consist of Miguel playing his accordion, Pedro plucking his harp, and two huge señoras with faces as old and wrinkled as the circus tents they were wearing (which looked as though they could have been traditional Spanish costumes about the time of Carlos V), twirling about aimlessly like a couple of barges lost in the night. I tried the Brasilia one night. I was told it was the hottest place in town. I'm no expert but I can tell you that ladies' night at the Cinque Ports Club in Uckfield is hotter than that. Most unusual thing of all, especially for South America, come nine o'clock at night and the whole place is deserted. Even at weekends. As an indication of how desperate life is in Asunción: the only swinging place to go at weekends – and that's Sunday nights only – is the British pub. After what happened to me in the British pub in La Paz – we got bombed with CS gas by the riot police – I vowed never to go to a British pub overseas ever again. It's too dangerous. So I never tried it.

The following day – because there are literally so many exciting things to do in Asunción – I went to a football match. And I hate football matches almost as much as I hate craft fairs. The World Cup it was not. Neither was it anything like I imagined South American football to be. In fact, it was more Wigan reserves at home, on a wet Wednesday evening, losing 10–0. The pitch looked like a training ground for a firing squad. There were deep ruts all over the place followed by untidy mounds of earth. The stands were empty. Instead the huge crowd of about thirty of us huddled behind this rickety-looking old wooden archway with a net behind it. What's more it was raining. No sooner had the match started than one of the players was substituted. So short were they of red shirts that as he left, he took off his own and gave it to the player coming on to take his place. I left shortly afterwards. If I was going to be miserable, I thought, I could be miserable with another slab of Chateaubriand and a couple of bottles of vintage Rioja. At least I would be dry. Outside.

That night on television, however, it was the match of the day. The bar in the hotel was packed. Every move, every dribble, every shot for the goal was cheered to the imitation-glass chandeliers. There was even a fight between two retired matadors who looked as though they'd be only too pleased to crush your castanets without thinking when the man in black with the whistle sent off a man in red.

As I was leaving the bar this well-dressed gorilla shuffled up to me. He looked like he'd been trying out a trial batch of elephant steroids.

'You watching football?'

'Si.'

No point denying it.

'You like football players?'

'Er?'

'You buy football player?'

'Er?'

He was running a smuggling operation. Babies? He could sell me babies. Kids? He could sell me kids. Kids that play football. That would be extra. If you're in the baby business, Asunción, I discovered, is the place to be. Flash a couple of hundred-dollar bills at your friendly neighbourhood well-dressed gorilla and you'll be offered any number of children. Sometimes by the parents. More often than not by a friend, a cousin, a sister, even the babysitter. The price: around US$400. Cheaper if you throw in a sweater, a radio, maybe even a portable television. Worrying about getting the baby out of the country? Don't. Airline and airport security staff know better than to ask a distressed, nervous mother whether the child she is carrying in her arms is hers or not. This is Spain, don't forget.

To the north of Asunción is Concepción, which doesn't seem to have given birth to anything, or at least anything of any consequence. Keep going and eventually you hit the border with Bolivia and Brazil. Bolivia is OK. But beware the border with Brazil. The Moonies are moving in. They are supposed to be building their own 2-million-acre Moonie Garden of Eden – or should it be Garden of Moonie Eden? – along the border. Either way I'm not interested. To me, the Moonies are crazy. I've seen them operating in South Korea and various other parts of the world. While there are obviously more dangerous and far more sinister organisations in the world, they seem a bit too creepy for me. I don't mind His Universal Reverence Sun Myung Moon living in a US$14 million apartment in New York. I don't even mind him dodging taxes. But I reckon he's pushing his luck when he not only claims to be 'the Saviour, the Messiah, and King of

Kings of all humanity' but says he was told he was by 'Jesus, Muhammad, the Buddha and God'. Luckily there was no way I could get up to the border to drop in on the Saviour, the Messiah and King etc., so I didn't have to risk upsetting him by deciding not to go. Well, you never know do you? All the same, can you see Jesus, Muhammad, the Buddha and God agreeing on anything, let alone on His Universal Whatever He Calls Himself?

The east is Paraguari, around 30–40 per cent of the population, scrub, savanna grass, thorn bushes, rolling pastures, dense subtropical forest, the Rio Parana, practically non-stop rain and on the border with Brazil, Ciudad de Este, the biggest official and unofficial smuggling operation this side of our local village boot fair. Population: normally, one hundred and seventy-five thousand. On a good day, the sun shining, shops open, everybody ravin' to spend, anything up to two hundred and fifty thousand.

Originally called Puerto President Stroessner – it was changed after the super-sophisticated Paraguayans realised it gave rise to any number of snide remarks, silly comments and downright filthy innuendoes – it's more a super-smuggling *supermercado* with thousands and thousands and thousands of little shops, stalls and wooden boxes selling everything from the latest bootleg compact discs and notebooks to black balaclava helmets and any kind of gun you can think of. No questions asked. *Muchas gracias*. Next please.

I went into one gun shop on the main drag below a mass of neon signs. There laid out on the counter was everything a terrorist could possibly dream of: a Beretta 9mm automatic, a Colt .25, an Ingram 'spray-and-pray' sub-machine gun complete with silencer, an Uzi 9mm and a Walther PPK, again with silencer.

I told the very helpful Indian gentleman behind the counter

that the British army were having problems with their SA80–A, which they claimed was fine except that it kept jamming and sticking in dusty conditions – like those experienced when fighting a war in a desert. Whenever they moved into the front line, the first thing they had to do after jumping out of the helicopter, apart from dodging enemy fire, was to oil their guns so that they were ready for action. Not all their enemies, however, appreciated this, and sometimes they had various problems to overcome. Like trying not to get killed.

I didn't dare tell him that the army also had problems with their Challenger tanks. They had discovered that for some reason tanks designed to operate in a war in northern Europe were no good trying to plough through the sandy deserts of the Middle East. I thought he might think I was making it up and throw me out of the shop. Instead he invited me to his office out the back. At first I thought he was either going to introduce me to two MI5 agents who had been following me since I arrived in town or throw me to the local mob. But no such luck. For them, I mean, not me. Instead he wanted to show me a new line they were keeping for special customers: a Bushmaster XM15 E2S Shorty. Just under 1 m long, 6 lbs in weight, it was the answer to a terrorist's prayer. It could hit an apricot, he told me, from a quarter of a mile away. An apricot? Terrorist speak for the area between the top of the spine and the brain. A single bullet through the apricot, and that's it. Far more effective, though not as beloved by movie producers, than a bullet straight between the eyes or to the side of the forehead.

I tut-tutted, the way they do in the films. He showed me a Robar RC50, which he said could pierce an armoured car or truck. It could also blow a helicopter out of the sky up to a mile away.

I tut-tutted again. This time he showed me a Barret 82 A1. He said it was so fast, so powerful, it could fire through five or six different buildings to reach its target.

Prices? We didn't talk detail. But for decent quantities, he said, we'd be talking around US$500 a unit. No licences. No questions. Delivery, extra. Depending on precisely where, it could be extra, extra or even extra.

I told him I would have to check and come back.

As I left the shop I looked at the twelve-or-so-storey building opposite. On the roof was a mosque. MI5 agents? I didn't see one. But I was approached by a huge sunburned dork, who looked as though he enjoyed nothing better than chewing on human placenta.

'Oh no,' I thought, 'This is—'

He asked me if I needed to bribe a customs officer to get anything out of the country. He could fix it: US$500. A passport? Did I need a passport? US$1000.

I promised to come back to him. He asked me for my card. I gave him one of a bundle I keep in my wallet for such occasions. It belonged either to the First Secretary at the British Embassy in Asunción or to my local horse vet. I hope now it was the one belonging to the First Secretary. I'd hate anything to happen to my local horse vet.

I wandered in and out of the stores. They were selling everything. Computers. Every electronic what-do-you-call-them you could think of. Perfumes. Ray-Bans for US$10. Genuine Nike everything. Fried sweet potato and beef. In any currency you like.

Say, there are five thousand to ten thousand stalls, shops and stores. Say each one is holding on average US$1 million worth of stock. That's US$5–$10 billion worth of stock in total. Say they're turning over the stock once a month, which would be on the low side. That's total annual business of US$60–$120 billion, ten times Paraguay's official Gross Domestic Product. But this, don't forget, is no hick town. It's in Paraguay. It's riddled with corruption. Politicians are facing a string of corruption charges – what else? Some have just been discovered with *their* own secret landing strip. Half the cars and vans on the streets of Paraguay are said to have been stolen or reported stolen in Brazil and made their way through Ciudad de Este.

Then there's drugs. Not Paraguayan – Paraguay produces few illegal drugs – but Bolivian. The Americans, who are not always reliable when it comes to figures, reckon over 40 tons of cocaine come through Paraguay every year from Bolivia on their way up to the States and on to Europe. A fair slice of that is bound to come through Ciudad de Este.

Double my guestimate of US$60–$120 billion to US$120–$240 billion. If that doesn't mean it's not also a centre for worldwide terrorism, I'll eat my SA80–A2. There's no point keeping it in case I get attacked. It'll never work.

They're my figures, of course. Arthur Andersen of happy memory would obviously make out that the whole place is one gigantic loss, that nobody is making any money and that the whole thing should be wrapped up once the stock options have been cashed in.

Before I left I thought I'd better buy something. I treated myself to a genuine, guaranteed, US-hospital-approved blood pressure testing kit for US$7, which fell apart the moment I took it out of the box. Which didn't do much for my blood pressure I can tell you.

After Ciudad de Este we drove over the bridge across the River Parana on the edge of town and into Brazil. No papers. No passports. No checkpoints. The whole town, Pto Yguazu, was really a preparation for Ciudad del Este. There were huge posters everywhere advertising everything electrical and otherwise. Behind the town were huge warehouses the size of aircraft hangars ready to restock anything at a moment's notice.

I asked my driver to take me to their Lider Palace Hotel. He refused. He told me he used to be the private chauffeur to *les plus grands* Rothschilds in Paris so I suppose it was not surprising he did as he not his passengers wanted. Instead he took me to what he said would be a dining experience '*uniquement*'. It was. We went to what looked like a fast-food chain called Boka Loka. They charged not by what food you ordered but by the weight.

On the way back, what with the driver regaling me with intimate tales of the Rothschilds at work and play – he told me when he got married they fired him. They only trusted the '*célibataires*'. Which seemed odd. I'd have thought it would be the other way round. But who am I to argue with Rothschild logic? – we almost missed Luz e Esperanza, a genuine traditional Amish village just outside Estigarribia. Which seemed far more Amish than the Amish villages you come across in the States. No restaurants. No hotels. No huge superstores.

We also called in at San Bernardino, which looks like an Alpine village built on the shores of Lake Como by Germans, for Germans. The kind of place where they can let their lederhosen down, scatter their towels and feel at home. The hotels were more modern German. Lean. Spare. Adequate. The slightest suggestion of gingerbread. The restaurants and bars, however, were traditional German. German names. German food. German beer. One of the restaurants even had the colours of the German flag flowing gaily, or rather, sternly, all around the walls. A case, perhaps, of a fridge too far.

I went there on a wet, miserable day in July when the place was practically empty. But you can imagine what it's like on a hot, packed summer's day in August when the air is full of Wiener Schnitzel. Steins are overflowing. The talk is all about the good old days. Which is why I went there on a wet, miserable day in July. *Prost!*

South, on the border with Argentina is Encarnación, named after the greatest incarnation of all time: The Birth of the Mighty German Nation. A big German region, it's a bit like Wagner: it's not as bad as it sounds. It's also apparently not as bad as it looks providing you can get inside the houses because, according to who you talk to, a good few of the 479 Picassos, 347 Mirós, 290 Chagalls, 225 Dalís, 196 Dürers, 190 Renoirs, 168 Rembrandts and 150 Warhols that have gone walkabout from the world's art galleries are supposed to be hiding damp patches on the walls of a good few of the houses in the area.

The birthplace of General Stroessner, even today they still hold big street parties in Encarnación on his birthday. They do the same thing in Asunción, where the police are only too pleased to stop the traffic, block off the streets and arrest anyone not playing 'Happy Birthday' on their hooter. In Encarnación, however, it's a genuine traditional German birthday party. A bit dated. Most of the songs are from the '40s, the 1840s, '*Hohe Tanner*', '*O Deutschland Hoch in Ehren*', '*Ich hab' mich Ergeben*', and the like. But still for some reason they sing only the first (and elsewhere, especially in Germany, frowned-upon) verse of '*Deutschland, Deutschland über Alles*'.

Up until recently I was told it was also about the only place in the world where Germans tend not to use their surnames, especially when being introduced to strangers. They've also apparently just started getting used to Mozart and Bizet although I was told cassettes and DVDs of the likes of Mendelssohn, Offenbach, Mahler, Schönberg, not to mention Wellesz, Schreker and Ullmann are not too hot.

Was that unusual, I asked one slew-eyed Schnickel Fritz with a hausfrau the size of the *Bismarck*.

'No.' He jumped to attention. 'It is the same in any German city with a strong sense of German history.'

His hausfrau said nothing.

'She makes very good Schwartzwälder Kirschtorte,' he added.

The real fun in Paraguay, however, is out to the west: the vast, deserted Chaco, one of the roughest, toughest environments in the world. It's also the most German: real traditional, old-fashioned, Plattdeutsch-speaking German. Because it's Mennonite country. This is where the strict, God-fearing, pacifist, anti-military, Bible-punching Mennonites came from Germany via Canada in the 1930s, then in the late 1940s from Germany via Ukraine to live their own life, follow their own faith, cultivate their ranches away from the rest of the world and build their kind of heaven here on earth – although judging by the temperatures, which can be as high as 40 degrees Celsius in the middle of summer, it's no wonder they gave up their ban on drinking beer soon after they arrived there. It seemed to me to be more like hell on earth than anything else.

But whether it's heaven or hell, there's no doubting their Old Testament enthusiasm, not so much for the Book of Esther or the Book of Ruth, let alone the Song of Songs, but for killing anything that moves.

There are other smaller Mennonite settlements in other parts of the country. But this is the Big Bertha of them all: over 250,000 square kilometres, about the same size as Poland. Population: about ten thousand including the Indians. Most of them tend to be big, tough, muscly, able to throw an ox over their shoulder and knock back a full stein of beer at the same time. The men are the same.

Being eager to escape from the world, they also made it impossible to get to. No trains. No planes. The only airport in the whole of the region is at Estigarribia, but that's only for Paraguayan military flights and it's closed anyway. The only alternative was the bus. I went to the bus station in Asunción. Nobody could tell me when the bus left, how long it took or if there was a bus at all. I spotted this old-fashioned couple who looked as though they had come out of the Book of Exodus. The old man had a heavy raincoat on, big boots and a Stetson. His wife – she could only have been his wife – was small, dumpy, a black scarf pulled tightly over her head. On the bench beside them was a lump of bread, a huge lump of meat and a thermos flask. In my bad German I asked if they knew anything about the bus to Filadelfia.

'*Ja*,' they said.

They gave me the time the bus left, the gate it left from and how long it took.

'*Zwölf Stunden siebenundreisig Minuten.*'

The bus journey was, *Mein Gott*! Why did I ever think of doing such a thing? It was boring. Hardly anybody said a word to anybody. It was also as hot as hell. Maybe not 40 Celsius. But hot, hot, hot.

Heading out from Asunción, it was like crossing the Sahara. At first it was pleasant, friendly, trees, grass, savanna, the occasional pond or lake. Then, gradually, scrub, thorn, forest. Finally in the far north up near the border with Bolivia it becomes desert.

We stopped once. At a Paraguayan equivalent of McDonalds. It was all beer and sandwiches as thick as the Old Testament. Everybody I saw seemed to have an extra-high forehead. A traditional Guaycuru Indian who spoke snatches of American with a German-Spanish accent told me the Germans were crazy. They drove like maniacs. Probably because there is nothing in the Bible about 4×4s.

Filadelfia, when I finally got there, was not only tiny – population, 5000 – it was so neat and tidy it looked as though it could keep any housepainter so busy he wouldn't have time to dream of looking for areas in which to expand. Not only that but they know how to wage a desert war. The rough, sandy tracks between the houses – there were no proper streets – they swept three times a day. It was also home to twenty-one species of parrot and a parakeet who could at the click of a jackboot sing '*Unter dem Lindenbaum*'.

If this is a strict Protestant German heaven, I thought, it's not for me.

As there were no hotels – they're not mentioned in the Bible either – I stayed in a primitive but very well-painted bungalow owned by my friend Adolf. Well, I say 'my friend'. He was the only person on the bus who spoke to me. And, no, he did not have a black postage-stamp moustache.

One day I spent visiting one of the big local farms. When they first came here in the 1920s there was nothing; well, nothing except jungle. From Brazil they came in their hundreds down the River Paraguay by boat and landed at the border. They then had to hack their way 250 miles – well, they wanted somewhere in the middle of nowhere – to where they established their base, Filadelfia. Dozens died on the way.

Originally, it was all mills and cotton. Today it's a big farming/ranching success story. They supply milk not only to themselves but the whole of Paraguay. Similarly meat. Hence the price of chateaubriand. Because production is booming, it is bringing its own problems: commercial and religious. Commercial: because of the quantities they are producing they are continually searching for new outlets. They even export to Germany. Religious: inevitably, as they become more commercial, they have to mix more and more with the outside world. Buyers rarely come to them. The result is that today it's not unusual to see Mennonites not only waiting at the bus station but wandering around Asunción, doing business and visiting the occasional choperia.

Some – the older, stricter members – regret what's happening. They fear it might be the beginning of the end. The younger ones welcome it. Not because they want to change their way of life but because they feel it is the end of the beginning. They're established. They're successful. But they need new blood. Maybe there was something about all those high foreheads after all.

But inevitably things are not working out quite the way they expected. From the beginning the Mennonites were all for one and one for all. They were a community. They lived as a community. They worked as a community. They shared the goodies as a community. Now they are becoming more relaxed. While some of them maintain the old ways, more and more of the younger Mennonites are working and making money for themselves and contributing to the community. Admittedly substantially. But it's not the same thing.

Tourism is also rearing its ugly backpack. Whisper it not but this is one of the few places left in the world where without Chacoing too much money around, a word in the right *Ohr*, or rather ear, and you can hunt, trap and stuff anything in sight: jaguar, puma, some local boa constrictor, which can grow up to 5 or 6 metres in length, not to mention deer, wild pig and anything that didn't know the Old Testament by heart; and have it sent back to you to hang on the ceiling above your bed or wherever it would annoy your wife the most.

Adolf told me he was thinking of organising hunting trips for rich foreigners. *Warum nicht?* He wanted to experiment, see how it would go, have a trial run. Would I accompany him and some friends?

'*Warum nicht?*'

Adolf came armed to the teeth. About the only thing he didn't have slung over his shoulders was a 55-ton Tiger Tank. Hermann brought a huge hunting knife. He believed in doing things the old-fashioned way. Joseph was going to skin whatever came his way for a group of big German hunters back home in the *Vaterland*. Adolf was in charge so he insisted we swept out like a Panzer division to the east without, I have to say, much success. Not that he ever admitted it.

I left them when they were about to cut their losses and switch their attention towards the west.

We didn't catch anything. Not even German measles.

When I got back to Asunción my clothes were so filthy and,

no doubt, full of Woolly Bear beetle larvae that I sent them straight off to the laundry. Back they came even filthier than before. Which tells you something about Asunción. But I wouldn't have missed it for anything. The tramping through the scrub in single file. The cleanliness. The strict attention to detail. The way they had of making me laugh with the joke about Hermann's wife just giving birth to their eleventh child. Adolf asking him what he was going to call it. 'Alice,' he said. 'Why Alice?' said Adolf and Hermann saying, 'When I saw it I said, *Das ist Alles. Gut ja?' Ja, Hermann, sehr gut.*

Then there was Hermann's joke about Joseph.

'Joseph. He like Attila the Hun. Attila the Hun, he break, how you say, blood wessel on wedding night. Joseph, he also break blood wessel on wedding night.'

Ja, Hermann, sehr gut.

But more than anything was the routine before lights out. We'd sing three verses of '*Unter dem Lindenbaum*'. They would then retire promptly to their camp and I would retire to mine.

'This is *mein Kampf*, Adolf,' I would shout every evening.

'*Ja, Englander. Ihren "Kampf"*,' he would yell back.

Wunderbar.

Kigali

- You switch the radio on. You hear wild blood-curdling voices screaming for people to go to the street where you live. The crowds who are already there need more help. To murder you, your family and families like yours.
- You go out of your house. It has been daubed with red paint. You see crowds coming towards you. They are going to kill you and your family. Because you know they won't just kill you outright – they'll butcher you, leaving you to suffer and die in horrendous agony – you decide to kill your family yourself to ensure they die quickly.
- The killers, your next-door neighbours for twenty years, the family across the street whose children have played with your children since they were born, are outside your house. To save your family you tie them up and throw them in the latrines in the garden. Then you jump in yourself.

Rwanda is one genocidal horror after another, another and another. From 6 April 1994 to 18 July 1994 – ninety days – the Hutus turned against the Tutsis and relentlessly, cold-bloodedly, mercilessly, tortured, raped, blinded, hacked to pieces, butchered, massacred 700,000, 800,000, 900,000 perhaps even a million people; one in seven of the population: 10,000 a day, over 400 an hour, seven a minute.

It was the biggest and most intensive killing spree of modern times. The worst outbreak of genocide since the Holocaust and the Nazis.

It was also sponsored by the government. The government told the prefects what to do. The prefects told the local mayors. The mayors told the local people. Reports were then fed back up the system. From mayors to prefects. From prefects to Prime Minister. The message was always the same: there was work to do – in other words, killing. The tools to be used were machetes, firearms, clubs, hammers, anything the Hutus could lay their hands on. First, the military were to move in with the police. If they had machine guns, mortars, hand grenades, they were to use them. Then it was the turn of the civilians to finish the job. Finally came the administrators or civil servants. It was their job to clean up, bury the dead, divide up the empty properties, distribute the loot. Then move on to the next killing field.

The politicians stood on the sidelines shouting out encouragement. If prefects and mayors were slow to act they spurred them on. If the killings were running behind schedule, they called for reinforcements: old, retired soldiers, ex-policemen, anybody who could hold a machete or be persuaded one way or another to butcher a fellow human being.

The local radio station joined in. Day after day they urged Hutus 'to fill up' Tutsi graves. They launched what must be the most horrifying phone-in programme of all time. If you know where Tutsis are hiding, phone us, they pleaded with their listeners. We will tell the killers where to go. They even told them how to kill the Tutsis.

'Do not kill these *inyenzi* [cockroaches] with a bullet,' they screamed at their listeners. 'Cut them to pieces with a machete.'

Not that the announcers neglected their job as disc jockeys. Except that even the records they played called for the 'total extermination of the Tutsi. To spare any of them would be a present that the Hutu could ill afford.'

As the killing progressed, the Hutus became more efficient at it. Instead of killing the Tutsis one by one in their homes, they rounded them up and killed them in groups. At Kacyru, for example, Hutu troops herded together over four thousand Tutsis and then threw grenades at them until they were all dead. They also instituted stricter controls over the killers. No longer were Tutsis allowed to escape in return for money or sexual favours. They were to be killed just the same. So too was anybody – Tutsi, Hutu or whoever – who could testify against them.

The world did nothing. Nobody said a word. Nobody suggested intervening. Not one of the 120 countries that were signatories to the UN Convention on the Prevention and Punishment of the Crime of Genocide as much as raised an eyebrow.

The US, guardian of democracy, champion of the rights of man, advocate of a world free from oppression, did nothing. Secretary of State Warren Christopher didn't even know where Rwanda was. He had to get an atlas to find out where it was when he sat down with his top advisers to discuss the crisis. Presidential candidate Senator Robert Dole dismissed the whole thing as of no import. 'I don't think we have any national interest there,' he declared grandly. Clinton, when he was not otherwise engaged, did everything he could to avoid calling it genocide. If he called it genocide he might have to do something about it. Instead, because eighteen US soldiers had just died in Somalia and he didn't want to commit any more US troops to sorting out Africa's problems, he claimed it was only 'acts of genocide that may have occurred'.

Tony Blair in spite of all his grand speeches and lectures on morality said nothing (probably because he couldn't solve the problem by going to war with anybody).

Worst of all, however, were – surprise, surprise – our friends, the French. They could have stopped the whole thing before it began. They were closer to the Hutu government than anybody else. They also – how they could do this is unbelievable – continued to ship in arms throughout the whole of the sorry business. Finally, the French being the French, at the end of it all they gloriously denied they had any responsibility at all for what had happened.

The UN was almost as bad. Originally they moved in in 1990. Tutsi exiles in Uganda, who had formed themselves into the Rwanda Patriotic Front, marched back home, sparking a civil war. The Hutu government arrested thousands of Tutsis they said were 'accomplices'. On 8 October the Rwandan army massacred one thousand Tutsis. Between 11 and 13 October they massacred another four hundred. Belgium and France sent in troops to protect and evacuate their nationals. At the end of the month Belgium withdrew its troops. The French remained. Things, however, got worse and worse. More Tutsis were uprooted and displaced. More Tutsis were massacred. Ceasefires were signed and ceasefires were broken. One human rights investigator after another condemned the Hutus. The Hutus, of course, denied everything. There were no death squads. There were no massacres. Nothing was planned in advance.

In 1993 the fighting got worse then suddenly peace broke out. Two thousand five hundred UN troops arrived to keep the peace, which they did until the massacres began all over again. Then unbelievably on 21 April 1994, with the killings well under way and with already around one hundred thousand Tutsi lives lost, the Security Council voted to slash the UN force that was there to keep both sides apart from 2500 to just 270 lightly armed soldiers. Their orders: to fire only in self-defence.

The UN commander, General Romero Dallaire, a Canadian, was told he could exceed his mandate in one respect and one respect only: helping to evacuate foreign nationals. Not a word about helping the Tutsi escape the oncoming slaughter, even though as far as I can recall the UN exists not just to protect the lives of escaping foreign nationals but all peoples of the world regardless. Later the General recalled that when he received his orders, 'My force was standing knee-deep in mutilated bodies, surrounded by the guttural moans of dying people, looking into the eyes of children bleeding to death with their wounds burning in the sun and being invaded by maggots and flies. I found myself walking through villages where the only sign of life was a goat or a chicken or a songbird as all the people were dead, their bodies being eaten by voracious packs of wild dogs.'

But orders are orders. He did as he was told. Finally, however, with the massacres continuing and the bodies piling higher and higher, the UN decided to try again to put a stop to the bloodshed. They voted to send in a UN force to keep both sides apart. Clinton decided to send fifty armoured personnel carriers as his contribution. But first he insisted that he was paid US$15 million for the hire of the transport planes to ship them out before he gave the go-ahead. Can you believe it? Hundreds of thousands of people are being mercilessly hacked to pieces and the President of the richest nation in the world is haggling over a few dollars. And they are the ones who are refusing to pay billions of dollars in arrears on their membership fees to the UN.

Although, to be fair, Tony Blair didn't even get as far as arguing about the morality of what was or was not happening.

Tiny, landlocked Rwanda is the Tibet of Africa. It's around 3000 feet above sea level. It's practically nothing but mountains. In fact, because it's so high, the eagles skim the top of your car. Some of them fly so low you can see the colour of their eyes. Bloodshot. Rwanda is also not surprisingly a country of young people and old women.

The capital, Kigali, which should be renamed Killgali, is

nightmares. Everywhere you turn, everywhere you go is nightmares, monstrous, horrifying nightmares. In spite of everything the country has been through, the horrifying scenes that have taken place there, the unbelievable agonies and atrocities, it's just like France. Dirty. Filthy. Disgusting.

In theory you're supposed to be able to tell the difference between the Hutus and the Tutsis. The Hutus are supposed to be average: average height, average weight, average build. The Tutsis are supposed to be as tall and thin as bean posts. A bit like the Senegalese. In practice, because of intermarriage, interbreeding, it's not as simple as that. The result is: shake someone by the hand, you can't tell whether he was a killer or a survivor. Buy someone a drink. Did he butcher someone to death? Did he escape death by hiding for days on end at the bottom of a latrine? Climb into a cab and drive off into the night. You can't tell whether the driver ferried people to their death or whether he risked his life driving friends and family to safety.

On the other hand, Killgali is safe. It's as if everybody is too exhausted even to think of stepping out of line.

The fancy four-star Hôtel des Mille Collines is as smart today as any four-star hotel in the world. The restaurant is not only fabulous, it's French fabulous. Thick white tablecloths. Silver cutlery. Elegant champagne glasses. Huge, sparkling wine glasses. A menu that would put Gordon Ramsay to shame. A wine list the length of the Old Testament. Whenever I stay there the waiters seem to spend almost as much time making certain everything is placed oh-so-precisely on the table as I spend tucking into the food.

The first evening I went there, I was in the restaurant. In the far corner was a young couple who were practically gouging each other's tonsils out. Italians. Behind me a group of French businessmen, napkins tucked under their chins, were talking about the evils of globalisation they had discovered while travelling the world visiting one subsidiary company after another. Sitting at a table almost but not quite opposite me was a young guy, thirty-ish, wearing a baseball cap on back to front, T-shirt, jeans, big bumpers. He was drinking Coke, packed with enough ice to sink the *Titanic*, and eating his French fries with the fork in his right hand. Being English and naturally hesitant before speaking to someone to whom I have not been formally introduced, I waited until I had finished my delicious Jambon de Bayonne. Not to mention the second bottle of Fleurie.

'So which part of the States are you from?' I looked up and asked him as casually as one does.

He stared at me wide-eyed in amazement.

'How did you know I was American?' he growled.

I hadn't the heart to tell him.

Yet during the massacres, for three months over a thousand people, Tutsis as well as Hutus, opposed to the killings packed into this very hotel for safety. Inside, they lived dozens of people to a room. From the windows they could see the gangs breaking into people's homes around the hotel, butchering whole families and then moving on to the next.

For food, they relied on what the hotel had stashed away and any supplies they could get from outside when the gangs had moved on. For drink, they drank the water in the hotel swimming pool. From his office, day after day after day, the manager Paul Rusesabagina sent faxes to the French Ministry of Foreign Affairs, the King of Belgium, Bill Clinton. Tony Blair he didn't bother with. Which is probably just as well. If he got a reply he wouldn't have understood what he was saying.

He pleaded with them: 'We escaped from the massacres nationwide. We are a group of children, women, people of all categories: lawyers, medical doctors, Human Rights Commission members, students, American Embassy employees, businessmen etc. – and all of us are calling for HELP. Without your intervention hundreds of innocent survivors could be killed in a few hours.'

No reply. Nix. Nuttin.

For days, weeks then months, they lived in fear that their time had come, that the gangs would burst into the hotel and slaughter everybody there. But that day never came.

Other places were not so lucky.

Go to the Cathedral. It's a long, shiny brown brick barn of a building with fancy wooden rafters. At the start of the killing it was packed with people searching for safety. What happened? One morning one of the priests came carrying a gun. With him were some Hutu killers. Calmly he walked through the church pointing out the Tutsis, who were then taken outside and butchered.

Talk to the men and women sitting at the back of the church. They tell you similar stories. At Nyange over two thousand Tutsis packed inside a church for safety. The priest ordered bulldozers to smash it and the Tutsis inside to pieces. At the sprawling Seventh Day Adventist complex at Mugonero over five thousand Tutsis sought refuge. They wrote to the pastor: 'How are you? We wish you strength in all the problems you are facing and we wish to inform you that tomorrow we will be killed with our families. We, therefore, ask you to intervene on our behalf with the mayor.' Back came the reply: 'A solution has been found for your problem. You must die.' The following day they were slaughtered. Every one of them.

Early one morning I went to the Kimironko prison, home to thousands of the killers awaiting trial. I expected a huge, secure fortress of a place. Instead it was an open compound surrounded by flimsy barriers and barbed wire. More temporary prisoner of war camp than Brixton or Wandsworth or Wormwood Scrubs. Nothing at all like Guantánamo Bay.

I was not the only one there. All around the camp families were shouting across to the prisoners dressed in what looked like bright pink pyjamas, throwing food across to them, probably also tobacco and God knows what else. There were guards. But they didn't seem interested in what was going on. (Although if somebody had tried to escape they would no doubt have shot first and thought about it afterwards.)

The main gates were closed. During the killings, they were open. If prisoners were not helping with the killings, they were helping with the cleaning up and the burying of the dead. Within a few days of the killing ending, they were closed again. Behind them this time were ordinary men who one day for one reason or another suddenly went out and killed not an unknown enemy, not somebody intent on killing their families, not somebody destroying their homes, their property, everything they had lived and worked for – but their next-door neighbours, people they had been living alongside all their lives. Killing somebody who is trying to kill you is one thing. But killing, butchering, massacring people you have lived with all your life must be completely different. Maybe they were forced to do it. Kill or be killed. Kill or we'll kill your family. Maybe they did it without thinking. Maybe they enjoyed it.

A Tutsi selling scraps of food and drink told me that the government bribed the Hutus to kill them. To the young, the unemployed, they promised money, homes, even farms belonging to murdered Tutsis. To others they offered drink, drugs, whatever they wanted. To businessmen they offered shops, offices, businesses that used to be owned by Tutsi businessmen. To farmers they offered animals, crops, machinery that used to belong to Tutsi farmers. To those who didn't want to kill they offered them the choice: kill or be killed.

Another guy hustling food and drink – I couldn't tell whether he was a Hutu or a Tutsi – told me people simply did as they were told. The government told them. Their local mayor told them. The radio told them. Even their churches told them. They did as they were told.

'Even kill your friends?'

'Even kill your friends.' He wiped his face with his hands. 'We always did as we were told. It is our custom.'

As I wandered up to the prison gates a young policeman ambled over to me. My first thought I admit was, Not the pink pyjamas. Although to tell the truth they wouldn't have been the first pink pyjamas I've been in. He asked me if I would like to visit the old President. I said, Yes, of course. I could think of one or two questions I'd like to ask him. Off he went. Within two minutes he was back. Apologies. But the old President didn't want to see me.

So now we know where I stand in the natural order of things. Below a prisoner on trial for genocide.

Behind the prison is a village built for widows left behind by the massacre which is an example of the steps the present Rwanda government have taken to help the survivors of the massacres and to make certain nothing like it ever happens again. They've formed help organisations. They've started organisations to take care of anything up to half a million orphans. They've started self-help classes for women in everything from bricklaying to nursing. They've also done everything they can to get women involved in politics: helping to organise elections, voting in elections, standing in elections. They've even set up women-only elections. Women can elect their own women-only local councils that operate side by side with existing local councils. On a national level, women can also elect their own women Members of Parliament. However, putting the women-only village next to the prison didn't strike me as one of the most enlightened steps taken by the government. Every day the widows have nothing to do but look at the men who killed their husbands, their children, their families.

One old Tutsi lady told me that not all Hutus were bad. Some shielded and protected Tutsis. Some helped them escape.

To other people's houses. To the bush. To surrounding countries. Her brother had survived because for the duration of the massacres his Hutu friends kept him hidden in a hole in their garden. It wasn't pleasant. It wasn't comfortable. But he survived. What's more so did the Hutus. Others who had been found harbouring Tutsis had been killed.

I walked back to the Mille Collines. Somehow at that particular moment I didn't fancy climbing into a car with a complete stranger.

Suddenly it occurred to me: no dogs. After the massacres were over the UN came in and shot all the dogs. The dogs had been eating the bodies that were lying all over the place in their thousands. There was an acute risk that if they didn't shoot them, God only knows what would happen to the survivors. The diseases they would catch. The germs that would kill them.

But what on earth made the Hutus turn on the Tutsis? Some people say it's in their blood. From time immemorial the Hutus have hated the Tutsis and the Tutsis have hated the Hutus. One day the Hutus would swoop on the Tutsis and cut them to shreds. The next day the Tutsis would swoop on the Hutus and cut them to shreds. It's just one of those things. Like the British and the French. Except in this case they squeezed their hundred years' war into as many days. The strange thing is, most unlike the British and the French, they all speak the same language, share the same territory and follow the same traditions.

While first the Germans and then the Belgians, neither of whom are known for being the world's most enlightened colonialists, were running the show, they let them get on with it; until 1 January 1961, when the Belgians tried to put a stop to the whole thing. They abolished the Tutsi monarchy and declared Rwanda a republic. From now on, they said, Rwanda would elect its own leaders and its people would live together as one. Which was rich coming from a country that is itself divided every which way by language, by religion, by customs, and can only survive by having two of everything.

Everybody was against the idea. The Hutus. The Tutsis. The Twas, who make up less than 1 per cent of the population and generally manage to keep out of the way of the big two. Even the United Nations was against the idea. They said all the Belgians had done was replace the dictatorship of one group of people with the dictatorship of another. Instead of the dictators being Belgian, the dictators would be either Hutus or Tutsis. Belgium couldn't have cared less. In 1962 they gave Rwanda its independence and returned home to their own bitterly divided country.

The first independent president was Grégoire Kayibanda. No prizes for guessing which side of the killing fields he came from. Tutsis, or at least those Tutsis who could flee, fled. Those who stayed behind were thrown out of their jobs. Ethnic quotas were introduced. Companies, colleges, universities could only hire Tutsis up to 9 per cent of the total number of employees and no more. It even became government policy that the Hutu majority would murder the Tutsi minority. The Tutsis, however, swallowed it all. At least they weren't being massacred. In any case, if they were massacred, it would be the Hutus' turn next.

In 1968 their turn came. Tutsi exiles who had fled to Uganda and formed themselves into the Rwanda Patriotic Front invaded the country and tried to overthrow the government. The government, with the aid of Belgium and Zaire, retaliated. Thousands of Tutsis were killed. The UN then stepped in to keep both sides apart.

In the early 1990s came the dress rehearsals for the Hutu fightback. Suddenly death squads arrived on the scene. They would roll up to a group of houses, a village, part of a town and kill every Tutsi in sight. They used the national radio to identify their killing fields, call on Hutus to kill their Tutsi neighbours or be killed themselves.

On 4 August 1993 President Habyarimana signed a peace agreement bringing to an end the killing. His Hutu backers cried treason. He was aiding and abetting the Tutsis.

Even more UN troops arrived to keep the two sides apart.

On 3 April 1994 Radio Rwanda, a Hutu radio station, warned listeners that in the next few days 'there will be a little something here in Kigali and also on April 7 and 8 you will hear the sound of bullets or grenades exploding'.

The 'little something' happened on 6 April. President Habyarimana's Falcon 50 jet was shot down over Killgali. It crashed into the grounds of his palace. There were no survivors.

The killing began shortly afterwards; first, Hutus who were opposed to any massacre, then the Tutsis, then anyone who got in their way.

'You cockroaches. You must know you are made of flesh,' sneered Radio Rwanda. 'We won't allow you to kill. We will kill you instead.'

The radio urged them on. Kill. Kill. Kill, it screamed at them. Have no mercy. Not even for women and children.

One of the most inflammatory broadcasters of all was a woman, Valerie Bemeriki, who is accused of hosting one of the most horrifying radio phone-in programmes it's possible to imagine. In between shrieking at listeners to 'fill up' the Tutsi graves, she pleaded with them to call in and reveal where the Tutsis were hiding so that they could be hunted down and killed. Some Hutus even offered to pay for several Tutsi heads.

How the Hutus thought they could get away with it, or rather how the leaders of the Hutus thought they could get away with it, I have no idea – although I suppose a fair number of them not to mention a huge number of ordinary Hutus have got away with it.

To ensure, however, that as few Hutus got away with it as

possible, the United Nations set up the International Criminal Tribunal for Rwanda. Its objective: to demonstrate that the world will no longer look the other way; to remind even the world's strongest, toughest, most ruthless dictators that even the strong, tough and ruthless must obey the law or pay the consequences.

Trouble is, the International Criminal Tribunal for Rwanda is not only outside Rwanda – it's in Tanzania, in Arusha, on the southern slopes of Mount Meru – it's also out of this world.

As I was queuing up for one security check after another just to get into the International Conference Centre that houses the court, let alone the court itself, I came across no end of Rwandans who told me the Court had not lived up to its billing. It had let them down. It was in the wrong place. The genocide took place in Rwanda. The trials should take place in Rwanda. Because it's not in Rwanda but in Tanzania, it was once removed. Rwandans didn't see justice being done. It was taking too long. Justice was supposed to be swift. People were forgetting what had happened. Witnesses were dying, because it was taking too long. Political and military leaders in other countries might be tempted to wage war on different ethnic groups because they saw the tribunal was largely ineffectual.

'With over 135,000 people in gaol awaiting trial, barely a thousand cases being tried every year. Work out for yourself how long it's going to take,' an eager student activist type told me.

It's also inefficient. Theoneste Bagosora, the army colonel accused of being the mastermind behind the massacres – he is said to have seized power after the death of President Habyarimana in the plane crash, promising everyone 'an apocalypse' – was in gaol for six years before he was finally brought to trial. Then when he was, the trial was postponed for six months for the want of a simple translation of just two documents.

As we shuffled our way along the corridors there were plenty of other criticisms.

One old man, who said he'd lost over a hundred relatives and friends, told me that officials investigating alleged cases of genocide have themselves been accused of committing genocide.

The leaders who gave the orders should be sentenced to death, not the men who carried out their orders, another man butted in. The people found guilty and imprisoned for life should not be allowed to live in better conditions than the victims who managed to survive.

I also came across Tutsis, who had lost their husbands, wives, children, homes – everything. They were hungry, dirty, desperately trying to survive in burnt-out houses and shops, slums. The Hutus who had carried out the killings were back in their homes with their families.

On the other hand one Tutsi woman told me that when her daughter got married they invited to the wedding Hutus who had killed her husband.

'If we didn't invite them, we would have nobody at the wedding,' she said. 'That would be worse.'

Then there's the cost. In eight years the Tribunal has convicted only eight people, three of whom pleaded guilty. The bill: over US$70 million a conviction.

Finally we reached the fourth floor of the Conference Centre. We shuffle our way along the corridor and into courtroom number two. I thought it was going to be serious, sombre and forbidding, all dark wood, dim lighting and a black cloth, the size of a handkerchief, thrown casually on the judge's bench. Instead it was like a tennis club committee room designed by IKEA. The public gallery was worse than standing in the dock itself. It was about 20 metres long and completely surrounded by a thick sheet of bulletproof glass, which is in itself a valuable admission by the authorities that they are less than 100 per cent confident in their own security procedures. At the far end of the committee room, up on high, looking down on everybody, were three red-robed judges. Before them, a row of black-robed clerks. On the left, the accused and the bewigged defence counsel. On the right, the bewigged prosecutor and his assistant prosecutors. Facing the judges is the witness box.

I'd no sooner got into the public gallery and settled down behind the bulletproof glass when for some reason we were all shuffled out again. I wondered whether there was a security scare. A smart, well-dressed-but-not-quite-Gucci woman told me it happened all the time. She turned out to be an interpreter.

'It's horrible,' she told me. 'I have had to learn so many new words and phrases since I have been here. The French they use here is not the French we were taught at university.'

As I shuffled back along the corridor and back down outside the building I heard still more criticism. The Prime Minister at the time of the massacres, Jean Kambanda, and most of his cabinet were in gaol. Only Kambanda had been brought to court. He had pleaded guilty. Why hadn't the others been brought to court? A former army officer, Bernard Ntuyahaga, had been accused of murdering ten Belgian peacekeepers. But he had been released. Still awaiting trial were eleven ministers, a whole bunch of military types, senior Church leaders, intellectuals, as well as the odd one or two journalists. When were they going to appear in court?

The critics obviously had a point. Within a couple of months the government decided the most efficient way of dealing with the problem of trying and sentencing so many suspected mass murderers was to turn the clock back and set up *gacacas*, village courts all over the country where local judges and local juries could try local suspects. The guilty would be condemned. The innocent would be set free.

On the surface it seems a good idea. It should certainly clear the backlog of cases far more quickly and much more cheaply than at present. Except. Except. Except.

It means setting up ten thousand village courts, selecting and training two hundred and eighty judges. It means relying on the integrity and honesty of local people to try local people. No score settling. No victimisation. No framing innocent people. It means local people having the courage to come forward in their own villages without protection to testify against their neighbours.

'It is not possible. It is asking too much,' one bewildered civil servant told me. 'But what can we do? We have over one hundred and twenty thousand prisoners awaiting trial. We cannot let them go. We must do something.'

Back in Killgali I asked your typical French-educated civil servant if he thought the local courts would work.

'People should not be proud nor should they be ashamed of what they are. They are what they are. If they are Hutus, they are Hutus. If they are Tutsis, they are Tutsis. Everybody has to learn to accept the facts of who they are and live peacefully with everybody else,' he said.

Whatever that means.

Another non-French-educated civil servant was more understandable. The new government, he said, comprised both Hutus and Tutsis. The first thing they did was to abolish the system of ethnic identity cards – even though everybody probably knew who everybody was anyway. That done, they had now started rebuilding from the bottom up. It was a long process.

But don't be fooled. The killing continues. There are still Hutus who believe they did no wrong, they didn't kill enough Tutsis, they should continue killing them. Once the massacres were over, those murderers who could, fled. To Uganda. To Burundi. To Congo. Their aim is still to wipe out the Tutsis, recapture power then encourage people throughout Africa to rise up and massacre their neighbours, burn down government buildings, attack schools, ambush vehicles and free anyone suspected of genocide.

In Uganda they call themselves the Army for the Liberation of Rwanda. From their hideouts in the Rwenzori Mountains in the west of the country, they attack villages, swoop down on government offices and steal whatever they can lay their hands on. They've also attacked and killed foreign tourists. And whenever they get the chance, they kill Tutsis.

In Congo they call themselves Armed People for the Liberation of Rwanda. In a country torn by civil war, where there is no such thing as the law they do whatever they like. Attacking villages. Raping. Pillaging. And whenever they get the chance, they kill Tutsis.

In Burundi, it's almost a replay. Attacking. Stealing. Raping. Pillaging. And whenever they get the chance, they kill Tutsis.

My last evening in Killgali: the hotel is full of fat, varicose-veined old biddies going on and on about the gorillas in Volcanoes National Park. Massacres? What massacres? Genocide? What genocide? All they were interested in was sweating and panting their way halfway up a mountain while munching their organic carrot sticks, to cough and sneeze and breathe all kinds of potentially deadly germs over a bunch of innocent gorillas.

Diane Fossey, I can tell you, has a lot to answer for. If she was really interested in helping the gorillas, protecting them from the ravages of the modern world, especially the most varicose-veined members of it, she should have kept quiet about them. Not help to turn them into a wheezing, panting, middle-aged has-beens' tourist attraction. *Gorillas in the Mist*? The amount of fags she got through every day, it was probably cigarette smoke.

No. I didn't go and see them. For the same reason I didn't go to the Galapagos Islands. The only way to preserve gorillas and their unique way of life is for nobody but nobody to go and gawk at them and risk killing them off not with a bullet but by infecting them with colds, flu, measles, polio, scabies and a whole host of other bacteria.

To escape – I don't particularly want to catch their bacteria either – I did my usual. I made for the bar. Mr America was there in his back-to-front baseball cap, T-shirt, jeans and bumpers. He was insisting to the waiter that if he ordered a Coke, he wanted it brought to his table. In the bottle. Unopened. He was frightened of being poisoned.

I nod weakly and sit in the farthest possible corner away from him.

One of the waiters brings me the wine list. Old habits die hard. I always go for the wine first then the food.

The waiter is not exactly tall but he's not exactly short either. He's not fat but he's not slim.

'So are you a Hutu or a Tutsi?' I ask him.

'I'm a Rwandan,' he says.

Kampala

Uganda is where it all started. Along the banks of Lake Victoria. Some even say it was in Kasensero, a tiny fishing village up in the west towards the border with Tanzania. In 1986. Go to Kasensero today and most people will tell you that truck drivers and traders brought it across the border about ten years before. At the time Uganda and Tanzania were practically at war. Everybody was smuggling everything. Everybody was struggling to survive. Women were the first to be affected. Then the children. They began losing weight. People called it the 'slims disease'. Then the young men living in the huts on the beach. Single. Alone. Working in the fishing boats by day. Hanging round the bars by night.

At first families tried to care for the sick. But as more and more people became infected it became more and more difficult. Those who were sick were left to die. Those who were not, and those who thought they were not, fled. To other villages in Uganda. To Tanzania. To Zaire.

Today it is the biggest killer of all time, the worst epidemic in history. Over 20 million have already died. Forty million people are infected. A further 5 million are infected every year. At the very least around 68 million men, women and children will die of AIDS in the next twenty years. In sixteen countries in sub-Saharan Africa one in ten are infected. In seven, one in five. Over 95 per cent of the world's AIDS orphans are African.

In Namibia by 2010 life expectancy will be thirty-four. In Swaziland it will be thirty-three. In Botswana, the country with the highest rate of infection, life expectancy will be around thirty years and falling. Across the whole of Africa life expectancy will be back at levels that have not been seen since the end of the nineteenth century. What's more, children born in 2010 will, in many countries, have a life expectancy of only twenty-seven. Five countries – Botswana, Mozambique, Lesotho, Swaziland and South Africa – will have negative population growth. The dying will outnumber the children being born.

With over six thousand people a day now dying of AIDS, over 2 million a year, eventually over half the population of Africa will be wiped out by the disease. As if that's not horrifying enough, even more horrifying is the fact that only 4 per cent of all sufferers can obtain treatment.

Today Kasensero is back to the way it was before AIDS struck. The fishing business is booming. The rows of wooden huts on the beach are still full of young men. The trucks still trundle backwards and forwards to Tanzania and Zaire and goodness knows where else. But this time with the highest infection rates in the world everybody knows what it's all about. Except one man I met who was wandering up and down and looking at the fishing boats. He told me there was no such thing as AIDS. It was a rumour spread by Americans in order to sell condoms.

Not that people are not still dying of AIDS.

Not that they are not still living with the consequences. That is, the old and infirm. Usually women. For most of the younger generation, their sons and daughters, are dead.

Not that it has changed their way of life at all. Sex is still virtually indiscriminate, if that's not a contradiction in terms. Polygamy is rife. Even worse, age-old traditions continue: like circumcision, when a single knife can be used on hundreds of boys during just one ceremony in one village. And then used again and again on goodness knows how many other boys in how many other villages.

Wherever you go you seem to see grandmothers, great-grandmothers – who knows how old they are? – desperately struggling to bring up three, four, maybe five children. With nothing at all. No money. No food. The occasional food parcel. It's unbelievable.

Sure there are aid organisations in the area doing fantastic work. But even though the problem may be off the front pages it's getting worse and it's going to continue getting worse. People are still dying of AIDS. Some say anything up to 40 per cent of all women are infected. The number of children orphaned – infected and not infected – is increasing all the time. Aid organisations are unable to cope. Hospitals. Clinics. Orphanages. They are giving up in despair. Almost.

In one hospital I saw no end of people with vacant eyes, pink lips, ashy skin, shrunken bodies, covered in boils, lying on straw mats on the floor, dying day by day under a rough hand-painted sign advertising coffins. Those that can't afford coffins – and most AIDS victims and their families in Uganda cannot afford coffins – go home to their villages to die. By public transport. Get on a public bus outside a hospital in Uganda and it's not unusual to see people stepping over a virtual skeleton curled up on the floor by the door. Once back in their villages, if they have survived the bus journey, they can be buried: maybe wrapped in tree bark if there is someone to care for them, otherwise in the rags in which they died.

Then, of course, there are all the implications. If AIDS has wiped out almost a whole generation in Africa, not only will there be fewer farmers cultivating less land and producing less crops but also fewer workers in the towns and cities. In Uganda what few successful companies they have are finding it virtually impossible to recruit good people. When they find them they recruit two to do the job of one. In case one dies. When they can't find people, good or bad, production suffers, the company suffers, employment suffers, maybe the company goes bust.

Now the scary bit. If so many people are dying of AIDS; if so many farms and businesses are finding it impossible to find people; if food companies are going to find it difficult to produce and distribute enough food; if drugs and medical supplies companies are going to find it difficult to manufacture drugs and medical supplies; if schools cannot find enough teachers; if by the year 2005, as many people estimate, there are going to be in sub-Saharan Africa 1 million, maybe 2 million orphans under the age of fifteen, desperately poor, disadvantaged, quite possibly already sick, with no hope of a job, no future, what's going to happen to the already overstretched, desperately underfunded, already grossly corrupt police, security and military forces in Africa? Because logic dictates that if the forces of law and order in a country break down, what order there is will break down. Then what?

One government official told me Uganda had nothing to fear. The number of people who were HIV positive had been miraculously slashed under President Museveni from 30 per cent in 1990 to 6.1 per cent today. I checked the figures with the London School of Hygiene and Tropical Medicine. The figures, they told me, were loaded. They came not from the whole population but from testing pregnant women seeking treatment at urban health clinics. Which is hardly representative of the population as a whole.

I asked one Ugandan government minister whether the figures were correct or not, what plans they were drawing up for such a situation. He told me AIDS was a judgement of God.

'If God means us to suffer and die from AIDS, we will suffer and die from it. If he means us not to suffer and die, we will not suffer and die. Taking precautions, therefore, is wrong. It is frustrating the will of God.'

Well, that's all right then. A firm hand on the tiller for the rough squalls ahead.

I asked a tribal chief the same question.

The Kingdom of Buganda, one of Uganda's largest traditional monarchies, he told me, had the matter well in hand. For every man who remains a virgin until his early twenties, they will give him a few head of cattle. For every woman, a fridge or an oven.

I first saw the beginnings of AIDS in west Africa. Then the talk was of Zaire, Kimbale National Park, Uganda, green monkeys, *Pan troglodytes*, wild cats, infected animals being killed for human consumption. Nobody seemed to know what it was. Except that it was deadly and it was growing. Then gradually it began to take hold. Each time I went back to Zaire, Togo, Benin, and, of course, South Africa – all the countries that denied they had it – more and more of my friends, colleagues, fellow slaves had died. Or just disappeared. Most people said it was TB, malaria, sleeping sickness – or that they had just died.

Over the last ten years more and more countries have started to try to come to grips with it. But it's impossible. They have no money. What money they might have had has long since disappeared. They have no facilities. What hospitals they have are already desperate and full to overcrowding. Rightly or wrongly, AIDS victims are pushed to the back of the long, long queue. Invariably what happens is that they crawl into a corner in their homes, back in their village – or just anywhere – and wait to die.

Not that AIDS is the only killer in Africa. There are plenty of others. It's just that AIDS is the biggest. Take sleeping sickness. Over three hundred thousand people die of it every year. Most of them like AIDS victims, alone, in a corner. The drugs companies are not even bothering to find a cure for it.

'Look,' one big drug company official told me. 'Its simple.

We're a public company. We've got shareholders, the stock exchange, analysts, brokers on our backs. Employees want wage rises. What would you do? Develop high-priced, highly profitable drugs for the 80–85 per cent of the world that can afford to pay for them or develop drugs for Africa, 1 per cent of our market, which can't afford to pay for them?'

I was going to explain that to my friend, a teacher who lived just outside the capital, Kampala. But by the time I got there he was dead.

As if being the birthplace of AIDS is not enough for one country to bear, poor landlocked Uganda has plenty more to put up with. Being discovered by the British. Labelled by Winston Churchill the 'Pearl of Africa'. First choice of the Zionists for their Promised Land. Location for *The African Queen*. The raid on Entebbe. Idi Amin, who in nine bloody years, while the world looked the other way, was responsible for the murder of more than three hundred thousand people. The inspiration for *Private Eye*'s famous euphemism 'Ugandan relations', which was apparently inspired by a famous one-legged Ugandan diplomat on the run – if such a thing is possible – from Idi Amin, a famous woman journalist and an infamous upstairs room in a London house where people had gathered supposedly to discuss Ugandan relations.

I first went to Uganda around 1976. It was a couple of weeks after a group of overnight Israeli visitors shot up Entebbe airport the way they do and made off with a plane and its passengers. The plane I was in stayed parked on the tarmac long enough for me to find out where I was: -NT--BE. Which in itself, given the times we were then living in, was an achievement. It was also long enough to see that the terminal building, such as it was, was hardly there; that an awful lot of cleaning up had to be done and that perhaps it wasn't such a bad thing to be stuck on the tarmac and not allowed to get out of the plane after all.

Years later I went back. Things had changed dramatically. Partly because it was a different airport. A new Entebbe airport had been built just up the runway from the old -NT--BE airport.

In the distance was Lake Victoria, source of the Victoria Nile and the largest lake in Africa, the greatest of Africa's Great Lakes. But all was not as peaceful as it seemed.

Beware, I was warned before I had left the airport: if you don't get snared by the weeds, the arms and the legs will get you.

The lake is gradually being strangled by a dense mat of twisted and tangled water hyacinth, which, if anything, is more twisted and more tangled than Uganda's own government bureaucracy. In fact in many places it is so matted and so dense that not only government ministers but even the lowliest peasants and journalists can walk on the water.

The arms and legs turned out to be more of a problem. Wander around the lake and you're likely to trip over one or the other. In the six months before my visit, forty people had been killed by man-eating crocodiles. Bits and pieces were being found all over the place. Worse still, bits and pieces were dropping out of the air. Not because of flying crocodiles but because of a Gulfstream GI jet. It hit a man as it was taking off from Goma, Zaire and splattered bits of his body all the way to Entebbe. When a leg landed in the playground of a school at Lubandi, a fishing village, the children fled in panic. The police were called. They immediately put the leg in a polythene bag and filed it at the local police station with a note, 'This leg is a sensitive case that carries international concern so do not bury it too soon.'

Legs apart, if that's the correct phrase, the surrounding countryside is, unusually for Africa, a green and very pleasant land. The climate is not too hot, not too cold. The people are calm, quiet, reserved, maybe a touch nervous and hesitant. In fact, most of them are so calm, quiet, reserved, nervous and hesitant that you often wonder whether they understood what you were saying. The answer is, they did. That's just the way they are. Hence Churchill's praise in his potboiling *My African Journey*: 'For magnificence, for variety of form and colour, for profusion of brilliant life – plant, bird, insect, reptile, beast – for the vast scale, Uganda is truly the pearl of Africa.'

Most expats who've left for one reason or another tend to agree. Almost without exception they regret the day either they had to leave or decided it was time to leave. The capital, Kampala, is much the same: calm, quiet, reserved. Nothing like Lagos or Kinshasa or Jo'burg, where every second you expect to be your last. Named after Kasozi K'mpala, which means either 'the hill of antelopes' or 'the seven hills' depending on whom you talk to, this is where in 1890 Frederick D. Lugard, British civil servant extraordinaire, first planted his desk and started writing things in triplicate; in triplicate, in triplicate; rather than down in the 'wet and dirty hollow' where the local chief, the Kabaka, no doubt for reasons of his own, had suggested he should go.

As if that wasn't insult enough to the ruler of the country, courteous, respectful British civil servant that he was, Lugard put off visiting the Kabaka, who was used to people bowing and scraping and kneeling before him, until the following day when he turned up as any British civil servant would when paying homage to a foreign dignitary: in his pyjama jacket (admittedly with brass buttons added for the occasion and a pair of what he described as 'comparatively sound Melton cords'). To add insult to injury, if that was possible, he took his own chair along with him so that there would be no nonsense about a swashbuckling British civil servant having to stand in front of the royal presence any longer than was necessary.

(Had he to pay his respects to the present Kabaka, Lugard probably wouldn't have bothered to turn up. For His

Excellency, King of the 8-million-strong Bugandans, the country's largest ethnic group, is Cambridge dropout and former South London door-to-door double-glazing salesman, Ronald Mutebi.)

Having done the necessary minimum, Lugard, who claimed that 'it was the dream of every Ugandese to possess an opera glass and a white ass', swashed and buckled his way across east Africa hunting down the slave traders on Lake Nyasa before conquering Uganda almost singlehanded, persuading the big chief, the Mwanga, to give in without a fight, tracking down the Muslims, marching across country to the west, surviving the ensuing civil war and finally peacefully putting the country back together again.

As if that wasn't enough to keep him occupied, he wrote his Ugandan memoirs, *The Rise of Our East African Empire*, which when it was published in 1893 got rave reviews from practically everyone. *The Times* said that it was 'the most important contribution that has yet been made to the history of East Africa'. After it was published it was discovered that the honest, upright, incorruptible Lugard had approached *The Times*'s honest, upright, incorruptible lady book reviewer prior to publication and suggested that he would be more than pleased if she said she liked his book. She might be more than pleased too, he hinted. The editor, Flora Shaw, when she found out about the approach and the perhaps not too subtle suggestion, railed against Lugard for trying to interfere with their precious editorial independence, the freedom of the press and everything editors are always going on about. She also decided to get her revenge on her honest, upright, incorruptible lady book reviewer. A couple of years later she married Lugard. Which says a lot for her editorial independence. From Lugard's point of view, it was a hell of a way to get a good review. And something I will most definitely bear in mind.

Go to the British Fort established by Lugard and they won't

let you near the place. It's the site of a new mosque being built by the good Colonel Gaddafi for his Muslim brothers in Uganda.

First the security guards who are crawling all over the mosque – which is more half-built than half-finished – told me I had to get permission from the boss before they could open the metal gates barring my entry.

'The boss?'

For a moment I thought they meant the Colonel himself. In Africa, let me tell you, that would not have been a surprise. Instead they meant the boss of the building site, who turned out to be some official in the hospital down the road. I thanked everybody profusely, shook as many hands as I could, and headed for the hospital.

'No way,' said the boss, who looked part doctor, part secret service man and part terrified about taking any decision at all.

'No way?' I queried.

'No way,' he repeated. 'National security.'

'National security,' I couldn't help but splutter. Even after a million years in Africa there are still some obvious things that come as a complete surprise. 'But the ruins are over a hundred years old. They—'

'National security,' he repeated.

'So who will give me permission?'

'The Voice of Africa.' (The all-Africa radio station.) 'The director there. He will give you permission.'

I didn't say a word.

All I can tell you is I did as I was bid. I went to the Voice of Africa. They didn't know what the Gaddafi I was talking about. But they promised to do their best to get me permission to visit the hundred-year-old ruins.

Knowing how concerned disinterested radio stations are about questions of national security, I took a turn around the city, which I soon wished I hadn't because it's nowhere near as good as its publicity. It's full of too many memories.

First, the hotels. The Sheraton Hotel was once the Apolo, after Apolo Milton Obote. It was said that he used to come here with his victims and throw them off the roof. Somehow I didn't feel like a drink. Next the Nile Hotel, previously the Nile Gardens, once a favourite torture centre for Amin's enemies. Didn't feel like a drink there either. I tried the deserted, practically derelict railway station. I met no end of Indians whose grandfathers and great-grandfathers were rounded up in their thousands by the British in India and shipped out to east Africa to build the 500-mile railway line from Mombasa to Kampala to open up the interior. Didn't feel like a drink there either.

I also checked out the Kasubi Royal Tombs – one thousand years old. A sacred site in the eyes of all Bugandans. A place of reverence. Except they had recently woken up to discover that part of the site had been bought by a fuel company. But, Uganda being Uganda, nobody knew who had sold it to them. Nobody was owning up either.

'Shocking,' Mr Rainbow, the director, told me. 'It's like somebody selling your Westminster Abbey.'

I went back to Voice of Africa.

'Excuse me. I wonder if—'

'No.'

'Thank you.'

Some say Uganda is a big success story. The President, Yoweri Museveni, is supposed to be one of the African greats.

'Because he's like Mandela?' I asked one serious African professor who looked as though he enjoyed nothing more than a good chew on human placenta.

'No,' I was firmly told. 'Because his name begins with the letter *M*. Like . . .'

Mathieu Kerekou (Benin);
Mbasogo (Equatorial Guinea);
Mbeki (South Africa);

Meles Zenawi (Ethiopia);
Mkapa (Tanzania);
Moi (Kenya);
Muammar Gaddafi (Libya);
Mubarak (Egypt);
Mugabe (Zimbabwe);
Muluzi (Malawi).

Of course, why didn't I think of that?

Museveni waged a popular, well-organised guerrilla war and in January 1986, after Amin fled to exile in Saudi Arabia, entered Kampala and seized power. He turned the country around. He gave it a new constitution, an independent judiciary, a free press. An ex-Marxist revolutionary, he became one of capitalism's biggest supporters. The economy began to boom. Inflation began falling. The Asians came back. Or at least some of them. Nile breweries started up again. Exports – 75 per cent of which is coffee – began rising.

Then he should have quit when he was at the top. Like Mandela. But he stayed on. Inevitably things turned sour.

Sure, they now have more than their fair share of Mercedes. Sure, there are some fancy new buildings in Kampala squeezed between the tin shacks and the cripples lying on the pavement. Sure, it takes only two and a half hours in the morning and three hours in the evening to stop-go-stop-stop-go drive past Makerere University, the oldest and some – usually University spokesmen – say the most prestigious university in east Africa. Sure, there are not so many power failures and telephone breakdowns as there used to be. Now it's one or the other. If the power is on, the telephones are off. If the phones are on, the power is off.

The economy is also suffering big time. In spite of everything, all the hype, all the promise, it's still one of the poorest countries in the world: annual per capita income is around

US$200; two-thirds of the population lives on nothing or next to nothing.

The government welshes on one bill after another: it's contribution to the East Africa Community, Organisation for African Unity, its annual subscription to *West Africa* magazine. Its embassies, where they are still open, spend half their time dodging their bills, desperately trying to stop the gas, electricity and water from being cut off and plugging gaping holes in the roof to stop the rainwater from pouring in.

There's no money for the police. In Kampala, which is plagued with not only small- but also big-time robberies involving the use of some heavy weaponry, the anti-robbery squad not only has no bulletproof vests, it has no transport. Neither does the CID. The whole police force has only six cars. All of them riddled with bullets. Not surprisingly they can barely cope. If they manage to turn up at the scene of the crime the same week it has taken place either those responsible have disappeared or they've been caught, stripped and beaten by mobs in the street. In April 2002 the police practically had to shut up shop altogether. They'd run out of money. The government, conscious of what it could mean to the gentlemen in balaclava helmets with heavy weaponry, immediately voted them Ugandan Shillings 809 million instead of the Ugandan Shillings 2 billion they should have got. In other words, they were robbed.

It's the same story in the hospitals. Talk to the doctors at the dirty, dingy, dilapidated Mulago Hospital, almost opposite the brand-new, sparkling Ministry of Health, with the car park full of fancy sports utility vehicles, gleaming gold letters on the gate and lifts that actually work. The doctors will tell you they need Ugandan Shillings 1 billion a year to provide three meals a day to their 1500 and more patients, which is a derisory couple of cents per patient per meal. All they receive from the government is Ugandan Shillings 300 million.

'So what do you do?' I asked one doctor, an Asian, whose family were thrown out by Amin. They went to England, bought a newsagents in Leicester and started all over again.

'What can we do? We only give patients one meal a day,' he said.

'But can patients survive on one meal a day?'

'They survive,' he said. 'They have to. Like the man who had his right leg amputated. When he came round after the operation the first thing he said to me was, Doctor, can you find somebody to buy my right shoe? They survive.'

Obviously so does the Leicester sense of humour.

Not being able to pay the police and hospitals is shocking. Even more shocking was the way the government paid for President Clinton's barnstorming visit for a regional summit of east and central African leaders at which he lavished praise on Museveni: by stopping all government employees' salaries for three months. If the Americans knew that was the price of getting Clinton a couple of positive headlines in the world's press, they didn't say so. Neither did they mention to the Ugandans that although Clinton was forever going on about the immense steps Uganda had made in healthcare, the State Department had warned his party not to kiss anyone during the entire trip and to keep their lips 'pursed' in the shower.

Finally, as is always the case in Uganda, the Asians. Many of them may have come back but few have received compensation for their homes, their offices, their factories, their farms, their land. Government officials say it's because they cannot prove they owned their homes, their offices, their factories, their farms, their land. Others say their property was not seized by the government but sold by the Asians before they left. The Asians say it's the age-old Africa problem. But what can they do?

One Asian family I first met in London had problems

claiming compensation for a boot and shoe factory they owned. They had all the papers. But it didn't seem to make much difference. Government officials said it didn't mean a thing. They could have stolen the papers. They could have forged them. The fact that the factory made boots for the military and had been taken over by a bunch of officers didn't help matters either.

Whether they've got their rightful compensation or not the Asians who have come back seem to be more low-key than ever. Sure you can see the dukas (the tiny Indian shops) all over the place. The big companies, however, are usually hiding behind non-Asian names, sometimes even Ugandan names, and you can bet your life the extra-smart guys are operating behind local partners.

Oh yes, and that puddle at the junction between Sir Apollo Kagwa Road, one of the city's busiest roads, and Kyadondo Road is no longer a puddle. It's a huge ocean of water. Something else they didn't have the money to sort out.

I decided to try Africa Radio again.

'Excuse me—'

'No.'

'Thank you.'

As for 'the rocks and weeds of a corrupt system' that Museveni promised to clear away and replace with the 'mustard seed of freedom and democracy', they're still very much there. Government ministries continue to just lose over US$20 million a year. Where it goes, nobody seems to know or care. In spite of a law compelling politicians to declare not only their own personal wealth but also that of their wife or husband and every child under eighteen, nobody bothers. Local councils invariably place all their contracts with local councillors.

Talk to practically anybody in any of the top restaurants in Kampala – the Fang Fang in Communications House, Kampala Road, the Haandi in Commercial Plaza on Lower

Kampala Road – and you hear amazing stories about Museveni's much trumpeted privatisation programme.

- An Ethiopian company was in the running to take over one of the city's top hotels. They were heavily pressurised to hand over the necessary readies to facilitate the deal.
- A Malaysian company had bought a finance company over the heads of a group of Ugandans for a fraction of what it was worth.
- A food company had been sold not to the highest bidder, a Kenyan company, but to the second-highest bidder, in which, quite by chance, someone with connections had a controlling interest. Within minutes, against all the rules, they resold the company to another one of the bidders realising no doubt a handsome profit and a big slice of the new much enlarged company.

Wander around Nakasero fruit and vegetable market in downtown Kampala, or any market in the country come to that, and practically everything for sale is copied, counterfeit or plain rotten: chewing gum, food, clothing, CDs. Last time I was there, there was a blue pork scare. Blue (that is, old) pork was being peddled in the markets and on the streets even though the government had warned everybody it could be dangerous.

I picked up one book on a bookstall that must have been the one hundred thousandth copy produced by a clockwork photocopier. The text was so blurry that I thought my eyes were going.

Treat yourself to a couple of head-blowing killer waragis in Club Silk on Second Street or Happyland on Masaka Road. Within two minutes you can be the proud possessor of a university degree. Any university degree. From any university in the world. Road licences. Passports. Gun licences. All kinds of immigration documents. They take a little longer to arrange. Say, the time it takes to knock back three or four waragis.

It's not quite as bad as River Road or, even worse, Kirinyaga Road in Nairobi, where, if you talk to the right people, you can get counterfeit anything you like: packaging for expensive drugs, title deeds, MBA certificates from the university of your choice as well as Kenyan, Ugandan, Tanzanian and even US currency. But it's *almost*.

Add everything together, and corruption, some people estimate, is costing the country way over US$200 million a year, which would make a lot of difference, you must admit, to the police, the hospitals, not to mention the people still living in ramshackle houses along by the Kampala–Port Bill railway line.

I went back to the radio station.

'Erm . . .'

'No.'

'Thanks.'

But what about the important things in life?

I spent one afternoon in the Otimbar in the middle of a mass of shacks on the outskirts of Kampala with five other broken-down married men, sitting around a huge pot of thick, brown sludgy millet beer sipping it slowly through a long wooden straw, contemplating our woes.

One evening I was in the fancy-looking parliament building, which looks like a library in Milton Keynes.

We all agreed on the same things. Is Uganda a democracy? Well, yes. Providing you believe in what they call decision-making by consensus. Is there a government and an opposition? Well, er, yes. But they believe in a spirit of all-inclusiveness. How about freedom of speech? Of course, providing everybody else agrees with everyone else. So it's really a one-party state? A one-party state? No. A one-movement state? Yes. Providing, of course, Museveni agrees? Providing Museveni agrees.

At Makerere University, over a couple of bottles of pombe, a banana beer, which tasted like banana skins crushed in petrol, and roast pork – pombe gives you the hangover, the roast pork cures it (at least that's the theory) – I not only heard the usual enlightened professors you find in any university in the world praising the doubtful virtues of Milton Obote and Idi Amin, I also saw students wearing Obote and Amin T-shirts. Which, I will admit, was a shock.

One professor was praising Idi Amin to the skies. He was a natural leader. He started off as a street boy. He was a Kakwa, one of the smallest and generally regarded as one of the most pathetic tribes in the country. He grew up on the streets of Jinja, about 100 miles from Kampala and home to the King's African Rifles. One day, he was spotted hanging around the barracks. Because of his size – his body not his brains – he was immediately volunteered. Within a couple of years he was Uganda's national heavyweight champion. He was sent out to fight the Mau Mau, which he did with his gloves off. Come 1962 when the Brits up and quit he was a general and a deputy commander of the army. Not because the British thought he was fit for the job but because they didn't. That way they thought they would be invited back to run the show. Fiendishly clever, the Brits, what! Except it didn't happen that way.

Milton Obote, a heavy-drinking Langi like most of the army, became prime minister. For eight years he survived, although many of his subjects did not. In 1966 he abolished the monarchy. He ordered his army commander, Idi Amin, to attack the palace. King Mutesa II, father of Ronald the Cambridge drop-out, the failed double-glazing salesman, escaped by climbing over the walls of the palace. Three weeks later he appeared in Burundi. He was flown to London where he died three years later in Bermondsey, penniless, an alcoholic. His umbilical cord, however, lives on. Carefully preserved for use in Bugandan state ceremonies.

In January 1971 Amin is accused by the press of grabbing

for himself all the cash, gold, ivory and whatever given him by guerrillas trying to oust Mobutu from the then Zaire next door. Obote calls for Amin and asks him to explain himself in writing, obviously thinking that Kakwas can neither read nor write. Ever confident in the superiority of the Langis over the rest of creation Obote flies off to a Commonwealth conference in Singapore. Amin decides this is his chance. Before you can say, 'Goodbye Prime Minister. Don't worry. I'll look after everything while you're away,' he and his fellow Kakwas, backed by the British and the Israelis, who were scared Obote was going Communist, have seized power. The Langi and the Acholi now have to take orders from the despised Kakwas. Those that are left that is. Amin and his fellow Kakwas wiped out most of the key players when they took over.

Up until then, said the professor, Amin was a leader.

From then on it got worse and worse and worse. While Amin became President then Marshal then Field Marshal then President Field Marshal for Life, Conqueror of the British Empire or some such nonsense, over two hundred and fifty thousand people were brutally tortured and murdered.

Most British expats left of their own accord. Asians, who at one time owned up to 90 per cent of the country's businesses, left because they had to. In 1972 Amin just threw them out.

The country went from bad to worse to worse to My God, is John Prescott really running this place? In 1978 Amin attacked Tanzania. Quiet, peace-loving Julius Nyerere turned nasty. He sent his troops to attack Kampala. The day they marched in Amin escaped to Libya. From Libya to Saudi Arabia.

Said the professor, 'Who says Museveni is a great leader? The country is still not back to the position it was in 1972 when Amin threw out all the Asians.'

Yes. But . . .

Having solved the problem of Idi Amin, we started speculating about the bombs that were going off at the time in Kampala.

Some said they were obviously the work of an Islamic rebel group, which seems to me a bit far-fetched. Why would Islamic fundamentalists target Uganda? Why, given the pattern of other Islamic bomb attacks, would it be so small-scale? Others said the bombs were more likely to be the responsibility of the opposition Allied Democratic Forces, which included Islamic fundamentalists among its supporters.

I went to see if my luck had changed at the radio station.

'No.'

I decided to do a Lugard and head up-country. Not to see the mountain gorillas I hasten to add. If they're such rare, precious creatures then it's wrong to do anything that could upset them or jeopardise them in any way at all. They should be left wholly and totally alone. The mere thought of people prepared to pay £600 to see them, to bribe guards to let them closer than the recommended 15-foot exclusion zone they are supposed to observe around the gorillas just because they want to play David Attenborough, is a nonsense. If people want to help the gorillas survive they should leave them alone and instead hand over their £600 to guarantee they're left in peace and quiet.

Instead I thought I'd try and see the black and white rhinos: black rhinos on the west bank of the White Nile and white rhinos on the east bank. They were *almost* completely wiped out during Amin's reign of terror. Now they are on their way back. Whether Yemeni tribesmen will go back to using rhino horn instead of antelope horn or wood and the Chinese will stick to their counterfeit Viagra is, of course, the big question.

I also wanted to check out the rapidly shrinking part of Lake Victoria that borders Kenya and Tanzania and is still open to shipping and fishing. The question the Ugandans keep asking themselves is how come Kenya takes twice as much fish from the lake and has more filleting and processing plants than Uganda and Tanzania combined when the lake is split up between them 6 per cent to Kenya, 45 per cent to Uganda and 49 per cent to Tanzania? Smart guys, the Ugandans.

But I didn't do either. I didn't take enough money with me. Sure, I had dollars, but I mean real money, Ugandan money. Not just shillings, but bundles of shillings. A beer? That'll cost you three and a half bundles. Change? What are you talking about change? Food and drink? At least ten, maybe twelve bundles. Fuel? Maybe twenty, twenty-five. Change? What are you talking about change? In other places you need so many bundles to buy anything, you have to buy and sell by weight. A filthy glass of filthy water? That's 5½ lbs of notes please.

In a shack by the side of the road somewhere up towards Masindi I told one villager who could only afford half a filthy glass of filthy water that it was the same in Germany after the war. Money was worth so little they needed a wheelbarrow load to buy a loaf of bread.

'They were lucky,' he said. 'They had wheelbarrows. We have nothing.'

Further on I came across a village in which I saw women cooking bananas and making soup out of nothing at all. Around them men were making shoes out of burnt-out shreds of rubber tyres. In one hut they showed me what they called their DIY toilet roll factory. They collected unused bits of toilet roll from all over. They then unrolled and re-rolled them again with other unused bits to make complete rolls. The complete rolls they then sold back to a brother, a sister or even the cousin of a friend at the hotels. Not the most exciting job in the world. But at least it was helping them to survive.

After that the driver refused to go any further. Not because I'd already run out of money. But because he said it was too dangerous.

Cattle rustlers, he said, were in the area. If it got nasty they could wipe out whole villages, kill anything up to two hundred people at a time, so desperate were they to get their hands on any cattle.

That's not all, he said. Ugandan and Rwandan rebels were still on the loose. They had just killed nearly one hundred people, including eight foreign tourists: four Brits, two Americans and two New Zealanders. They left notes on their bodies saying they did not want British or American tourists on their land because they were on President Museveni's side and not on theirs.

Then there was the Lord's Resistance Army. Even after thirteen years, Museveni, the great guerrilla leader, has still not crushed or found a political solution to the Lord's Resistance Army, which is, they say, backed and supplied with weapons by Sudan because Uganda backs Sudan's own home-grown rebel army, the Sudanese People's Liberation Army. In fact if Museveni weren't Museveni, I'd begin to think suspicious thoughts about why he hasn't defeated them by now.

Said to be forty-five thousand strong – it used to be called the Holy Spirit Army when it was run by Alice Lakwenya who was forced to flee across the border into Kenya – today it is led by a former altar boy Rasta Joseph Kony who wears dreadlocks, dresses in women's clothing and claims he is possessed not only by the Holy Spirit but also by a Chinese general and an Italian priest. As if that's not enough, he also says he speaks directly to God. It's not for me to say who God does or does not talk to, but if that's what you've got to do to be able to speak directly to God what hope is there for the rest of us sober-suited, tie-wearing, boring, short-back-and-sides members of the congregation?

Mr Rasta Joseph Kony's aims? Simple. To wipe out the satanic government of President Museveni.

How he and his army have survived so long I can't understand. It's not a well-equipped, fast-moving modern army. Nobody knows for sure but a fair number of the fighters are reckoned to be children. Maybe five thousand. Maybe ten thousand. Some as young as six. If that's not bad enough they are all abducted from their homes and villages and initiated into the army by being forced to bludgeon to death anyone trying to escape or surrender and then taught how to become natural born killers: how to mine main roads, ambush trucks and convoys, attack village markets, raid and loot churches and destroy and set fire to whole villages.

Given the options – possible capture, possible freedom – I agreed with the driver. We turned round and headed for safety.

Back in Kampala, I went to the radio station.

'No.'

That evening I'm drowning my sorrows in the dank, musty, seedy bar of the so-called Grand Imperial Hotel, which looks more like a Masonic lodge in Leamington Spa, complete with cosy pictures of English country churches, happy fishermen busy mending their nets and tanks of goldfish going round and round in circles. In one corner a group of Ugandans were talking about Idi Amin, the way I guess people in Leamington Spa talk about Mrs Thatcher. In another a group of Indians were talking money. What else?

Suddenly in come a group of Brits who told me they were members of the City of London Territorial Army Regiment. They were celebrating the end of a TA exercise at Archers Post, some secret military training ground near Impala in northern Kenya. We ordered drinks all round.

If what they told me is true – and what they told me all tied up together – it's unbelievable.

The previous Friday evening they were in the UK. They were

told to stand by. At two or three o'clock in the morning they were picked up from their homes by unmarked cars, driven to, they think, an airbase near Oxford, given a kitbag and an envelope that they were told to open when they landed and bundled aboard an unmarked transport plane.

They were flown, they guessed, for five or six hours and then told to parachute out. When they landed they were in rough open country. It was hot. They had no papers. No documents. They were in military uniform. And unarmed. They opened their envelopes. Inside they found an unmarked map with just two reference points. They had to make their way from Point A to Point B. Attached to the map was a note that said they could use any means they wanted. If they were caught, however, they were on their own. Oh yes, and while making their way from Point A to Point B they would face 'friendly fire'.

One of the group told me he guessed where they were. He'd been born and brought up in Kenya, spent all his spare time out hunting in the outback, and knew the place like the back of his hand. He led them from Point A to Point B not by the direct route but by old bush trails he remembered. He thought it would be safer. It was only when they got close to Point B, another unmarked military base, that they realised 'friendly fire' meant live ammunition.

Not only did they survive, they got into the camp and then, the way things go, they decided that instead of staying put and getting a pat on the back for good behaviour they would commandeer a plane and fly to Kampala.

'Well, why not?'

'They told us to use any means at our disposal.'

'If we get caught we'll spill the beans,' they told me. 'Bet the press would like to know Tony Blair's government is dropping British troops from unmarked planes into another country's territory, telling them to do whatever they have to do and to hell with the consequences. Make a good story.'

I tried to interest the local radio station.
'No.'
'And what about—'
'No.'

Lilongwe

> A huge sparkling lake, an infinitely varied landscape and some of the friendliest people on earth, all make Malawi a superb choice of destination for tourists. From the lush green tea estates of Thyolo and Mulanje to the white sand beaches of Lake Malawi, to the zebra and antelope grazed highlands of the Nyika Plateau, Malawi is a stunningly picturesque country with more scenic diversity than most people realise.
>
> Malawi tourist brochure

The babies were stick-thin. Their skin was shiny and wrinkly. They had huge potbellies. What little hair they had was thin and wispy. I was told they were suffering from non-stop diarrhoea.

One kid who had collapsed on the ground had pale, dry skin. His eyelids were puffed up. He had yellow palms, the result of living on mango leaves. He looked as though he had swollen feet.

The adults were worse than skeletons. Exhausted. Apathetic. Barely able to speak let alone move. One old man, who looked a million years old, told me in a long, slow, dying whisper that he was trying to look after three tiny grandchildren. Everybody else in his family was dead. They were trying to survive by eating leaves, bits of grass, tree stems, scraps of bark, sawdust.

Long ago they had dug up the seeds for next year's harvest. He couldn't remember the last time he had had any maize beer.

Two old women who looked like inmates of a concentration camp were desperately trying to dig up the roots of a shrub of a banana tree to make some kind of porridge.

'It'll make them sick,' said the doctor with me. 'But what can they do?'

I was with a group of French technical advisers who were planning to distribute food to the starving. They were talking about logistics, distribution patterns, secure holding centres. Aid had been promised by the European Union, the Dutch, the Japanese, the Canadians, even the British. It wouldn't begin to arrive for five, maybe six months. They wanted everything to be in place so that when it arrived, it could be distributed throughout the country as quickly as possible.

'But why five, maybe six months?' I asked. 'By that time won't they all be dead?'

He shrugged a Gallic shrug.

'Administration,' he sighed.

Twenty minutes away in the capital, Lilongwe, however, the government was still denying that in a country that can easily feed itself there was any kind of food crisis at all.

> Malawi is sometimes referred to as 'Africa for beginners' because relative to other African nations, it is safe, cheap, local transport is good and English is widely spoken. Add to this its compact size and you've got a popular destination for do-it-yourself travellers and backpackers.
>
> Holiday magazine article

Malawi, a land-locked sliver of a country, has everything.

Running the length of it, from north to south, is the Rift Valley, so called because of the rift between the rich and the poor. The rich live up in the cool of the hills. The poor live down in the middle of the valley where at times temperatures can melt your eyeballs. Which surprised me. I had always thought that because it was in the Rift Valley that they had found the oldest human bones ever discovered, the name had something to do with the nature of the relationship that has existed since the beginning of time between men and women. But there's no point falling out over it.

Starting in Mozambique, the valley stretches for over 4000 miles, running through Malawi, Tanzania, Kenya, Ethiopia and across the Red Sea into the Jordan Valley in Israel, which is, of course, the cause of many more rifts in the world. It was here in the Rift Valley near Karonga, by Lake Malawi, that in 1992 archaeologists discovered a 2.5-million-year-old jawbone belonging to *Homo rudolphensis*: *Homo* because the jawbone was remarkably intact, suggesting minimial use which in turn suggested it as belonging to man; *rudolphensis* because the archaeologist who found it had been working for so long in the red-hot sun that his colleagues had, for some reason I cannot imagine, started to call him Rudolph.

Malawi also boasts the third-largest lake in Africa: 300 miles long at its longest point, 40 miles wide at its widest point. It flows into the River Shire and from there down to the Zambesi. To the local Chichewas it was *nyanja*. To Arab traders it was *nyasa*. To marine biologists, it's the Galapagos Islands. As the finches inspired Darwin so out of the millions of different tropical fish in the lake the cichlid fish inspire marine biologists. Apparently different groups of cichlids have been isolated in different areas for so long that they've developed different characteristics. There are over three hundred and fifty other types of fish unique to the lake, including the mouth-breeding chambo fish, so called because the mouth of the female fish is so big that in times of danger all her little fish shelter inside it. I'm not saying a word.

To tourists, however, and unlike most African lakes, it has

everything. Sandy beaches. Bars. Fish eagles. There's even an old steamer, the *Ilala*, which chugs up and down it. It was also here on the shores of Lake Nyasa just over one hundred years ago that Chief Mataka out-Disneyed Disney and created the world's very first theme park: an Arab city, complete with dhows, coconut groves and even mangoes. He made his poor subjects dress up in Arab clothes, eat Arab food and drink whatever they could drink when he wasn't looking.

Then along came the man who was to successfully destroy for ever the lives of the local people: failed explorer, failed missionary, off-duty father and brother, Dr Livingstone. The area he called Nyasaland and the lake, Lake Nyasa. Which it remained until 1966 when with independence Nyasaland became Malawi and the lake, Lake Malawi, a local Chichewa word for 'God save us from interfering, failed Scottish missionaries'.

Much more fun than Livingstone was the local British Consul, Harry Johnston, who drew up a treaty with the local Chief Jumbe, a notorious Arab slave trader, to put an end to the whole sorry business. Johnston suggested to the Foreign Office back in Whitehall that they might thank the old slave trader by sending him a present from Queen Victoria herself. Out came a complete and genuine Staffordshire toilet set engraved V.R.I. Come the presentation, Johnston confided to his diary, 'There was an awkward moment; in the array set forth on Jumbe's great veranda were two vessels not specially ordered by me but supplied almost mechanically in those days with any complete toilet service. "And what are these for?" said the delighted old man: and himself supplying the answer, "I know! One for rice and one for curry!" And to that honourable function they were apportioned in the meal that followed.'

Malawi, deservedly known as the warm heart of Africa due to the friendliness and charm of its people, offers the visitors diversity and outstanding natural beauty.

Hotel chain advertisement

Today Malawi is one of the poorest, most indebted, AIDS-ravaged – one in five, they say, suffer from HIV – famine-stricken countries in the world. A million families live on less than US$50 a year. Debt is higher than their GDP. Unemployment is 40 per cent officially. God knows what it is unofficially. Inflation is around 50 per cent and zooming. With almost 42 deaths per 1000 live births, its child mortality rate is 35 per cent higher than the average rate for less developed countries. Over 50 per cent of all children who survive are stunted by hunger. Life expectancy is next to nothing.

Worse still, if that's possible, in Kasungu, in Nkhotaka, in Ntchisi, in Dowa, in Mchinji, all over the country, over seven million people out of a total population of ten million are slowly and surely starving to death.

Not only is there no food, there is *nothing* to help them.

Clinics long ago ran out of blood to give the dying to try to revive them. Instead they have fallen back on an apparently tried and tested remedy: mashed bananas, which are rich in sodium and potassium.

'But now we're even running out of bananas,' one nurse told me.

What few hospitals there are, are turning away the starving because they can't squeeze any more into their already overcrowded wards and corridors and outhouses. The big problem, one matron who was almost as thin as her patients told me, was whether to boil all the maize for the starving or use some of it to try and trap the monkeys who were ravaging it for food for themselves.

'The crocodile eggs went years ago,' she said.

So, too, had all the tiny black piglets you usually see all over

Africa scavenging around in the rubbish and digging up whatever they can find.

But even if you're in hospital it's no guarantee you'll be taken care of. Most lack even minimal healthcare facilities let alone food. Even when there is food there's no guarantee patients will get any. Another matron, who had a bit more weight on her, told me that as things have got worse, they've found more and more outsiders in the hospitals pretending to be patients or pretending to be visiting patients just to get at the food. So, too, were some of the staff. The patients don't complain because they at least get the leftovers, which is more than they were getting back home in the bush.

I was just twenty minutes from the capital, Lilongwe.

> The atmosphere is highly conducive to interaction between locals and travellers, while a selection of restaurants and bars serve backpacker staples such as pizzas and banana pancakes not to mention the notorious space cakes that regularly land overindulgent travellers in hospital.
>
> Travel magazine article

In another time, and perhaps another place, Lilongwe, or LL as we locals say, would be the perfect garden city. It's small. It's all trees, bougainvillea, oleander, red hibiscus, marigolds, blue acanta and green rolling lawns. The government buildings and offices are all tucked away out of sight. The town centre itself is neat and compact. It's almost like small artificial American country community meets Africa.

Except it's practically empty. The roads are deserted. There's the occasional car or truck. Now and then you see somebody pushing a broken-down bicycle. Why on earth the government slapped giant 'Resist Corruption' posters all over the place I cannot imagine. There's hardly anyone around to see them. In fact, there are so few people around that if the government wants to get its message across they could write to them all individually. It would be cheaper.

Offices are still and silent. Unlike in other African countries you wait all alone for hours on end for Ministers who never come.

The shops are half empty. Many have closed down. Hungry people don't buy fancy furniture, fancy clothes or fancy anything. If they have anything fancy they are more interested in selling it than adding to it. It won't be long before the Big Mama shop becomes the Little Daughter market stall.

Banks are deserted. Even the gaily decorated Central Bank doesn't look as though it has two ten-kwatcha notes to rub together.

The markets, even the big one along Malangalanga Lodge Road, which seemed to sell nothing but shoes, were like an off-day at a car boot sale. Some stallholders were trying to sell wild, exotic, expensive luxuries such as onions, tomatoes, red peppers, chunks of bread. Everything that can be is smuggled across the border to Zambia and Mozambique. As for the stallholders, most of them look like virtual skeletons, eyes half-closed, motionless, expressions blank, hardly able to swat away the flies. Just waiting, waiting, waiting. For customers who would never come. Stretched out underneath one stall I saw a shrivelled-up, greasy bundle of rags shaking with what must have been malaria.

The only place I saw any action was at the Friday and Saturday night raves at the Lilongwe Hotel. But even then, they were not your usual African Friday and Saturday night raves. Try as they might, the odd few couples couldn't seem to work up the enthusiasm. Either that or they could no longer rely on their regular lump of dagga, the super-strong African marijuana, the essential ingredient for any night out on the town.

It was the same story at the Tilipano Leisure Centre at Lumbadzi Trading Centre, which before the famine was famous for its ever co-operative waitresses, its resident Boogie Express band, its surrounding chalets and its non-stop supply of Ziboda, a favourite local hash. When I dropped by – purely and simply in the interests of research – it was more like a female vicar's tea party than the wildest place in town.

As for the hotels, they were all nearly deserted. Many's the time I had dining rooms and restaurants to myself. Once I had a quick guilty lunch at the outdoor restaurant in the Sunbird Lilongwe. There was me, a particularly scratchy hairball waitress and, staring at me, a sign that read Do Not Feed the Fish, which seemed a cruel joke from all points of view.

Here and there, however, I did come across some enthusiasm. Whenever hunger and poverty become more and more desperate, so, too, do the con-men, crooks and tricksters.

Out in the country, apart from the starving and the dying, I seemed to stumble across nothing but witches and sorcerers and all kinds of healers and preachers plying their trade. Some say it's sick. They're taking advantage of the weak. They're after their money. Others say they're bringing help and peace and, more importantly, hope. The trouble begins when witchcraft spills over into killings and even cannibalism.

Malanga village down in the south is said to be a black magic hotspot for witches. The scratchy hairball waitress told me there were around two thousand to three thousand in the area. One, a young man in his late twenties, who wore flowing white robes and carried a Bible in one hand, claimed to have cured over three thousand people. Another, a woman in her early thirties, boasted that she had her own black magic aircraft made of old wicker baskets and various assorted tools and equipment. Some people said that she killed people, mashed them up and sold the meat as if it were batter.

'So have you eaten human meat?' I nervously asked the waitress who had just served me my lunch.

She smacked her thin, skinny lips together.

'It is good,' she grinned. 'Very good. Better than ordinary meat.' She paused as if remembering the delights. 'Delicious.'

Was she telling me the truth?

How can you tell if any woman is ever telling the truth?

Even more amazing was the story she then told me of Nema, a twelve-year-old girl from Chilobwe. By day, she's a model pupil at Ntonya Private Primary School. By night, they say, she preaches and heals the sick. First it was her mother who was suffering from foot fungus. Then it was her sister suffering from malaria. Next a cousin with stomach pains.

'Miracles?' I said.

'Sure,' she said.

I didn't even think of disagreeing.

In towns, the tricks are more down-to-earth, more practical. The most popular seemed to be not Find the Lady but Find the Matchstick. One matchstick under one box.

Shuffle them around. Guess where the matchstick is and say goodbye to what little money you've got left.

Lie, cheat or steal, however, and you'll be either strung up, set alight or hacked to pieces. Or even all three.

As a result Lilongwe is one of the safest cities in Africa. No pickpockets. No muggings. No violent attacks. I thought it was because of a strong police presence, the fear of arrest, the tyranny of the courts. No way. The police work only mornings. There's not enough money to pay them for the rest of the day. But when they do work they make up for it. Inside Lilongwe police headquarters, I was told again and again, it was terrifying.

'Almost akin to the days of Idi Amin,' a retired school teacher told me.

The business capital, Blantyre, up in the Shire Highlands and named after David Livingstone's birthplace in Scotland, I always used to think was a cross between Nairobi and Harare. That's when the phones are working. When the phones are not working – because thieves keep stealing the telephone cables – it's more like Nairobi. As for Blantyre airport, it's fantastic. Whenever I land there I'm always collected by a grand old gentleman wearing a rather faded blazer and sports trousers and taken to the VIP lounge. He settles me down, gets me a drink and then runs off to sort out my tickets and my passport. A great guy. But why he does it I have no idea.

Livingstonia, however, is different again. Founded by Scottish missionaries to celebrate, I mean commemorate the death in 1874 of the old Scottish fraud himself, it is more Deadstonia than anything else. Built on the shores of Loch or rather Lake Nyasa, which the old failure stumbled across in October 1859 convinced, like he was about everything, that it was the source of the Nile, it was at one time the largest town in east Africa. It was also home in 1875 to the biggest hospital, the biggest secondary school, the biggest teacher training college, the biggest seminary and the biggest pile of shoes, socks and shorts south of the equator. Shoes, socks and shorts because the first thing uppermost in the mind of the kilt-wearing Scottish missionaries was to get everybody in shorts as quickly as possible. Although why shorts should be a God-given item of clothing for the Africans but not for the Scots themselves is something I've never fully understood. Every year that goes by, however, it becomes more and more like Scotland. Scotland in the eighteenth and nineteenth centuries when the crofts were falling down, towns were being cleared and the natives were fleeing.

Behind the museum, which has more photographs of white men in pith helmets than there are pound coins in the average sporran, are the remains of what I was told was a once proud Scottish triumph. I thought it was bound to be something or other about Sir Alex Ferguson. Instead it turned out to be Ephesians 2:14 which, let's face it, is from a book whose words are almost as important as those of Sir Alex.

Apparently during Malawi's violent struggle for independence

– so much for the notice the locals took of the old fraud's branch of Christianity – the British dropped an empty tear gas grenade on Livingstonia. A message inside told the locals that if they were safe they should arrange a pile of white stones in the form of an *I*, presumably for Independence. If they were not, they should arrange the stones in the shape of a *V*, presumably for Victory. The Scots, of course, couldn't read, or they were upset by the fact that the empty grenade was English and not Scottish. They arranged the stones to read Ephesians 2:14. The following day the pilots saw the stones, thought it was part of the result of a match between Ephesians and Manchester United and left them to get on with it.

Another thing I don't understand is that around Livingstonia nobody mentions William Livingstone, who ran the place while his brother was on walkabout, and because of his attitude, his behaviour and the way he continually mistreated the Africans was overthrown and beheaded in an uprising led by John Chilembe in 1915. Funny that.

Talking of Livingstone, and who can't when you're talking about Malawi, life on the *Ilala*, which chugs up and down Lake Malawi, has also changed because of the famine. Named after the ferry that Livingstone's porters carried on their backs across the rapids on the Zambesi river, hardly anyone today travels in her mahogany-fitted cabins let alone sleeps on deck as she makes her way from Monkey Bay to Chilinda with its long sandy beaches on the eastern shore of the lake, to Makanjila and Fort Maguire, named after the big cheese who was one of Cecil Rhodes's lieutenants, Rochefort Maguire. From there she swings to the south-western side of the lake, which Livingstone said looked like the 'boot' of Italy. How he thought it looked like the boot of Italy I have no idea. It looks nothing like it. He was either on the blink or he was never there. From there she sails north-east past the Maleri Islands, north to Nankambi Point and then north-west to Nkhotakota, once the largest village in central Africa and a major trading centre for slaves. From Nkhotakota she crosses again back to the eastern shore to Mtengula in Mozambique. From Mtengula she makes for Malawi again and Nkhata Bay, Usisya, Ruarwe, Chiweta and Chilumba in the far north.

I was tempted to make the trip. But I heard so many delightful stories about rats and lake flies, which, as the moon rises, start up out of the larvae in the lake and swirl around by the million in huge clouds, not to mention typhus, that I decided against it. But one day. One day.

Back on dry land it was the same story wherever else I went. Famine. The effects of famine.

If the schools are open, the parents who can send their children to school, don't. They are frightened in case they catch cholera from the other kids. The graduates that are left are forced to study abroad. Both of them. The rest have to make do with the very latest literature distributed by the British Council proclaiming Isabard Kingdom Brunel to be Engineer of the Year.

Industry is pretty basic. One company, Press Corporation Ltd, seems to practically run the place. It's in banking, agriculture, fishing, pharmaceuticals, brewing and retail. But it's pretty much a part-time job. There's an energy sector but it's hardly energetic. Telecoms is hardly communicating . . .

As for travel and tourism, well, they say Tanzania is fantastic. There are few hotels. What hotels there are, are more closed than they are open. The game reserves are shrinking fast. There is so much sand and dust that even the vultures have started walking around looking for their next meal. The animals are also going hungry. Lions are escaping and killing people for food. Elephants and hippos are breaking out and destroying desperately needed crops. Even the anti-poaching squads in their tatty battle fatigues and their rusty old AK-47s are turning against the elephants and hippos in their desperate search for food.

To tell you how bad it is, even the prisoners in Chichiri Maximum Prison have been reduced to one meal a day instead of two.

The only business doing well is the funeral business. Almost every other person I met out in the bush who wasn't suffering from AIDS was busy collecting the dead and burying them as best they could. For a fit man to dig a six-foot hole is a struggle. For a poor, thin, desperately hungry man it's impossible.

In the towns it was more aggressive. The professional funeral parlours were busy fighting off the amateurs.

'These amateurs, they are thugs,' one particularly thuggish-looking so-called professional told me when I came across him propping up a bar in LL in the traditional Irish funeral manner. 'They turn up at houses. They turn up at hospitals. They turn up at mortuaries with vans to take away the bodies. Sometimes the vans are refrigerated. Sometimes they are not. Sometimes they bribe doctors and nurses for the bodies. Sometimes they just steal them.'

I heard in South Africa, similar stories, where even though thousands were dying of AIDS, the President maintained all was well.

In Pretoria, outside their impressive hilltop parliament building, I met by chance one professional funeral director who told me that he had even heard of the amateurs in and around some of the townships burning down people's homes if they refused to let them bury their dead. As for the coffins, they used to be grand, elaborate affairs, wood, lots of fancy decoration. But no more. The coffin makers couldn't keep up with demand. Instead the more upmarket establishments went for cheap, wood-grain-printed cardboard. The downmarket ones for whatever they could get, if they could get anything. In most cases it was just the rags the poor victim lived and died in.

> So often in Africa people are reluctant to be photographed – sometimes taking drastic evasive action when a lens is pointed in their direction – or demanding dollars. Malawi is different. As a photographer your problem is more likely to be ridding your composition of excess, youthful humanity which inevitably gathers in front of a camera.
>
> US holiday magazine article

Drought. Floods. Famine. Even the clothes-loving tsetse fly. If it laid its eggs in your long, thick khaki shorts at night, and the following morning if, in the mad dash of things, you leapt into them without checking, the larvae could be busy nibbling your valuables by lunchtime.

Malawi has had the lot. But the thing that finally broke them was corruption, the government's complete and total mismanagement of the country.

Some blame their first President, the crocodile king, His Excellency The Life President Ngwazi Dr Hastings Kamuzu Banda, who for thirty years until 1994, when the West finally pulled the plug, ruled the place with the verve and zest and enthusiasm of an unreconstructed fascist.

He built a 300-room State House at a cost of US$100 million. With his, er, wife, Mama Tamanda Kadzamira, he set up the enormous, sprawling Press Group of companies, long run by British and South African expats, which at one time controlled more than one-third of the economy. Wearing his regulation black Homburg, his three-piece black suit, his dark glasses and carrying a lion-hair fly-whisk, he would tour the country in a pillar-box red, open-top Rolls-Royce, followed wherever he went by his very own pillar-box-red-shirted Young Pioneers and on special occasions by pillar-box-red-bedecked women wearing fancy Banda dresses, banning everything and everybody under the sun.

He banned Orwell, Baldwin, Malamud, Hemingway,

Tennessee Williams, Donleavy, Graham Greene, Zola and even Wole Soyinka, not to mention over one thousand three hundred and fifty different books.

He banned Jack Mapenje, the country's best poet, their only surgeon and hundreds of others who he thought disagreed with him, his policies, the time of day.

He banned long hair, ham radios, cartoons, guns and television. Under Banda, Malawi was the only country in central and southern Africa not to have television.

He banned anyone who sang or even whistled a pop song called 'Cecilia' by, I am told, some slobberheads called Simon and Garfunkel because of the refrain:

Cecilia
I'm down on my knees
I'm begging you please
To come home.

Innocent enough you would have thought. Except 'Cecilia' was the name of Mama Tamanda Kadzamira. However, it wasn't long before all kinds of 'different' versions were being sung all over the country.

He banned miniskirts. According to the Decency Dress Act 1973, Section 2(a), any woman 'dressed in any clothing which . . . causes . . . to be exposed to view any part of her body between the lower level of her kneecaps and her waist or any under-garment covering such part' could be thrown in gaol. What she was allowed or not allowed to wear above her waist wasn't specified. And the ban was universal. All women, regardless of their age or status, had to wear long skirts. Including women rock-climbers.

He banned anyone who even hinted that he was really born in February 1898 and not 1906 as his official biography says.

The only thing I can forgive him for is he also banned Paul Theroux. Trouble is he deported him. He didn't throw him in gaol.

When he wasn't banning people, Banda also acted as Minister of External Affairs, Minister of Justice, Minister of Works and Supplies, Minister of Agriculture and in his spare time Commander-in-Chief of the Armed Forces.

But even in those days all was not well. Famine was a problem. Over three hundred children per thousand were dying before they were five years old, the same number that were dying in Ethiopia during their great famine.

The West, however, loved him, even though he boasted he had killed his opponents, because he shunned the Soviets.

The World Bank loved him because he repaid all his debts on time.

Mrs Thatcher even went to visit him.

South Africa loved him. During Apartheid he backed them. So pleased were they, they built him an airport terminal at LL.

Israel and Taiwan loved him because he also recognised them when the rest of the world was scared to do so.

Why he ended up the way he did is a mystery. He was born near Kasungu in the tobacco heartland of Central Malawi. He took the name Hastings after the missionary who baptised him at the Livingstonia mission school. He then walked 1000 miles to South Africa. On the way he stopped off in Rhodesia and got a job as a hospital porter. Next he studied medicine in Edinburgh, and graduated in the States with grades as high as 99.45 per cent. His ambition: to return home and work in a hospital in the bush. He applied for such a post. Back came the reply: it was his. Except that he had to undertake not to mix socially with any European doctors or nurses who might be in the same hospital. He turned it down. The reason: a surgeon, he maintained, couldn't operate as a surgeon if he couldn't invite fellow surgeons and doctors into his office to discuss their patients and offer them a cup of coffee.

He ended up in London, became a GP, suffered the agonies of the National Health Service. In 1959 he returned home, fought for independence, was imprisoned, released, and in 1963 became Prime Minister and led the country to independence the following year.

When he was finally voted out of office over thirty years later, he was arrested, accused of the murder in 1983 of three cabinet ministers and put under house arrest. He died in 1997.

> The hotel's patio restaurant is renowned for its international cuisine and intimate ambience. Guests seeking after dinner entertainment will find a live band at the hotel bar, seven nights a week.
>
> Malawi tourist brochure

Even though he never used the 300-room State House built by Banda, I blame the chubby, jovial Bakili Muluzi Chatonda wa Chatonda, the Conqueror of the Conqueror, the man who beat Banda to become President in 1994.

In some ways he's like Banda. Wherever he goes his glee club goes too, M'bumba women singing and dancing his praises. 'Who is your President!' sings one half of them. 'Bakili, Bakili,' sings back the other half. The men, they form guards of honour, bow and scrape and laugh at all his little jokes.

On the other hand, you have to say that things have got a million times worse under him. He says it's all been got up by the international press. There were one or two shortages. A few people were unfortunately suffering. The problem was under control. The international press says, What about the limos?

The first time I went to Malawi I hardly saw one. The next time they were about as common as lake flies on Lake Malawi. Not only that but each government minister was also being given

2000 litres of fuel every month. Free. Enough to drive 10,000 miles, the whole of the length of Africa. Twice. Or, if you prefer, enough to build forty classrooms. In fact, it had got so bad that even the ethically driven British government and its Deputy Prime Minister, who cannot move without the aid of at least two Jags, decided to make the hesitant, nervous suggestion that unless something was quite possibly considered they very well might be minded to give thought to the millions they every year push into the pockets of government ministers, I mean, donate in aid.

The result: the President, would you believe, promptly fired the whole government. Some say it was because they wanted to stick with the super-smooth Mercedes. Others say it was because a number of ministers took notice of what the Deputy Prime Minister said and wanted to ditch their single Mercs for two Jags. Either way, they were on the bus home and the government Mercs were up for sale, with the President proclaiming loudly that the government would ensure that the proceeds went directly to a wide range of poverty-reduction programmes. Whose poverty-reduction and whose programmes were not specified.

I asked the government official if he could let me have the details when they were announced. But he didn't hold out much hope. The information was hidden in the Presidency, which was, he told me, five miles away 'as the crow walks'.

After limos came the Land Rovers. Why were eighty-odd government Land Rovers bought not from the official franchise holder but from another dealer? Nobody would say.

The President then says he is dedicated to serving the people of Malawi. Malawi has one of the most vibrant democracies in Africa. His critics say, OK. Why have journalists critical of his policies been beaten up? Why have judges been impeached? Why have opposition MPs and human-rights activists been subject to regular harassment? Why does he ignore the court ruling that says his ban on street demonstrations is unconstitutional? Why does he want to change the Constitution so that he can serve three terms instead of two?

The President says he is doing everything in his power to solve the problems the country is facing and there is no man better able to do it than him. His critics say, OK. So why, after years of providing Malawi with one of the world's largest aid flows per capita, are donors now pulling out when the situation is getting so much worse by the day? Why has the UK suspended budget support? Why have the Danes pulled out? Why has even UNICEF stopped funding the Save the Children Fund Malawi, the largest and oldest charity in the country? Not only that, why did it even demand the return of the Toyota truck it had given them? Run the country on a proper basis, establish proper management controls, root out corruption, they say, then we'll come back.

Finally the President says genetically modified crops are wrong. He refuses to distribute to the starving crops

- the World Food Programme, the World Health Organisation, the Food and Agriculture Organisation say is safe,
- the European Commission says is safe,
- Greenpeace says countries should accept if they are the only alternative to starvation,
- that have passed US food safety and environmental impact testing, the most vigorous in the world,
- that millions of Americans have been chomping every day since 1995 without any harm. Well, not too much harm.

His critics say:

- Tell that to the babies who are as thin as sticks, whose skin is all shiny and wrinkly, who have enormous potbellies and who are suffering from non-stop diarrhoea.

- Tell that to the kids collapsed on the ground, their eyelids puffed up, their palms yellow from eating mango leaves, their feet beginning to swell.
- Tell that to the adults who are worse than skeletons, who are exhausted, apathetic, who can barely speak let alone move.
- Tell that to the old man desperately trying to look after three tiny grandchildren by feeding them leaves, bits of grass, tree stems, scraps of bark and even sawdust.
- Tell that to the seven million people slowly dying of starvation.

Malawi has a Lilongwe to go.

Port Louis

The land of the dodo is no longer the land of the dodo. It's the rest of Africa that's the dodo. Over the last twenty years Mauritius, where the dodo found fame when it became the first species to be completely wiped out by man – the last one was eaten by shipwrecked Dutch sailors in 1662. Who can blame them after all that Edam? – has turned itself very much into a booming do-do country of the future. Not only is it home to more five-star hotels and resorts than anywhere else in the world – charter flights are definitely out – it also has more upmarket restaurants. Their fried wasp larvae is fantastic. Mauritius is also Africa's most successful economy, the top of the World Economic Forum's Africa Competitive Report and the place to go if you want to make money in Africa. Legally, that is. In fact, it's the nearest Africa has come to producing anything like Singapore is to south-east Asia or Hong Kong is to China.

The capital, Port Louis, looks and feels like an Asian Tiger. It's like a tiny enclave – it covers only 45 square kilometres – squeezed between the coast and a surrounding semicircle of mountains. During the day there are so many people tearing around that you're lucky to see anything. Its population of around one hundred and fifty thousand almost doubles in size. It's like Singapore with a human face, Hong Kong without the humidity.

The main square, the Place d'Armes, immediately facing the sea might sound French but it definitely feels British. Solid. Four square. Respectable. So, too, are Government House, the Supreme Court and all the banks around it.

The Waterfront, with its bars and restaurants, is more American. It wouldn't look out of place in Baltimore or any one of a dozen recently restored, rebuilt, refurbished US waterside cities. But the real fun, as always, are the back streets and the racecourse. The back streets, especially Chinatown, is where all the real money is made from, they say, importing brown sugar from India. Brown sugar? Drugs. Don't you know anything? The racecourse, which is just about in the centre of town, is equally addictive and probably responsible for destroying more lives, admittedly in a far more exciting way. One of the oldest racecourses in the world – it was founded in 1812 – the thing I like about it is that if you lose all your money you haven't got far to walk back to your hotel. Not that I gamble. I gambled only once in my life. Never again.

On the business front, its factories are among the best in the world, churning out crisp cotton shirts for trendsetters like Marks and Spencer, cuddly woollen sweaters for House of Fraser and Austin Reed and everything it's best not to imagine for Miss Selfridge.

It's a major supplier to the worldwide jewellery industry. They make the millions of tiny bits and pieces that go to make your rings, ear-rings, brooches, all the nonsense you hang round your neck, stick up your nose or use to pierce all kinds of places. They also do women's jewellery.

Publishing: they do all the clever, technical pre-production work for major worldwide publishers. Type setting. Layouts. Proofing. Boring low-tech printing is done elsewhere.

Gambling. Want to bet on American baseball? One of the biggest American baseball betting companies is based in – where? – Mauritius.

A tiny volcanic island off Madagascar, off the east coast of Africa – Mombasa, Kenya is around 1800 kilometres and thirty years away. At least. It's where Africa, Europe and Asia come together: Hindus, 51 per cent of the population; Muslims, 21 per cent; Chinese, 2 per cent; and everyone and everything else, 26 per cent.

First came the Arabs around 975. Then the Portuguese, who used it as a pit stop on the way to and from Goa. Then the Dutch, who used it as a base for slaves they were shipping in and out of Madagascar, Mozambique and Indonesia. Next came the French, who in their forever self-effacing way called it the Isle de France. But they didn't bother trying to run the place. They got Swiss mercenaries to do that for them. They were too busy tucking into fruit bat curry and Creole grilled lobsters and knocking back the champagne. Finally came the British, who not only dumped the fruit bat curry and the Creole grilled lobsters for fish 'n' chips, they reverted to the island's old name, Mauritius, not because it's the true historical name – it is, in fact, Dutch. It was named after Prince Maurice of Nassau, the Stadtholder of Holland – but because it wasn't French. But then the British have always hated the Dutch less than they hate the French. In 1968 they got rid of it altogether. It still looks and feels as though it is part of France.

The women wear saris, the salwar-kameez, the traditional Chinese blue trousers and sweat top, and the workers among them the more common Armani and Versace and Yves St Laurent.

The men – the usual story – wear whatever they can buy with the little money they have left to spend on themselves after their wives have blown it on themselves.

The Mauritians speak not only English but also the more exotic Hindi, Bhojpuri, a Hindi-Creole mix, Tamil, Urdu, Hakka, Cantonese, Marathi, Telugu, Gujarati and, of course, I nearly forgot, French. So, too, is the legal system and the humble Morris Minor, which you still see from time to time chugging along the streets, French bread sticking out the rear window. For some inexplicable reason they call it La Morris Boeuf.

Their homes, however, are not French. They're Norman and Breton and occasionally a complete *dîner de chien*.

The food is Indian, Creole, Muslim, Chinese and – I nearly forgot again – French. It's not unusual for breakfast to be a sandwich Creole washed down with home-grown vanilla-flavoured tea; for lunch to be dim sum followed by venison curry; and for dinner to be smoked marlin with dhal puri, Indian flat bread stuffed with curried lentils. All washed down with – what else? – French wine. On special occasions, I swear, they gather around a table, napkins over their heads and wolf down steaming bucketfuls of tiny marinated ortolans. With dhal puri and lashings of French wine, of course.

For the less important things of life, they go to Christian churches, Hindu temples, Muslim mosques, Chinese pagodas and celebrate all the religious festivals under whoever created the sun: Christmas; the Hindu festivals of Maha Shivratree and Diwali; the Tamil Yhaipoosam Cavadee, when the more enthusiastic devotees stab, skewer and thrust all kinds of things into various parts of their body; the Muslim feast of Id-ul-Fitr to mark the end of Ramadan; the Chinese New Year complete with dragon and fireworks; and every evening around Happy Hour, St Patrick's Day.

The British influence? They drive on the left. Occasionally you might find someone who can do bacon and eggs. With dhal puri.

Mauritius has also got boring things like one of the most successful ports in the world, a fast-growing industrial sector and a reputation for very upmarket tourism.

The port is booming. Before the opening of the Suez Canal in 1869, Mauritius was already a major port capable of handling over two hundred sailing ships at a time. Today it's even more so. It can accommodate not only all the current generation of giant ships and supertankers but also all the next generation of super-giant ships and super-supertankers as well. What's more, it's got all the warehousing and cold-storage facilities that go with it.

The industrial sector, which is geared almost wholly to exporting, is up there alongside the port facilities. If it's hi-tech, if it's high value added, if it's worldwide, they've got it. Manufacturing. Servicing. Finance. Even consultancy. Foreign companies are falling over themselves to get in. Partly because of all those Creole grilled lobsters. Partly because it works. Manufacture in Mauritius, you get immediate access to Europe and the US. You also make money. In some cases, a lot of money.

When it comes to tourism, it has all the advantages. No snakes. No mosquitoes. No malaria. No crowds of tourists. Almost no cheap hotels. But then that's always been the case. Mark Twain raved about the place. 'You gather the idea that Mauritius was made first and then Heaven was copied after Mauritius,' he said in that pithy, folksy way of his. Martin Amis tried much the same thing when he went to Mauritius. He called it 'a palpably Edenic transformation'. Which doesn't sound quite the same, does it? But then he was probably having trouble with his teeth at the time.

Trouble is, if Mark Twain came back today, he'd find Heaven a little bit more infinite. There must be over 100 luxury-luxury hotels on the island. When I first got there, however, I couldn't get near any of them. I had to spend my time kicking my heels at a scruffy bungalow hotel near the airport full of drunken aircraft engineers. Which airline were they working for? It's better if you don't know.

When I finally made it, I found I couldn't afford it. Mauritian hotels are not only upmarket and exclusive, they are out-of-this-world expensive. Your run-of-the-mill bottle of Bollinger at breakfast, for example, costs more than the airfare to get there.

But while Mauritius has been building up its port, its industrial sector and establishing itself as the world's upmarket tourist spot, it has not neglected the essentials. Education is free. Literacy is 100 per cent. Per capita income is around US$4000, the highest in Africa. Unemployment is practically zero. Life expectancy is seventy years, again the highest in Africa. Although maybe it's because they have concentrated on building up its port, its industrial sector and its upmarket tourism that education is free. That literacy is 100 per cent. That per capita income is around US$4000, the highest in Africa. That unemployment is practically zero. That life expectancy is seventy years, again the highest in Africa.

Thirty years ago, however, it was nothing. It was almost wholly dependent on sugar. If the sugar business collapsed it would have been caned. The only thing it could rely on were the millions of rocks and boulders of lava pushed up through the soil by the still-bubbling volcano underneath. Unemployment was 30 per cent. The different ethnic groups were beginning to get restless.

Then came the storms, which instead of wrecking the country made it what it is today. The sugar cane crop was virtually destroyed. Unemployment soared even higher. Racial tension increased still further. Mauritius was standing on the precipice.

Something had to be done.

Instead of crying help and running round the world blaming everybody else for their misfortune, they decided salvation lay in their own hands. They had to solve their own problems.

They decided to go into business. They decided to turn themselves into one huge export processing zone for manufacturers worldwide. Now there are export processing zones and export processing zones. The British-style export processing zone is a factory estate surrounded by barbed wire and patrolled by security guards with dogs that are invariably more intelligent than their handlers. Not only that, they're buried in red tape. Just to get in or out takes four or five forms, half an hour's interrogation and, depending on your luck or otherwise, a touch of the rubber glove. The Mauritian export processing zone, like Dutch export processing zones, is any factory anywhere in the country that exports 90 per cent or more of its production. What could be simpler? All controls are paperwork controls.

Next they tackled the service sector. They set themselves up as an offshore financial centre. They invited companies from anywhere in the world to use Mauritius as an offshore banking and investment centre. Instead of setting up an Indian company in India, for example, set up a company in Mauritius to do business in India and you pay only Mauritian tax rates not Indian tax rates. Today they have seven offshore banks, twenty-three offshore management companies, over seventy offshore funds and more than four thousand registered offshore companies.

Finally, and even more dramatically for an African country, they decided to ditch the bureaucracy – not that African bureaucracy ever works anyhow. They abolished all the rules and regulations that got in the way of doing business. Out went all the baloney about local ownership of companies, about minimum levels of local content in products. Tariffs they slashed to a nominal 0.03 per cent, the lowest in Africa. Corporation tax they abolished altogether. If you believe in free trade, they argued, you believe in free trade. Like pregnancy, there's no halfway house. Either you are or you're not.

They also – again amazing for Africa – abolished their army. No more huge expenditure on arms. No more problems keeping the military out of mischief. No more commissions and backhanders to politicians and generals and the second cousin to the ambassador in wherever.

The result: Mauritius boomed and is continuing to boom. The sugar industry is down from 90 per cent of GDP to around 25 per cent and falling. Industry, finance and tourism are not only taking its place but expanding the economy. Which, of course, means a whole set of other problems. Today Mauritius is trying to cope with the problem of success. Cheap labour is no longer cheap. Some manufacturers who came for the low prices are moving out to lower-cost countries. But, true to form, they're not panicking. They're fighting back. They are going even more upmarket, even more hi-tech. They're pushing education for all they're worth. At present less than 3 per cent of the population go to university. They want to double/treble that in no time at all. They have built an Informatics Park complete with all the latest whiz-bangs. And already it's paying dividends: hi-tech companies from around the world are moving in.

Tourism is the exception. Because they have gone as upmarket as they can go, the only way they can expand is by coming downmarket. Wander around some of the top of the top hotels and you can see their unfortunate problem.

The Royal Palm, the favourite hang-out of President Chirac, which he does all the time he's there, according to the French press, is so smooth and upmarket it should be called The Royal Calm. Even when you have fresh pineapple slices on a silver tray served by a maharajah in his best pressed tropical whites complete with topee you wouldn't know he was there.

Similarly Le Touessrok – or Le Toe-suck as it is known by the in-crowd since Fergie and what's-his-name honeymooned there, all those denials, divorces and reprints ago. The Residence is also up there: suites come complete with private butler. The more expensive suites come complete with more discreet private butlers. But whatever you do, don't go anywhere near Le Saint Géran at the very tip of the Belle Mare Peninsula. It's full of footballers. You're forever bumping into

Gary Lineker, Ian Wright, the guy who kept crying, Ruud Gullit and all the others. If that's not bad enough, there are hoards of footballers' wives. One had so much peroxide on her moustache my eyes were running. And I was at the other end of the bar. It's almost enough to make you wish you were at home.

If, therefore – Le Saint Géran apart – you fancy fresh pineapple slices served by a discreet butler, go there now. It won't last. Grand Baie will probably go the way of Ibiza, Goa or even Brighton. Le Paradis, with its long, sweeping driveways, thatched beach cottages, four restaurants and all the sports facilities and equipment you always dreamt of throwing in the sea, will no doubt become a Club Med. Even Spoon, the fifth-best restaurant in the world after El Bulli in Barcelona, Gordon Ramsay in London, French Laundry in California and Rockpool in Sydney according to a guide drawn up by fifty celebrities, chefs and food writers 'with a keen interest in food and travel', will probably start serving trigger fish and chips before long. Then they'll start expanding the airport, building a tunnel from Port Louis under the surrounding mountains to open up the rest of the island to tourists and turning Cap Malheureux, a tiny fishing village at the far northern tip of the island, into a downmarket tourist paradise. Although they'll have to do something about the name first.

But at least they'll be doing something, which is more than you can say for the rest of Africa. For while Mauritius has been switching away from sugar and joining the modern world, Africa has slipped further and further behind. Income per capita fell from US$665 to $474 in 2000. The number of Africans living on less than US$1 a day soars higher and higher. With one African child dying every three seconds, governments are still desperately struggling to provide even the most basic of basic healthcare, not to mention trying to cope with AIDS. Half the women and a third of the men in sub-Saharan Africa are illiterate. In Liberia and Sierra Leone it is an unbelievable 80 per cent. The fit, the educated, the middle classes, the rich are leaving. In spite of all the promises, foreign aid is drying up. Whisper it not, but Africa is poorer today than it was in the bad old colonial days.

Now at last Africa says it wants to catch up. Does it want to catch up the proven and successful Mauritius way? Of course not. It wants to do it the old and failed way. And it wants to use even more of our money – our money. Not theirs – to do so.

Last time I was in Mauritius, presidents Thabo Mbeki of South Africa, Abdoulaye Wade of Senegal, Abdulaziz Bouteflika of Algeria, and Olusegun Obasanjo of Nigeria, all recognised for their dedication to governing to the highest possible standards, their ability to do everything in their power for the good of their people, their unwavering belief in democracy, self-determination and human rights and, of course, their total stand against corruption in all its shapes and forms, launched what they called the New Partnership for Africa's Development.

Mbeki, the only man in the world who doesn't believe there is a link between HIV and AIDS.

Wade, who believes in self-determination for everyone apart from those living in Casamance, which wants to break away from Senegal.

Bouteflika, who believes in human rights for everybody apart from those the Algerian army decides do not have any rights.

And good old Obasanjo who was elected in 1999 on the promise that he would tackle the corruption that has crippled Nigeria, one of the world's top-ten oil producers, since independence in 1960, yet who presides over a government that gave US$10 million to the government of Niger in direct contravention of the constitution; made a US$13 million interest-free loan to the police force in Ghana when the Nigerian police were on strike because they were not being paid; and every year somehow loses over US$20 billion in oil revenue. They even lost the US$1 billion they recovered from the family of the late dictator General Abacha, which he stole when he was in office. Then when the Senate went into secret session to debate what happened – surprise, surprise – there was a power cut, the microphones didn't work and the whole thing had to be abandoned.

And what are these four presumably serious, sensible presidents proposing in their New Partnership for African Development, which they call NEPAD although I think it should be KNEEPAD because of the length of time everybody has been down on their knees begging African leaders to do something to develop their enormous human and natural resources?

First, our four serious, sensible presidents want every African country, rich or poor, to grow at the rate of 7–12 per cent every year to the year 2015. Are they out of their minds? Will somebody please tell these guys – who obviously wouldn't recognise a post-neoclassical endogenous growth theory if somebody gave it to them in a plain brown envelope – that nobody in the history of the world, let alone in the history of bogus targets, has hit these figures. Mauritius, the most successful economy in the whole of Africa, still only manages around 5.7 per cent growth a year. Since 1990 Africa's annual growth has struggled to a measly average of 2.6 per cent. How for the life of me, with ever-decreasing populations, weaker commodity prices, over US$150 billion a year being taken out of the back door and the increasing threat of famine and ever worsening poverty, are these countries going to suddenly treble their rate of growth to 7 per cent a year, let alone 12 per cent? And for every year till 2015?

In 1960 Senegal and South Korea both had GDP per head of US$230. Today South Korea has a GDP per head of US$8910.

Senegal's is just US$260. Fifty years ago South Korea's main export was human hair. Today it's up there with the leaders of the highest hi-tech. Senegal? Don't ask. What I'd like to know is if Senegal couldn't catch up over the last fifty years, how is it going to do so today, when it's even worse off and even further behind?

Second, our four serious, sensible presidents want Africa once and for all to stop putting its hands in the till, to stop fighting each other, to establish governments based on democratic principles, the rule of law and respect for human rights, and to provide its long-suffering inhabitants with food, shelter, healthcare and security. How are they suggesting they do this? They want African governments to voluntarily submit to criticism by other African governments and, where necessary, be punished for any infringements.

Come on. Pull the other one.

Apart from the big question – why does Africa need a deal: aid and trade concessions in return for good governance and less corruption, when other countries in other parts of the world don't? – even if African governments did submit to criticism, which must be as likely as Robert Mugabe climbing into bed with Mrs Thatcher, how on earth are our four serious, sensible presidents going to punish them if they're found guilty? By allowing them to commit only 50 per cent of human-rights abuses in the future? By reducing the margin by which they can be illegally elected? By allowing them to only steal 75 per cent of what they would normally steal?

Then there's the question of administration. How are they going to monitor every single one of the fifty-four countries in Africa? How are they going to decide whom they are going to criticise, the basis of the criticism, the punishment they are going to inflict, the timescale, whether the punishment has been inflicted?

The whole thing is Mickey Mouse. They'll need an organisation and a structure the size of half-a-dozen Organisations for African Unity – and, let's face it, the old Organisation for African Unity wasn't exactly the most efficient organisation on earth. Yet our four serious, sensible presidents are convinced. Do this they say and the foreign investment will come flooding in. Not just your usual level of foreign investment. But seven times the usual level of investment. In other words US$64 billion. A year.

For a hydroelectric dam on the Congo. For a fuel pipeline and road between Nigeria and Algeria. For a whole raft of dam projects in Nigeria. For a million other projects.

But there's not a word about Africa investing its own money in Africa. Why? Africans are not poor. There are probably more multi-billionaires in Africa than anywhere else in the world. The problem is that their money is not in Africa. It's in Switzerland. It's on Wall Street. It's helping to drive the American economy.

I know. I worked for the African Development Bank. I've dragged myself the length and breadth of the continent. I've visited fifty of the fifty-four countries in Africa, many of them several times over. I've been to companies, banks, factories, steelworks. I've visited every single African stock exchange. I've drunk champagne in the best and the worst government offices and departments, shovelled down buckets of caviar in ministers' homes and been entertained in I forget how many presidential palaces.

Similarly African ministries, government departments, banks, insurance companies, not to mention your run-of-the-mill public and private trading and industrial companies. They've all got pension funds. Where do their non-African advisers suggest they invest their funds? You've got it. In Wall Street. In Paris. In Frankfurt. In Zurich. And in London.

It's a nonsense. When we all started developing and growing, we all invested in our own backyard: the Europeans in Europe, the Americans in America, the Chinese in China. Not the Africans. Why? Because they know they can get better, safer, guaranteed returns by buying a slug of General Electric or Coca-Cola than by investing in a factory halfway up the Limpopo. They are also less likely to be cheated.

This has got to stop. Africa should not be helping us. It should be helping itself.

Instead of the Group of Eight playing footsie with NEPAD, they should be telling the Africans to establish an African Development and Reconstruction Fund to enable African investors – private, corporate and presidential – to invest in Africa. The fund should be confidential, tax-free, government-free. The rate of return should be guaranteed to ensure nobody loses out by switching out of Wall Street to downtown Ouagadougou. It's wrong, I know. Investment should be investment with all its attendant risks and rewards. But if that's the price we have to pay for bringing all that African money back to Africa so be it.

How do we help? Easy. Instead of just throwing more and more money at Africa and watching it disappear as we do at present, we agree through the World Bank to match every African dollar, Swiss franc, euro, pound or milk-bottle top put by Africans into the African Development and Reconstruction Fund.

How will the fund operate?

Easy. Instead of giving handouts to governments and businessmen, which as we all know doesn't work, the money should go direct to the African people in the form of vouchers: small amounts, redeemable over a one- or two-year period. African businessmen will then have to run like mad to help the people spend the money. African governments will have to run just as fast to make certain they collect their share of the taxes. But it will at least mean that desperately needed cash is injected directly into the African economy. Not through some corrupt, red-tape-bound, ever-delaying, grossly inefficient government department.

Once there is cash in the African economy things will happen. There'll be a rush for plastic buckets and hand basins. People will order picks, shovels, sheets of corrugated iron, water pumps. Women will want another length of material to wrap around themselves. Children might even get a pen or pencil.

Of course, some of the vouchers will be stolen or lost. Of course, people will be cheated. Of course, not all the money will be spent on African goods. That doesn't matter. The non-African goods will still have to be unloaded by Africans, transported by Africans, carried on their backs by Africans. The trucks and lorries will have to be serviced by Africans. Money will be pumped not only into the economy but throughout the economy.

It might not be the perfect scheme. But can you think of any other way of stimulating the African economy in such a short period of time?

As we all know, money creates money. Market traders and shopkeepers will expand. Employment will increase. Banks and transport will rush to keep pace. Businessmen, in turn, will demand that governments govern: provide the infrastructure, regulate the economy and begin planning for the future.

Debt relief. Fairer trade rules. Better access to richer markets. They are all fine. But face facts: until Africa has more money to spend it is stuck. It can't even begin to develop. Give everybody $100 or even more to spend in stages over, perhaps, a two- or three-year period and, oh boy, you'll soon see things happen. They'll be so busy wheeling and dealing they won't have time for the likes of NEPAD. That'll be the biggest relief of all.

But are our four serious, sensible presidents interested in investing their own money in Africa? What do you think? They don't just want foreigners to risk their money in Africa, they want to vet them before they do so. They want to sit in judgement on the project. Politicians who have no business experience, who have robbed their countries blind, who cannot ensure that every family in their own countries gets a clean bucket of water every day – they want to assess investment projects put forward by people, companies, organisations prepared to risk their own money?

Before our four serious, sensible presidents start assessing foreign investment projects, why don't they help the poor, small, struggling African businessman to invest in Africa? Why don't they start by abolishing the million and one petty rules and regulations and permits and authorisations and cosy little chats with the minister's brother-in-law that every African businessman has to face every day of his life? Why don't they give him some financial backing? Why don't they forget all the Western-style baloney about feasibility studies which only really benefits Western consultants? Why don't they hand out US$10,000, US$20,000, maybe even US$50,000 loans direct to African businessmen on the basis of good references, a track record and two pieces of paper outlining an idea?

I can think of any number of small African businessmen who would benefit by such a scheme. One is running his own mirror operation. He imports glass from France, coats it, frames it and sells it to local offices, hotels and government departments. He is helping to reduce exports, create jobs and build up the skills base. Another is importing motors from France and making his own large-size domestic refrigerators. Again he's cutting imports, creating jobs and building up the skills of local people. There are thousands like them. Help them.

As if giving them all the money in this world and the next is not enough, our four serious, sensible presidents also want the world to open up its markets to African products. Africa already has all the preferential trade arrangements they could wish for thanks to one Lomé Convention after another, under the Cotonou Agreements, under the American-African Growth and Opportunities Act. Africans accuse the world of using agricultural, health, safety and every other standard you can think of to keep them out of world markets. The truth is the Africans are not interested in or not able to break into world markets.

I've been on as many farms and in as many factories as I've had beautiful ice-cool glasses of Dom Pérignon with African ministers desperately worried about where the next brown envelope is coming from. The one thing the Africans want more than anything is for their crops to be collected and delivered on time to their local market before they rot. Stop crops from rotting by the side of the road, some experts claim, and you can forget access to markets. You would solve the food shortages and famines in Africa at a stroke.

I know. I've seen it. Again and again and again. There the crops are piled up by the side of the road. No protection from the heat and the dust or any little visitors that happen to be passing. The truck may or may not come on time. The crops may or may not be shovelled carefully onto the back of the lorry, which may or may not be in the cleanest and most hygienic condition suitable for delicate European palates. If the road to market is good, the truck may or may not break down. If the road to market is bad, the truck may or may not even get through. If it gets through, the crop may or may not be carefully dumped in the market next to a pile of rubbish. Finally, piled high in the glorious dirt and the dust of an African market place, completely unprotected from the sun and whatever else, these crops are then somehow expected to find their way miraculously to the world's dinner plates.

Take Uganda, for example. Every year the Coffee Marketing Board, which provides 75 per cent of the country's export earning, has to reject around five hundred thousand bags of coffee because they're not up to standard. Moreover, they reckon that up to 25 per cent of the whole coffee crop is not fit for export. Just imagine the difference it would make to Uganda's farmers – not to mention the economy – if they did not have to reject five hundred thousand bags of coffee every year and if they cut that 25 per cent export reject rate.

Access to world markets, if it means anything at all, means going back to before square one. Checking the land. Making certain it's accessible to customers and distribution centres. Growing the right crops at the right time in the right conditions. I know one big farm in Ghana that started growing tropical plants for Marks and Spencer. They did everything by the book. Marks and Spencer couldn't sell them. Housewives didn't like the natural African colours. They had to cover the whole farm with plastic sheeting to keep off the sun. Now they can sell them because housewives prefer the unnatural African colours.

Harvesting is the next problem. You can have access to all the markets you like but if you can't harvest your crop at the right time, without damaging or bruising it, wrap it, pack it, keep it in temperature-controlled conditions, deliver it to the market and ship it round the world so that it arrives better than when it was picked, you might as well stick to lying in the sun. To do this is not the work of a single day, it's probably a five-year programme.

Africans have also got to be introduced to the whole world of marketing. Identifying your buyers. Producing the products they want. Guaranteeing continuity of production and pricing. Meeting, negotiating and agreeing deals and buyers. Designing and preparing packaging. Agreeing shipping and delivery schedules. Advertising. Publicity. Even PR. Why, for example, do the individual tea growers, again in Uganda but it could be anywhere else in Africa, operate separately, have their own individual marketing strategies, auction their tea individually at the weekly tea auctions in Mombasa, Kenya, when they should have their own overall marketing organisation, buying their tea in Uganda at admittedly higher prices but marketing it world-wide as a Ugandan blend for up to four times more than they get for it at present? Other countries do it. The fact that Ugandans don't – is that the fault of the rest of the world or is it *their* fault?

The same applies to raw materials, semi-raw materials, bulk shipments, industrial products, semi-industrial products, even red roses for your buttonhole. Access to markets means nothing unless you do the job properly, to world standards and better than your competitors. But surely before the world opens up its markets to African products, Africa itself should open up its own markets to African products, reduce its own tariffs and subsidies. Our four serious, sensible presidents didn't even think of trying to expand and develop Africa's own existing, admittedly flimsy, export base. They should have come up with plans for boosting greater intra-African trade as well as trade with the rest of the world. A small increase in intra-African trade would work wonders.

Neither, incidentally, did our four serious, sensible presidents who place such huge store by democracy even think of discussing their grand plan with other African presidents, other African governments let alone the people of Africa before suddenly launching it on the world.

You don't think I'm taking our four presidents seriously? You're dead right I'm not. If they really wanted to know what was good for Africa, if they were really determined that their plan would not go the way of the Lagos Plan of Action for the Economic Development of Africa 1980–2000 and all the others produced over the last twenty years, they should have taken a trip to the booming, do-do island of Mauritius. They would have showed them how it's done. And more.

Dar es Salaam

I blame myself. If I'd have given the Horse and Groom a miss and spoken out when I had the chance, maybe Tanzania wouldn't have almost destroyed itself, people wouldn't have had to suffer as much as they have, it wouldn't have become one of the seven poorest nations on earth, and they wouldn't still now be struggling to survive.

A million years ago in a tiny terrace house in Merton in south London, I met their first President, Julius Nyerere, the Mwalimu, Swahili for 'teacher', probably the nicest, most pleasant, most innocent disaster to ever afflict Africa.

Tanzania, or Tanzanyka as it then was, was about to become independent. At the time I was grubbing about on local newspapers. One of the stars of our local council was an earnest, live-wire electrician called Maurice Foley, who went on to become a Labour MP, a junior minister in a string of different ministries, ending up as Deputy Director General for Development at the European Commission in Brussels. At the time he was big on Africa. He was working full-time for the Young Christian Workers. He was travelling all over the place for the World Assembly of Youth. He was also something to do with the mysterious Ariel Foundation, which always sounded to me like a cross between the Electrical Trade Union and Opus Dei. Nyerere was one of his contacts.

I was invited round to take tea and, of course, write it up

for the following week's newspaper. Local Councillor Meets Big African Chief. That kind of thing.

All I can remember is Nyerere, a slight man, about 5' 6", going on and on and on. Tanzania was bigger than France and Germany combined. It had fertile soil, rich deposits of nickel, cobalt, diamonds and oil. Then there was Mount Kilimanjaro, Africa's two largest game parks. Tanzanians were going to rule the world. Capitalism was the 'money economy'. It encouraged 'individual acquisitiveness and economic competition'. It was catastrophic to 'the African family social unit'. Instead he was going to collectivise everything in sight. The whole country would be turned into a nation of happy, peaceful village communities. *Ujamaa*, he called it, Kiswahili for 'family togetherness'. It would also be easier to provide healthcare, education, water to these happy bands of villagers if they were concentrated in one area instead of spread out all over the place. Small-scale industrial units, big businesses, banks, insurance companies, import-export companies would be nationalised. Government officials would work for practically nothing for the privilege of serving the poor.

'*Uhuru na Kazi,*' he kept saying. Not being the old Africa hand then that I am now I thought the cups of tea were getting to him and that he wanted the freedom to dodge out the back into the garden. Now I realise he was developing one of his favourite slogans: Freedom and Work.

Foley, I vaguely remember, agreed with every word, dashing in and out of the tiny sitting room with still more capitalist cups of tea and we'll-share-them-all-equally socialist biscuits.

I was just happy for the cup of tea, the couple of biscuits, the chance to fill our Newsman's Diary column without too much sweat and be slumped in my usual place at the bar in the Horse and Groom, Tooting Broadway, at 5.30 p.m. when they opened.

What I should have done, of course, was argued with him,

set him straight, told him what the real world was like. People want their own patch of dust. They want the responsibility and the freedom to work for themselves and their families. They don't want to be collectivised or nationalised. And as for government officials working for the privilege of – was he crazy? And, no, he didn't have to keep dodging out the back. Even Electrical Trade Union socialists had them inside.

But I didn't.

Within a couple of years Nyerere was president. Over 14 million peasants and their families, over 65 per cent of the population, were rounded up and herded into huge *ujamaas*, collective farms. If they didn't want to join in his great experiment, too bad. He called in the army. At gunpoint people were resettled in huge collective villages. To stop them from returning, their homes were burnt down. Talk about Stalin and his kulaks.

But worse was to come. Farmers were forced at gunpoint to plant crops they knew were unsuitable for the patch of soil they had been ordered to resettle on. The Chief Veterinary Officer of the Ministry of Livestock Development was summonsed before a special Central Committee and asked why he was keeping so many chickens. An area commissioner was asked why he owned a farm and spent so little time farming it.

Next Nyerere turned to business. Practically everything that moved he nationalised. Banks. Insurance companies. Import-export agencies. Anything that looked as though it could make money. It is said that during a break in the independence negotiations in London he went into the Gents with Kenyatta, who was at the time leading Kenya to independence. Kenyatta turned away from Nyerere to face the corner.

'There's no need to hide,' said Nyerere. 'We're both brothers.'

'Trouble with you, Julius,' said Kenyatta, 'is that whenever you see anything big you want to nationalise it.'

As for government officials, they did what government officials do all over Africa. They lied. They cheated. They did nothing. They put their hands in other people's pockets. The black market boomed.

But Nyerere blundered on. He declared Tanzania a one-party state. The mild-mannered man from the sitting room in south London who believed in democracy and freedom of expression now started arresting anyone who even thought about disagreeing with him. Wearing his version of a Chairman Mao suit, he now maintained that 'Democracy will create opposition among ourselves.' At one point the man who had proclaimed, 'Democratic reforms are naturally well-suited to African conditions. For me the characteristics of democracy are: the freedom of the individual, including freedom to criticise the government, and the opportunity to change it without worrying about being murdered,' had over three thousand political prisoners under lock and key.

To keep the army happy – vital for keeping his grip on the country – he opened special shops where they could buy all the capitalist essentials such as beer and fags for next to nothing.

Before long the country ran out of the non-capitalist essentials: sembe, maize flour, rice. Production of sisal, once the country's major export earner, plummeted to just one-tenth of what it used to be. Cashew nuts collapsed altogether. Fields, tended by the collectivised farmers, went riot. Everything grew in them except the crops that should have been growing in them. Half of the 330 state-run nationalised enterprises went bust. Schools, clinics and clean water became more and more of a distant dream. Schools were built, others half-built, most of them not at all. But they had no books, no paper, no pens, no teachers. Similarly clinics. At one time Tanzania had over one thousand doctors. But, thanks to the Mwalimu, they upped and left. Shops were empty. What's more, there were hardly any shelves left for the poor Tanzanians not to put any products on when they didn't arrive. Aid project after aid project crumbled into the dust.

But the great Mwalimu refused to accept that he was wrong, which probably accounts for the fact that at the time, according to Robert Holden, a British psychologist writing in the *Central African Journal of Medicine*, Tanzania was the scene of 'the longest laughter epidemic on record'. A teacher made a weak joke in a classroom in Buboka. The class fell about laughing. The rest of the school started howling. Come the end of the day, the children arrived home hooting with laughter. Parents and neighbours and next-door neighbours joined in. The whole town started rolling around. It spread to surrounding villages. So it continued for two whole weeks until the Red Cross was called in with special anti-laughter drugs – probably the latest famine statistics for Africa. The big laugh, of course, was that when it was all over nobody could remember what the teacher had said to start the whole thing off. Not even the teacher.

My bet is that it was probably something to do with Nyerere being the greatest political success story of all time. I know that after my session with him I can talk, but the crazy thing is that even though he destroyed his country, brought his people nothing but poverty and misery, left them after twenty-five years poorer and more desperate than they were at independence, he was hailed as a saviour. Sweden, Denmark, Norway backed him to the tune of over US$15 billion and continued to back him even when agricultural production was on the way down, the industrial sector was seizing up and people were going hungry. So too the World Bank. At one time they were making more loans to Tanzania than to any other country. Tanzanians were receiving more aid per head than anybody else in the whole of Africa. And it was all going down the collectivised drain.

Then guess what?

When he finally stepped down in 1985 after twenty-five years in power, the great Mwalimu admitted he'd got it all wrong. In his farewell speech he said, 'I failed. Let's admit it.' But then, politicians being what they are, with hunger and starvation staring him in the face, he was still not prepared to ditch his socialism. 'I will remain a socialist,' he said. 'Because I believe socialism is the best policy for poor countries.'

And one day my brother-in-law will buy me a drink.

As if he hadn't made the life of the poor Tanzanians miserable enough – many people call him Africa's Stalin – he then set about translating *Julius Caesar* and *The Merchant of Venice* into Swahili.

The only good thing about him was that of all African leaders he toppled Idi Amin but surprisingly refused to do anything against his own almost equally distasteful first vice-president, Sheikh Abeid Karume, the President or rather Dictator of Zanzibar who detained whomever he liked without trial and killed many more. But that, I suppose, is politics.

To the end still calling himself a peasant, he refused the trappings of power. He refused to allow any public holidays in his honour. He always wore a grey or black safari shirt over his trousers. He drove around in an old car with just his driver. He stopped at red lights. He never earned more than US$8000 a year. He retired to a one-storey house on a 100-hectare farm in Butiama on the eastern shore of Lake Victoria, where he was born. Towards the end he moved to a modest two-storey house on the beach overlooking the Indian Ocean on the Msasani peninsula in Dar es Salaam. But when he died, he died not like a poor man but in a private hospital in London.

Inevitably the tributes were two-handed. He was a shepherd boy who didn't understand farmers or farming. He was a Catholic who was almost a Marxist. His collectivisation policy was certainly as Stalinist as Stalin's. He was a champion of African freedom fighters who was a good friend of the West.

He was an all-powerful African leader who stepped down voluntarily. He was a genuine, honest, decent man, determined to do the best for his country. The problem was that he was an innocent. He didn't know what the real world was like. What he knew he knew from books. He was, as somebody once said, a 'great leader who made great mistakes'.

Some blamed Edinburgh where he studied and got his degree. Others blamed the likes of Maurice Foley, the whole Christian Socialism thing, the Fabians. Me? I blame myself – and Mateus Rosé. Apparently he was practically addicted to the stuff. He drank it every day of his life. No wonder he did what he did. The poor man must have been off his head. The pity of it is so many people had to suffer as a result.

Tanzania is like a blonde who is not only beautiful but brainy and rich as well. It has everything, the whole A to Z of whatever anyone could wish for in an African country. From Arusha and Mount Kilimanjaro, the highest mountain in Africa. To a dog being sentenced to death by hanging because it's called Immigration. To Ngorongoro and the Serengeti. To trains infested with huge, fat rats and to Zanzibar. Not to mention the likes of Stanley, Livingstone, Speke, Burton, Hemingway and . . . Freddie Mercury. Which is not surprising seeing as if it wasn't for Tanzania none of us would be here today. For it was in woodlands and marshes of the Olduvai Gorge on the edge of the Serengeti that our whole miserable existence began.

On 1 July 1959 Mary Leakey found the skull of an early hominid, *Australopithecus boisei* (*Zinjanthropus*) or to give it its correct name: a poor, pathetic, downtrodden male member of the human race. It was some 1.75 million years old. Which rules out David Attenborough. Just. At the time Mary Leakey was searching in the dried-up River Kolo for the odd thirty-thousand-year-old Stone Age rock painting. But you know how women find it difficult to concentrate on any one thing for any period of time. Next thing she was ruining it for everybody by finding *Australopithecus boisei*, so called because he had a six-pack in one hand and a remote control in the other and was going on and on about the match. The rest, as they say, is prehistory.

With its head start you would have thought Tanzania, give or take the curse of Mateus Rosé, would be the greatest country in the world. No way. It's about halfway between nothing and the depths of despair. Well, with 50 per cent of the population struggling to survive on less than US$1 a day they're hardly likely to be whooping it up. Maybe its because as soon as poor, pathetic, downtrodden *Australopithecus boisei* realised where he was, he was up and tramping north or south out of the place as fast as he could, which accounts for not only the length of the Rift Valley but the fact it is so much lower than the surrounding countryside. Those that were left were obviously the first to be afflicted by the curse of Mateus Rosé (some of which I drank actually tasted as if it were 1.75 million years old).

Today as a result Tanzania is around 800 kilometres of beach and red tape. Admittedly things are nowhere near as bad as they were under our great Mwalimu, but they are still bad. Few ministers seem to know what they are doing apart from putting their hand in the till – if it hasn't already been lifted. One day they decide this. The next day they decide the other. On the spur of the moment they will suddenly announce that a whole string of businesses have a month to up and quit. The next day they are introducing a five-year gaol sentence for winking – yes, winking – at a girl. Do it three times and under the terms of their Special Offences Provisions Bill you'll be there for life. Or, and this is one of the poorest nations on earth, they are flying toads – yes, toads – backwards and forwards to and from the States to see if they will survive if the precious electricity supplies used to power pumps to spray them with a cloud of water vapour are diverted instead to providing electricity for thousands of desperately poor people.

About the only thing they haven't done is to try and rename the Indian Ocean the Islamic Ocean, which when you think about it would be a sensible idea. More Islamic nations border it than India. On the other hand, maybe that's why they haven't done it. That and the fact there's no money in it for anyone.

As for civil servants, they are as helpful as the most unhelpful civil servants in the rest of Africa, although to be fair one civil servant at the Ministry of Finance did admit he didn't have time to concentrate on what he was supposed to be doing. He was busy trying to raise T. Shs 20 million (US$20,000), the amount he reckoned it was going to cost him to marry off his daughter. And, no, I didn't offer to help. He should have been doing the job he was supposed to be doing.

Somebody *must* be doing something. Maybe they are the guys who have already married off their daughters. Inflation was down from 30 per cent in 1995 to 6 per cent in 2000. Most of the state manufacturing companies have been sold. More sales are in the pipeline. Companies, privatised and already private, however, are still plagued by nuisance taxes. Utility costs are among the highest in the world. Not surprisingly their manufacturing sector – their biggest export earner is dried seaweed; every year they sell over 5000 tons of the stuff which ends up in everything from ice cream to shampoo – is tiny compared to, say, next-door Kenya, which sells to Tanzania fifteen times more than it buys from them. Half the population still exists on 65 cents a day. Where people have incomes, they are growing slowly. But at least they're growing. Investment is looking up. Main roads are being repaired.

Corruption, however, is still rife.

As for red tape, it's in a class of its own. In triplicate. Sign here, here and here. And we'll need your inside-leg measurement as well. To export just one container, for example, you have to fill in no fewer than twenty-one forms and then you still have to go down to the port and make certain the container they're shipping is yours, is going to the right place, is put on the right ship.

Some say it's because it was first a German colony. After the First World War, when according to good old colonial logic, a German town, Tabora, fell to Belgian troops, Tanzania became a British mandate. After the Second World War it became a trust territory, administered by the UN. In 1961 it became completely independent. As a result they are still wrestling with five different ways of doing things – let alone doing them properly: African, German, Belgian, UN, British.

Dar es Salaam, the capital, founded by Majid, the son of the first Sultan of Zanzibar, as a Haven of Peace, a fun-loving, live-for-today-for-tomorrow-we-could-all-be-back-home sunspot, is nowhere near the capital it should be. More Down the Drain than Haven of Peace. In fact, it's only in the last few years that it's begun to look anything like a town at all, let alone the capital of a country the size of France and Germany combined. Previously it was more a collection of shacks huddled around the kind of pretty run-down, out-of-date, inefficient port they stopped building when Conrad was still thinking of running away to sea. The only excitement was a toss-up between the neat and tidy Opanga Cemetery for the poor Tanzanian soldiers who died in the two World Wars and the New Africa Hotel, which was virtually home from home for any exiled freedom fighters the great Mwalimu took a shine to. In other words, all the would-be monsters, liars and biggest cheats of all time; I mean would-be African presidents.

Tanzania was the first country in the region to get its independence. Dar was an obvious meeting point. Today it's still small-town – the population is around 1.5 million – more Nairobi without the violence than, say, Cairo or Johannesburg. The streets are a mess. Most of the buildings are falling down.

The railway station is pretty much as it was when Dr Livingstone was catching trains there.

But that hasn't stopped the street traders, the kiosks, the shacks, the stalls. They are everywhere. On pavements. On walkways. In bus shelters. In car parks. In the lift going up to my room in the New Africa. In the minibar. Piled up on top of the stalls is everything you can or cannot imagine. Twisted roots. Lumps of bark. Tiny cowrie shells. A jar with clear liquid which, I swear, looks like paraffin. Tins of lion oil. Underneath, piles of elephant dung.

Beside one rickety stall I saw in Samora Avenue were stacks of bottles with greasy labels saying they contained water from the seven seas.

'From all the seven seas?' I wondered nervously.

The guy behind the stall looked at me as though I was about to embark on a dissertation on Cartesian dualism.

'From all the seven seas,' he replied as if he were discussing the most serious issue in the world – like who's buying the next round.

'So how do you know?'

'It says so on the label.'

Alongside the kiosks and shacks and stalls are Kilimanjaros of rubbish (although in some cases it's difficult to tell where the kiosks and shacks and stalls end and the rubbish begins).

Shacks and squats are everywhere. In alleyways. Alongside any building that looks as though it will still be standing after the next rainstorm. On the beach. Some say over 80 per cent of the city's population live in these shacks and squats. Which may or may not be true. All I know is, whether it's right or wrong, the most heartbreaking thing of all to see cooped up in dingy, dirty shacks are the Masai. First, because they traditionally inhabit a stretch of land, sometimes rich pasture, sometimes desert, the size of Germany. Second, they are your real tough guys. In the old days they had to kill a lion with their bare hands before they could be called a warrior. The fact that there are so few lions around today is proof of how many warriors there were. Third, instead of just sitting outside their huts and hitting the booze like so many other once proud tribes, they have tramped in their traditional skimpy red cloaks – and sometimes not even that – 1000 miles across Tanzania to Dar to find work. Not that the expensively besuited Tanzanian government in all its post-colonial majesty has a good word for them. They even staged a full-scale government debate to try to get them to cover up.

'Why should they?' shrieked one Member of Parliament. 'If Almighty God could stomach to see the entire anatomies of Adam and Eve in their complete nudity, is it not a little prudish for an African government to have fits merely by viewing a casually exhibited Masai buttock?'

Today the New Africa is more new than Africa. It's a big modern building complete with casino, a Romanian receptionist and empty rooms. There are so many hotels now in Dar, including a brand-new Holiday Inn and the swish upmarket Sea Cliff Hotel (where once I was attacked by locusts while having breakfast), they are finding it difficult to compete. Last time I was there they were offering so many discounts and special offers they ended up owing me money.

I suggested to the Romanian receptionist, who kept complaining there were no cinemas in town, that in order to get people back they start reminding the world of the old days when it was a second home to future African dictators and men intent on destroying their countries. She didn't think it was a good idea. But then women never think much of my ideas.

As for the port, it's worse than in the days of Conrad. It's a byword for theft – anything from casual pilfering to breaking into containers and disappearing with the lot. It's also so inefficient and so unbelievably expensive that in spite of its superb location – from Dar there is a rail link to Zambia, another to the north-west and on to Uganda, Congo, Burundi and even Rwanda, all landlocked countries, all desperate for safe, efficient access to the sea – it is losing out to the likes of Mombasa, Beira and Maputo and to a string of South African ports.

Just up the coast north of Dar is Bagamoyo, where things couldn't have been any worse. In fact, it's so unbelievable somebody should make a film of the place and get all the facts wrong.

Today it looks like a not-too-successful mission station: church, convent, seminary, a huddle of houses, a fish market, a sprawling hotel and bar and what looks like the beginnings of a small-scale luxury hotel, built they say by a Saudi businessman, with a small-scale mosque attached.

Forget the hotel and bar and the small-scale luxury hotel and the parts of town that look the way they looked when Dr Livingstone was a baby, this patch of dust has got more history than is good for it. In some ways it's got more history than the rest of the country put together.

Around one hundred and fifty years ago it was just that: a patch of dust. Then came Richard Burton and John Hanning Speke looking for the source of the Nile. Burton on a camel, Speke on a hiding to nothing. By the time they got back to Bags they were hardly speaking to each other. They had also failed to find the source of the Nile; or, if one of them had, he wasn't prepared to tell the other.

So, too, but not at the same time, came Stanley, and the likes of Hermann Wissmann, Oscar Baumann, Joseph Thompson and Verney Lovett Cameron. But because they were not doing it for Queen and country, or at least not for our Queen and country, they are not important.

And, of course, also came famous slave traders like Tippu Tip and hundreds of thousands of slaves.

In 1868 came the Germans or the French or whatever side Alsace was on at the time. A group of Roman Catholic priests founded what they called a Christian Freedom Village to house, care for and put together again ex-slaves. Within ten years they had handled over half a million of them. By 1880 they were teaching and training five hundred at a time. They had also started digging in. They built a chapel, which on 24 February 1874 became for ever famous when a bunch of around sixty Africans arrived, carrying what looked like a bundle of rags dangling from a pole.

'*Mwili wa David*,' they told the priests.

It was the body of Dr Livingstone or rather what was left of the body of Dr Livingstone. As soon as the great man breathed his last in Chitambo, a tiny village in present-day Zambia, all his internal organs had been removed and buried under a mabola plum tree. His name and the date of his death were carved on the trunk. The body itself was then stuffed with salt, soaked in brandy and left to pickle in the sun for a couple of weeks. To avoid the risk of attack by marauding tribesmen objecting to a dead body being carried across their territory, it was trussed up like a turkey. His legs were doubled up behind his back to make it look less like a dead body and more like, well, a dead body with its legs trussed up behind its back. The body was then wrapped up in calico, packed in bark, covered in rags and sealed in sailcloth, the seams tarred to make the whole thing watertight.

Led by his two loyal servants, Chuma and Susi, for nine months the group of sixty Africans had carried it over 2000 kilometres. Before them they had a drum, a Union Jack and the scarlet banner of the Sultan of Zanzibar.

Their reward? The usual British sign of appreciation: the cold shoulder. Chuma and Susi were not deemed suitable to be invited to Westminster Abbey for the funeral, which could not, of course, have taken place unless they had supplied the body. Such is the logic of imperialism.

As soon as the procession arrived at Bagamoyo, the priests told the porters to leave the body in the church porch. Whether this had anything to do with the maggots Livingstone had stuffed into a festering wound in his left shoulder caused by the jaws of a lion thirty years before or the fact he was a Scottish Presbyterian missionary who had never converted a single person to Christianity in the whole of his life, I have no idea. The following morning, however, he was in a freshly made wooden coffin and off on HMS *Vulture* to Zanzibar and then finally London, glory and a plot in Westminster Abbey.

But the poor priests shouldn't have bothered. Even though they took care of Livingstone and sent him on his way, even though they took in more and more slaves freed by the British up and down the coast, and even though the British agreed to cover their costs, they never received a penny.

'Subsidising missions,' declaimed Lord Derby – as they did in those days – when he first heard of such a preposterous idea, 'is something we have never done.'

And something they continued not to do. Next the British began to put it around that the priests were not buying slaves to rescue them but rather to trade in them – until the French consul slapped them down and told them to stop insulting the mission with their ridiculous insinuations. Quite right too, *Mon Excellence*.

But the British had still not done their worst.

The priests now built what they called a Fathers' House complete with cloistered verandas and arches, which is still standing today (although it looks very much like Alsace did after the Germans, the French and everybody else had trampled all over it).

Stanley turned up here, typical journalist, just as the priests were opening a bottle of champagne.

'Ah. Those Fathers understand life and appreciate its duration,' he wrote afterwards. What he didn't say was that the champagne was a single bottle and a Christmas present from the French consul. But since when have journalists been fair? On the other hand, maybe it was because the French consul gave them champagne that Bagamoyo was the first place in east Africa where coffee was planted.

In 1884 came the Germans. The local Sultan, they decided, should keep the land along the edge of the coast. All the interior, however, should be divided up between themselves and the British. But Dar es Salaam, although part of the Sultan's strip of land, would be German.

In 1915, 9 March to be precise, German East Africa was declared 'the ally of all Islam'. If Muslims fought against Germany and Austria they would be, it was announced, scourged by God.

Then in 1916 the British arrived. Offshore. With five battleships, the *Talbot*, the *Thistle*, the *Vengeance*, the *Severn*, the *Mersey*, and two armed whalers. To bomb the place to Kingdom Come. Bagamoyo, said the British, was German. Britain was at war with Germany. Therefore, peace-loving, hard-working, doing-nothing-but-good Bagamoyo, which had delivered one of Britain's greatest heroes to the British, must be bombed.

Facing the British were a small cannon, a machine gun, a big 4.1-calibre gun from the cruiser *Königsberg,* a three-barrelled revolver, three ornamental little cannons taken from the mission's garden, over two thousand innocent civilians and a black-and-white flag of neutrality that the priests had hoisted on to the church flagpole. Not that it did them much good. For five hours the British shelled the mission, hitting the church, the Fathers' House and numerous other buildings. Miraculously, nobody who sought refuge in the mission was wounded or killed. British troops, in what must be one of the most absurd victories of any war, then invaded and conquered the church, the Fathers' House and all the other buildings. They interrogated the priests. All the Germans were interned. Some in Egypt. Some even in India. The speed, the ruthlessness and the complete disregard of human rights with which it was carried out – you would have thought David Blunkett himself was in charge.

As for the Alsatian members of the clergy, some were interned, some were not. The chief priest objected. Priests were priests, he argued. As for the German priests, he was prepared to guarantee their conduct, even stand surety for them. The British turned him down.

'I am not able to modify the instructions conveyed to me by His Majesty's Government,' he was told curtly.

To which he replied, no doubt slightly less curtly, that he could not allow his missionaries to leave the missionary field assigned to them by the Holy See. But in vain. Even the Vicar of Christ cannot pull rank on His Majesty's Government.

Today Bagamoyo is more half-forgotten, half-derelict township than one of the most historic sites in Africa. The Scandinavians have built a big modern fisheries school and development centre, but there are now few fish to be caught off the coast and the fishermen can't afford to buy the fishing boats they are being trained to man. My God. I thought it was only the British who behaved like this.

For Dr Livingstone fans, of whom I am definitely not one, there is a big prefabricated church-hall-type building, the Kanisa La Anglikana, the old Anglican church, which boasts a sign, 'Through this door Dr David Livingstone passed.' Dead or alive, it doesn't say. Nor what he passed.

Just outside Bagamoyo is Kaole and the famous Kaole ruins. Well, in this part of the world they're famous because they are all that's left of one of a string of Swahili settlements established over a thousand years ago by the Arabs all along the east African coast from Somalia down to Mozambique. Today the buildings have all but disappeared. But you get the idea. Fancy houses with inner courtyards. Arabs wandering around in silks and sashes, jewelled silver daggers strapped to their waists, wheeling and dealing in gold, ivory, leopard skins, gum copal or if you prefer, gum Arabic and, naturally, the age-old favourite, slaves. In fact, it is so typically Swahili that when I went there the doorman was so upset because his supervisor had just left with the cash box, the key and the book of official receipts for visitors that if I didn't mind I would pay him cash for the privilege of looking around. If I wanted a receipt he could send it to me later.

Oh, the joys of living and working in Africa.

But if you think that's a killer, try Arusha, Tanzania's second-largest city. Now that's a real killer. In the old days it was not just swamp malaria but cerebral malaria. All a white man had to do was look at it and that was the end of him. Today it's still got its killer reputation. The malaria has gone but today it's home to the international tribunal investigating genocide in Rwanda. It's infected with international judges, jurists, lawyers, interpreters, translators and assorted international civil servants. Go into any bar or hotel and you're likely to hear Italian, French, German, even the occasional English.

Last time I was there I holed up in a tiny Italian hotel. It was hardly the Gritti Palace in Venice. But the lasagnes were fantastic. Trouble was, I had problems ordering the tiramisu for all the Italian human rights lawyers and their partly Versace-clad, long-legged legal assistants going on about their *mamma mias*. To escape, I asked a security guard at the International Court, who looked like he was smeared with liver spots, what was on offer. He suggested three things.

First, the houses of two widows of a man killed in a car accident years ago who had somehow turned themselves into a tourist attraction.

Second, head out for . . . if you're Kamba, Kilimajew; if

you're Chagga, Kilemakyaro; if you're Taita, Kayolaa; or if you're like me, Kilimanjaro. But I'd seen it more than enough times. Flying over the top of it. On one memorable occasion, three times in as many hours when I was flying or trying to fly to Kampala from Nairobi and the plane kept being turned back. Which I can tell you was pretty scary. Not because three times we boarded, three times we took off and three times we turned back. Not because of the Americans on board and the fuss they kept making which was pretty scary. But because every time we reboarded and took off they insisted on serving us cold baked beans slopped out of a huge tin into a tiny cardboard box of a plate. Ugh. An experience I wouldn't wish on anyone. Well, almost anyone.

Third, the Ngorongoro Crater. I opted for the Ngorongoro Crater. Not that safaris are my scene. As far as I'm concerned careless stalk costs lives. I can think of a million other things I'd rather be doing than battling my way through the bush just to watch a bunch of colombus monkeys picking nits out of each other's backsides or a pack of wild dogs signing a contract to appear in yet another BBC Wildlife Special.

I've also done more than my fair share in Tanzania. I've done two of the big three: the Serengeti and the Tarangire, and the smaller, more select Manyara. The wide-open, seemingly endless plains of the Serengeti are the place to go for big cats, especially cheetah. But I remember it more for the wildebeest in the southern end of the parks around Kusini: heads down, determined, starting off on the long trek to the Masai Mara, where even the more experienced driver can get lost in the mass of kopjes, ridges and valleys.

The Tarangire I remember for some of the largest elephant herds I've seen in Africa. So too the Manyara National Park, which is famous for its elephants and for the fact that when they die they seem to disappear off the face of the earth. Dead hippos I've seen. Bellies the size of a barrage balloon. Legs sticking up in the air. And dead almost everything else. But no dead elephants. No elephant graveyards. No elephant burial sites. No pile of elephant bones. Funny that. The number three national park, the Selous, is supposed to be the biggest protected game reserve in Africa.

The Ngorongoro, however, was the right choice if for no other reason than that I like all craters great and small and it was unbelievable. The approach. The setting. The size. The scale. The way you make your way slowly down into the crater itself. The mass of animals just lion in wait for you. It's as if you'd asked the Romans to build the Colosseum Mark II or, if you don't have that classical turn of mind, it's like something out of Hollywood. A real-life grown-up cross between *Jurassic Park* and *The Land that Time Forgot*. I also decided that instead of going by the air-conditioned, reinforced, super-sprung safari transport beloved of professional whoopi-do African explorers I'd go by *matutu*, your common-or-garden bush taxi. In other words, a battered, non-air-conditioned, non-reinforced, non-super-sprung Land Rover that was probably responsible for *Australophithecus boisei* being in the Olduvai Gorge in the first place.

The first time I went there the drive from Arusha was desperate. It was during the big drought in 2000 – the worst in fifty years – when the whole region looked like a moonscape. Because of the choking clouds of dust you couldn't even see the Masai tribesmen or whatever it was they were desperately trying to get to water before they dropped dead from thirst and/or exhaustion.

The last time things were almost back to normal. The grass was green. Crops were ripening. Mount Kilimanjaro could be glimpsed in the distance. The Masai were busy herding their cattle along the roads. No problems.

Then, suddenly in the distance, is Ngorongoro, a huge volcano. We start to climb. The mud track is wet and sticky because of the low clouds. There are thick trees either side. Some say leopards live in the trees. Slowly, slipping and sliding and skidding, we climb through the clouds. We are on the rim of the crater. Either side is thick cloud. We spend the night in one of the safari lodges on the rim.

After dinner I drag myself back to my room. I open the door. There looking at me from over the top of the sheets on the bed are these two beautiful, soft brown eyes, two little ears and the shyest smile you could imagine. It was a bush baby. Somehow or other it had got into my room while I was at dinner and made itself at home.

Come morning we begin our descent, slipping, sliding, skidding 600 metres down into the crater itself. First, we make our way through the trees near the rim of the crater. Then down we go through the grey clouds. Suddenly there is the crater. An almost perfect circle, 23 kilometres across, around 100 round miles of grassland packed, standing room only, with over twenty thousand animals. Large. Small. In-between. Virtually sealed into their own world. Not even the wildebeest here bother to go on their grand trek. And few other animals, except perhaps the occasional cheetah, try to break in. But with a name like that, I suppose, it's what you would expect.

You also know that, unlike a safari, you are going to see every single one of them. Guaranteed. One hundred per cent. The big five: lion, leopard, buffalo, elephant and rhino. Sure enough, there they are. Stretched out by the side of the road. Standing in the tall, lush grass. Ambling along. Huddled under a tree. There's even a rhino standing on the track in front of you.

Quick. Over there. Four o'clock. No, not the flamingos. They look like genetically modified turkeys with their feathers off. There are hippos, warthogs, a bunch of wildebeest.

Nine o'clock, zebras. Ostriches flapping around all over the place.

It's ten in the morning. In any other game reserve, by now

you would probably only have seen the backside of a Thompson gazelle disappearing into the bush. We drive to Lake Magadi on the floor of the crater. Long-crested eagles are circling overhead. More of those weird-looking flamingos. We sit by the lake. All it does is make me feel like having a long, cool drink.

We stop for lunch under a spreading acacia tree. We get out of the Land Rover, unload the food, the booze. A friendly rhino comes to take a look. Maybe it fancies the cheese, wants to try the wine.

Lunch over, we drive through the other half of the crater. By now I'm blasé. Not another bunch of lions. My God, leopards. More buffaloes. More elephants. Still more rhino. This is becoming a yawn-athon.

By mid-afternoon I'm making my way to another waterhole: the bar in the hotel. I've seen every animal there is to see. Twice, three, maybe even four times over. I've out-Hemingwayed Hemingway. Anywhere else it would have taken me a lifetime. And it's still not four o'clock. As far as I'm concerned, a crater love hath no man than the Ngorongoro.

Better still, the bar is empty. I don't have to put up with all those whoopi-do would-be adventurers in their brand-new, beautifully creased chinos, smothering themselves in anti-this and anti-that, gulping down handfuls of tablets to stop them catching nothing at all and going on and on about the two elephants they saw. My God, David Attenborough has got a lot to answer for.

Like Ngorongoro, but even better than Ngorongoro, is the spice island of Zanzibar. Stanley called it the Baghdad, Isfahan and Istanbul of east Africa. Livingstone called it Stinkibar, which tells you something about their different attitudes to Africa.

About 40 miles off the coast of Dar, it takes about three and a half days to get there by a Russian ferry piled high with television sets and mysterious sacks stacked all over the place. Judging by the number of times it breaks down and arrives late, I'm convinced it must be some kind of franchise operator set up by Virgin Trains. My own personal record is three weeks, two days and one hour, which I spent surrounded by Toss pots: 'Toss' being the name of the local detergent, pots the big white plastic containers it comes in. The dolphins that usually ride shotgun alongside the ferry gave up in boredom and left us alone. The dhows, however, make the trip in a couple of hours. But then I suppose they've had a shade more experience.

Like Ngorongoro, Zanzibar has its head in the clouds. It acts and behaves like a separate, sovereign, independent country. It has its own president, its own set of ministers, its own parliament. Thomas Pakenham worked himself up in a real tizzy in his book *The Scramble for Africa* about approaching Zanzibar: 'across the shimmering lagoon, one saw a city that might have been summoned by Aladdin's lamp, its arches and colonnades, towers and turrets, flags and flagpoles, reflected upwards in the frenzy of mirage'.

When I approached Zanzibar its Aladdin's lamp had most definitely gone out.

It also has its own Immigration and Emigration procedures. But finding them in the middle of a busy port in the middle of the night with trucks and cranes swinging backwards and forwards in the pitch dark is about as easy as a blind man finding a black hat in a dark room when it isn't there. But find them I did. Eventually. In a wooden hut tucked away at the far end of the port by the gates. Not that the Zanzibari porters were any use. I'm not saying they were a pain. It's just that I can understand why Stanley hanged half of them. The half that included the neck.

The Immigration and Emigration offices were hidden behind a solid wall of *papasi*, a local Kiswahili word for 'At your peril'. In other words, taxis, which is obvious enough when you think about it. Except that all I was thinking about at the time was avoiding the trucks, the cranes, the Indian Oceans of oil all over the place and whatever might leap out at me from behind a packing case in the dark. Not to mention the best way of getting my own back on that damned Russian ferry.

The funny thing is that Zanzibar is not a separate, sovereign, independent country at all. It has no right to its own president, its own set of ministers, its own parliament, let alone its own Immigration and Emigration procedures. It's as much part of Tanzania as Scotland is part of the United Kingdom. Well, at the moment.

On 26 April 1964, three months after the success of the Zanzibar revolution that saw seventeen thousand Arab and Indian traders massacred in a single night and the emergence of the Communist-backed Revolutionary Government of Zanzibar, it merged with the old British colony of Tanganyika to form the *United* Republic of Tanzania. One of the Mwalimu's more sensible ideas. But you would never think so by the way they behave.

Like Ngorongoro, it is also full of wild exotic creatures, no end of spice girls who really, really, really know what they want, and one or two wilder beasts as well if my memory serves me correctly. Why else would it be named after a million bars and nightclubs I've seen all over the world? It's even got more than its fair share of wild, untamed spirits.

Once, on the way over on the ferry, a British engineer told me he'd arrived back in Zanzibar after a trip to find his house crawling with witch doctors. They had broken in and sprinkled all kinds of unmentionable things all over the place, they told him, because they wanted to protect him. They wanted to rid his house of the evil spirits that were automatically turning his lights and radio and television sets on and off while he was away. For some reason, he told me, they were surprised he wasn't more grateful to them for their efforts. They were even more surprised when he showed them how the automatic on-and-off switches worked. The fact the house was opposite an ancient burial ground didn't help matters either.

Some of the creatures on Zanzibar can also be pretty ruthless. It's supposed to have a reputation for police brutality and corrupt judges and – shh – be a transit point for all kinds of goods apart from cloves and other spices. And the hotels are supposed to launder more than just the towels. All I can say is that every time my car was stopped by a policeman, I invariably found them very kind and courteous. The hotels I found empty apart from the small group of judges who were forever whooping it up in the dining room late into the night.

Richard Burton, the explorer and translator of *The Thousand and One Nights*, discovered it had a reputation for something else besides. In a brief footnote he boasts of having a big job in hand wandering around Zanzibar measuring the 'parts' of the local male population. Such were the size of the 'parts', he said, that traders refused to bring their wives with them to Zanzibar 'on account of the huge attractions and enormous temptations . . . offered therein'.

Such incidentals aside, Zanzibar is fantastic. It's Africa. It's Arab. It's Asia. It's Muslim. It's Christian. Oh yes, it's also a touch British. All rolled into one.

Forget Casablanca, forget Key West, forget the Rock and Fountain outside Chepstow. It's the kind of place to drop out, forget the world and do your own thing – and anybody else's come to that. Which is pretty much what the world has been doing for the last five thousand years give or take a couple more.

First came the Omanis. Way back around 5000 BC they were busy growing sorghum there and looking after their cattle. Come 3000 BC it was a trading stop between India and Mesopotamia. It had stone buildings, a thriving copper-smelting industry and the occasional spice girl. In 1828 back came the

Omanis again, this time for real. The big chief, Seyyid Said, made it his capital. From his point of view it was a perfect base from which to control his growing east African empire. It was an island. It had a large harbour to shelter his ships, the pride of which was his fully rigged three-deck, seventy-four-gun flagship called by the romantic name *Liverpool*. No doubt because it was full of beetles. It was also not Oman. It was green. It was pleasant. It was not too hot.

From the beginning he decided to spice things up. Every time a palm tree collapsed, he decreed that three clove trees should be planted in its place. It wasn't long before Zanzibar was the biggest producer of cloves in the world. He also decided to keep taxes to a minimum. The place boomed. It was the fastest-growing area on the east African coast.

Always keen to take immediate advantage of a good business proposition, the Brits moved in thirteen years later, eight years after the Arabs from all over the Persian Gulf, the Portuguese, Indians, Germans, Muslim refugees from Shiraz in Iran and even the Americans, who were probably chasing a regime change even in those days.

To keep the pot boiling, Said decided to expand by sending more and more trading caravans deep into the east African heartland searching for ivory, slaves and anything else he could sell to the rest of the world. In fact, it was most of the trails opened up by his caravans that all the famous British explorers followed when they were claiming that for the first time in the history of the world they were setting foot on territory upon which man had never set foot before. Soon from Zanzibar he was controlling over a million square miles of Africa (about 10 per cent of the continent), two palaces, seventy-five concubines and, oh yes, a couple of wives.

But it was not to last. The British took over as a result of a deal with the Germans. In return for Heligoland, a tiny island in the North Sea beloved of weather forecasters, the Germans handed over Zanzibar. Which was not a good idea. For Heligoland served as an important German naval base in both World Wars. Well done the Brits.

Next the British decided to abolish slavery. At the time Zanzibar was the trading and shopping centre for the whole of the east coast of Africa from Zambia and Malawi up through Congo, deep into Uganda and way up into Sudan. From all over slaves were rounded up and marched, carrying tons of ivory, ebony, animal skins on their backs, to the coast and then shipped across to Zanzibar in special slave dhows. Once in Zanzibar they were checked, priced, sold and shipped out.

The British decided they were going to be the first to be closed down.

Wander around Stone Town, the capital, and it's not difficult to imagine all this happening. In many ways you get the feeling it all happened yesterday. Whole areas haven't changed much since Aladdin gave up rubbing his lamp for other things. The back streets are scruffy, twisting little alleyways. If they still had camels they probably couldn't get them down them. Some of the houses – I use the term advisedly – with their cobbled courtyards look as though they have been collapsing for a thousand years and are still standing only because of their massive brass-studded doors. But don't be fooled, behind a couple of those massive brass-studded doors I discovered old-fashioned flats complete with huge Crabtree electric plugs, Twyford porcelain and no end of Lux soap.

The Sultan's Palace looks as though it was designed by an Italian overdosing on cardamom seeds. Instead it was designed by a Scotsman who was probably overdosing on cardamom seeds. It was once the tallest building in Africa. It also boasted the first lift in east Africa. Today it's known as the House of Wonders. The fact it has survived so long is a tribute to the skills of the British navy. In 1896 they tried to destroy the place.

They missed. It's also a wonder that in 1963, just three hours after Prince Philip declared Zanzibar independent, the whole show was overthrown by an illiterate Ugandan house painter and bricklayer, the self-styled Field Marshal John Okello. The Sultan, Seyyid Jamshid bin Abdullah bin Harub bin Thwain bin Said, escaped on his luxury yacht. Today it's still an eye-catcher, one of the tallest buildings on the island. But the wonder is no longer there. It's now full of old cars covered in dust sheets. As for the Sultan, the last I heard he was alive and well and living in Portsmouth.

The Sultan's Residence, now known as the Palace Museum, is more fun. It's almost like you imagine a sultan's residence should be. The ground floor is all history. The first floor is Zanzibar catching up with the outside world. The third floor is the Sultan's living quarters, which prove only one thing: he had a flat somewhere in town. Nobody could live in these conditions, especially with two wives.

Little is left of the once powerful Portuguese-built fort, Ngome Kongwe, probably because this is where all those Royal Navy shells fell that were aimed at the Sultan's Palace. What is left looks as though it could be a backdrop to a National Trust concert or money-raiser or both. Small. Nondescript. A touch pathetic.

More important, especially for alpha mails, is the post office and, of course, the House of Funguni. It was from the post office that Stanley and Livingstone, Burton and Speke, Cameron and Thomson sent their postcards saying: 'Wish you weren't here'; 'It's more difficult than we imagined'; 'Keep the home fires burning, we'll be back one day'. The House of Funguni, on the Bububu Road opposite the famous Msikiti Mabuluu (the Blue Mosque) is where David Livingstone set out from on his last expedition. Today it's the local tourist office, which doesn't strike me as terribly appropriate seeing as the doctor was a tourist who never returned home.

Best of all is the Anglican Cathedral with its tributes to flying boat commanders with names like Flag Commander The Hon. Richard Orlando Beaconsfield Bridgeman, no doubt known to his chums as Flag Commander The Hon. Richard Orlando Beaconsfield Bridgeman, who died fighting in Africa during the First World War. It is on the site of the old slave market.

Stand in front of the High Altar and you are standing on the very spot where the slaves were lashed before being put up for auction. If they screamed with pain they were regarded as weak, their price was marked down and they were destined for all the toughest, roughest jobs. If they didn't scream, they were regarded as strong, their price marked up and they were bizarrely destined often for a life of relative luxury as an overseer, a Mr Fix-it and sometimes even the head of household.

Look at the crucifix behind the altar. It's made from the tree under which Dr Livingstone's heart is buried in Zambia.

Wander around the church and see if you can spot the deliberate mistake. All the pillars are upside down. Usual story. The bishop agreed everything with the builders then off he went to some Mothers' Union meeting or other – you know how busy these bishops are. When he came back, the builders had put all the pillars in upside down. The plinth at the top. The fancy, twirly bit at the bottom.

'By mistake,' said the reverend bishop.

But rather than pull the whole thing down and start again, they decided to leave everything as it was. Presumably even in those days taking a builder to court was a time-consuming and costly process. Or maybe the good bishop left everything the way it was because he felt it symbolised the fact that the Anglican Church's very foundations were upside down anyway.

What puzzles me is how come the builders built the Anglican Church upside down but had no problem building all the Muslim mosques and prayer houses the right way up. Clever Muhammedans these Muslims.

For many people, however, the only place of worship on

the island is on Kenyatta Road: the home of someone called Freddie Mercury, who, I was told, had definitely nothing whatsoever to do with the Spice Girls.

Underneath St Monica's Hostel next door to the cathedral are some of the cells in which the slaves were kept until it was their time to be auctioned. Auctions over, most would be marched to the port and the waiting ships. The remainder kept behind to work on the ever-expanding plantations in Zanzibar. When I struggled down there for a look it was full of women, most of them wearing ankle chains as a fashion accessory. Next year, numbers tattooed on your arm?

At the other end of the spectrum is the block of flats on the edge of town built by the East Germans during Zanzibar's twenty-year love affair with communism, which staggered to an end in 1984. I won't describe them. You can't miss them. Crumbling plaster. Electric wires sticking out all over the place. Somewhere outside not to park your Trabant because it hasn't been delivered yet. It's bizarre. I've seen the same blocks of flats all over Eastern Europe. But in Zanzibar, it's unbelievable.

Now I know that I know nothing, as my wife has kept telling me these last seventy-three years, but I thought the spices for which Zanzibar is famous would be grown like vines or coffee beans or even roses or lavender: in long, neat straight lines, a strip of grass in between, everything orderly, tidy. No way. They're grown all over the place. A cardamom bush here. A black pepper flower there. A ginger nut by the side of the road. Cinnamon palms behind the shack. Clumps of chillies, lemon grass and nutmeg all over the place. Growing up a tree. Over the dead trunk of a tree. Under a mass of leaves.

They're also the easiest thing in the world to grow. Stick the thing in the soil. Go away and sit in the sun all day. Come back in six months', twelve months' time, it's ready to harvest. No regular care and attention needed as there is, say, for vines. They grow of their own accord. No disease. Insects can't stand spices. One sniff of a clove or a cardamom, let alone a black pepper, and they're off. No tight deadlines for harvesting. Harvest early and you get your money early. Harvest late and you get your money late. And bearing in mind the high cost of labour, the enormous start-up costs, the expensive machinery, the regular inputs . . . probably the biggest mark-up in the world. It's difficult to see where all the money that they make goes.

One spice girl, who looked so old and decrepit she probably remembers Posh before she became a coat-hanger, took me out to see her prize possession. We ambled through the scrub for about 300 miles. Suddenly she stopped in front of a tall, spindly tree. I thought she was going to have a heart attack. Instead she grabbed one of the flimsy branches, pulled it towards her and grabbed a gnarled handful of berries. She peeled one of them, squeezed the vivid fire-station-red juice on to the palm of her hand, then with a long, twisted finger rubbed it round and round her lips.

'Lipstick tree,' she cackled. 'Me now Spice Girl.'

Very Scary Spice.

Bissau

Forget the Crillon, the Gritti Palace, even the Forte Grand (so called because that's how much it costs to spend a night there).

Let's talk real hotels. In other words, African hotels. Trouble is, Africa being Africa, the five-star hotels are hotels in which you can literally see five stars through the holes in the ceiling.

In reverse order, therefore, zero-star African hotels are the likes of the 'Nellie' in Cape Town, as we regulars call it – The Mount Nelson to you – the Carlton in Johannesburg, The Nairobi Safari Club and the Mamounia in Marrakesh where I once spent hours waiting in reception for a big-time African businessman who told me he had checked in late the previous night and when he woke had found three doors: one to the toilet; one to the bathroom; and one with a sign on it saying, Do Not Disturb. He got out by ringing Reception and asking for somebody to come and rescue him. I also include the Hotel Atlantide in Gao on the banks of the Niger in Mali. My room, I remember, was enormous. It was like a cross between a chapel and a Turkish bath. The bar downstairs was like the bar in *The Hitchhiker's Guide to the Galaxy*.

One-star hotels are zero-star hotels trying too hard, like the Victoria Falls overlooking the Victoria Falls on the Zimbabwe side, where they don't just ooze sincerity they seem to excrete it. I somehow feel they don't deserve zero-star status for forever reminding us that our beloved Queen and Empress suffered one fall after another. Not that I can find any reference to any of them in the history books, English or Zimbabwean, which is not surprising given that Mr Mugabe has rewritten them so often.

Two-star hotels are hotels known for their wild life. The wild life inside the hotel. Not the wildlife outside in the surrounding streets or even safari parks. Not that I'm criticising them. Most of the two-star hotels I stay in all over Africa are invariably clean and neat and tidy. The rooms have been properly hosed down, the corrugated-iron sheets hammered back on the roof and a fresh pile of straw piled in the corner. If I have any criticism it's not even of the cockroaches. Staying in African hotels as often as I do, I've come to know and love so many of them over the years. They're like in-laws. No, that's not true. They're nothing like in-laws. They don't go for the blood. Once, God help me, I stayed in a two-star hotel in Kinshasa, Zaire, where, I swear, the cockroaches went around in hobnail boots. They made so much noise I couldn't hear the woodworms chewing on what was left of the building.

There are no cockroach problems in three-star hotels. Three-star hotels are too small even for cockroaches. If they *do* get in, they have to walk sideways. These three-star hotels are Africa's answer to boutique hotels. I'm not saying the rooms are small, it's just that they would fit into the shower tray at home. With room to spare. I stayed in one hotel in Cape Verde where the only way I could move around the room was to keep my arms up in the air.

As for the four-star hotels . . . well, they're not exactly on the Relais et Châteaux mystery tour I can tell you. Not that they don't have their individual appeal. Like that sweet smell of sweat, sewage, booze and cheap perfume. Like restaurants that are known for contributions to culinary delight such as amoebic dysentery and, for dessert, sandfly fever. Like taps that gurgle and spit great dollops of brown water then completely die on you before you can even think twice about putting your hands under them. Like spyholes in the bedroom door that follow you round the room. I stayed in a hotel in Ouagadougou, Burkina Faso, and every time I looked through the spyhole I could see a black eyepatch staring back at me.

Finally, come what to me are the tops, the ultimate, the five-star African hotels like the Hotel 24 de Setembro in Bissau, the capital of Guinea-Bissau, the tiny country, about the same size as Switzerland, squeezed up against and slowly being swallowed by next-door Senegal. Already Senegal has persuaded them to adopt the same CFA (Communauté Financière Africaine) currency they use, even though Guinea is not a Francophone country; to sign a defence agreement with them; to enter into a trade agreement with them even though more Senegalese trade comes into Guinea than Guinean into Senegal.

Two less likely neighbours I can hardly imagine. The Senegalese are seven-foot beanpoles. Even though Guinea is made up of over twenty different ethnic groups – plus the odd American who's gone native – most people's idea of a Guinean is a small, fragile figure with an innocent face, a trusting expression and a tiny pointed beard. Similarly, the men – although the further you disappear into the interior the bigger, tougher and broader they become.

The Senegalese are, in many ways, more French than the French. Their first President, Leopold Said Senghor, was a poet and a member of the Académie Française. The Guineans are peasants and fishermen and live in a one-time Portuguese colony.

The reason they're such friends seems to be – this will come as a shock – politics. Along the Guinea–Bissau–Senegal border are the rich, lush green fields of the Casamance, the largely agricultural area of the country, which for generations has been waging its own small war for independence. The Senegalese say *Non, non et non* again. By shuffling up more and more to the tiny Guineans, the giant Senegalese feel they will be able to stop them supporting the Casamance and their bid for independence and providing the rebels with a safe haven and the chance to recharge their batteries. Not to mention their weapons.

Not that Guinea-Bissau hasn't had its own problems. It fought the longest war of liberation in Africa. Whether that was because it was backed by the Russians and the Cubans, I don't know. At one stage, it was practically the revolutionary darling of the world. It was a pacemaker, even trendsetter for liberation movements. Instead of killing and moving on, as all the other liberation movements did, they established special liberated areas. Inside the liberated areas they built schools and hospitals and gave people and – more importantly – the rest of the world a picture of what life would be like after they took over.

Trouble is, it never happened. When the Guineans finally took over the Portuguese left them nothing but a handful of peanuts, a factory for peeling them, a brewery and a couple of university graduates. They didn't even have a doctor.

To make matters worse, as soon as they were left to themselves they could hardly agree on the time of day. And since then they have suffered a severe dose of Marxism, non-stop civil war, corruption, hunger, blackouts, the support of the Senegalese and a reputation for being at the bottom of the pile of least-developed countries in the world. Practically 90 per cent of the population lives, or rather tries to live, on less than US$1 a day.

For years it was shut off from the rest of the world. Tourism was non-existent. Business was not encouraged in any way at all. The only way in was to say you were with some charity or aid organisation, preferably from Sweden. For years I'd been going to Dakar but had never found time to take a look. Then on one trip all my meetings started to collapse . . . At last I had time to look next door.

I decided to take the scenic route. From Dakar through the Gambia and across the Casamance, maybe taking a look at the old Breton-style church on the island of Karaban, on to Ziguinchou, a couple of quick pernods in the Hotel Nema Kadior and then Farim on the border. Grab the ferry at Cachequ and head for the capital, Bissau.

I had everything arranged: the usual 4×4, a driver and two pockets full of presents to grease my way through the traditional African assortment of roadblocks, both official and unofficial; police checkpoints, both official and unofficial; and customs and immigration procedures, both . . . You've got the idea.

Then, suddenly, the day before I was to leave, a convoy of trucks crossing the Casamance was attacked by a group of freedom-loving people who desire nothing but the true independence of their homes and their homeland. In other words, terrorists demanding independence from Senegal. Three people were seriously injured, including the armed bodyguard who was there to protect them. He was immediately flown out by the military. Whether this was because of the extent of his injuries or the lack of the extent of the injuries he incurred in not protecting the people he was there to protect, nobody would say.

To the Senegalese press it was neither a desperate act by a group of freedom-loving etc. etc. nor an act of terrorism. Forever conscious that their first President, Léopold Sédar Senghor, was a poet and a member of the Académie Française, they catchily labeled it '*une tragédie antique digne de Sophocle ou de Thucydide, considéré par les Grecs comme le père de l'histoire.*'

Nonetheless I decided to take the plane, much, I will admit, against the advice of my family and friends.

The flight was uneventful. We even arrived ten minutes late, which is fantastic for Africa. Some flights I've been on have arrived ten days late. Normally at African airports, whether you arrive ten minutes late or ten days late, you are kept waiting for hours on end queuing up to pass through some Mickey Mouse health check where a man in a greasy white coat intently examines whatever piece of paper you give him whether it's upside down or not; immigration procedures where some dozy soldier makes a lot of fuss and bother about stamping some form he can't read; and then finally by Customs, who make a great show of pushing their greasy fingers into everything that doesn't pose the slightest threat to the security of their great nation.

Not so Guinea-Bissau. There they make you wait in temperatures of up to 40°C, huddled under the wing of the plane for some shade, for the arrival of a dilapidated six-seater bus to take you to their new super-deluxe modern terminal.

Now I know I shouldn't say this. But wait two hours for Immigration or wait in 40°C huddled under the wing of a plane for shade? I know which I would choose.

Once through Immigration and Customs – it was difficult to tell which was which. All kinds of people were grabbing my passport, my briefcase, my papers. Some in uniform, some not – it was outside to the taxi rank. I say taxi rank. On the one hand, there was this super-deluxe modern terminal building. A massive structure. Huge open halls. It looked like a cross between an empty sports stadium and a French bank manager's office. Outside it was Africa twenty years ago. There were hardly any taxis around. The taxis that were around had filthy black smoke billowing out of their exhausts – and their engines weren't even turned on.

I leapt into the nearest one. We did the usual French/Africa thing. The driver and I greeted each other like long-lost friends. We swore our undying loyalty to each other, La France and the next bottle of champagne. We agreed that we couldn't stand the Americans.

It was my first time in Bissau. I didn't have any reservations – well, apart from the usual.

'OK,' I said with a swagger. 'Take me to the best hotel in town.'

We chugged our way to the airport security barrier, spluttered past it and headed out into the pitch-black night. It was like fighting your way through the impenetrable prose of a John Prescott speech. That's not all. If you know Lagos, Dakar, Abidjan, even downtown Nattitangou, you will not believe me: the roads were empty. Nothing. Not even a donkey. I say roads. We drove along roads that were more pothole than road, past rough scrub, the usual desolate shacks, the occasional house. There was a mosque. And another. And another. More people seemed to be standing by the side of the road.

I wound down the window and looked out. I practically had a heart attack. There. Right in front of me. Staring straight at me. Just a couple of feet away. The barrel of a Russian tank. Except, when I got my breath back, I realised it was the barrel of a clapped-out, falling-to-pieces Russian tank. Now, I may not be everybody's perfect guest, but all the same – revolutionary or not – it's one hell of a way to welcome visitors to your country.

On we chugged to the most derelict Sheraton hotel I've seen in my life. Outside it looked to me as though it was either gently rotting into the bush or it was some new-style design for a prison produced by some fancy Florida designer who at the age of forty-seven has yet to wear anything but shorts, T-shirt and enormous pumps.

Inside, however, it was pure Soviet Union 1950. Low, dark, empty rooms. Huge empty sofas. Mysterious people wandering around in the shadows doing nothing in particular. Photographers photographing everything. A faceless empty restaurant. Lifts that didn't work. A bar where it took two people to serve me a glass of beer and another two to take my money. Shops that were always closed. And the clincher: nobody had any change for anything: escudos, CFA or even dollars. It was my own fault. Why I don't know, but I'd forgotten that African hotels are classified back to front. If I'd asked the cab driver for the worst hotel in town I might have ended up in somewhere like the Ritz-Carlton or the Drake in Chicago. As it was I ended up in this . . . this . . . this . . . In fact, it's so bad I can't believe Sheraton knows it still exists. Or if they do, that it is trading under their name.

Being a glutton for punishment – I was missing my regular sessions – I tried to check in.

Even though I could see all the keys staring me in the face, the fat old Guinean babushka told me in true Intourist style they were full.

'OK,' I said to the cab driver, 'take me to the worst hotel in town.'

'The worst hotel?'

'The worst hotel.'

On we chugged, past more shacks, past what looked as though it could have been a vast open-air market, past either a huge gun turret or a water tower, past the Presidence, which looked like it could do with some executive action, and through the gates into the Hotel 24 de Setembro. Except it wasn't my idea of a hotel. It was more like a one-time upmarket concentration camp. With curtains. And a Russian concentration camp at that.

In the centre was the reception block—I mean reception area. To the left was where strange men in uniforms twisted and broke legs, smashed skulls, tore open bodies and splashed hearts and lungs and livers all over the place: the kitchens. To the right, the, er, bar. Stretching out from the reception block were various anonymous-looking outbuildings, the long, low prisoners' shacks with broken and missing window panes, smashed-in doors and . . . yes, the guests' rooms.

I waited in line to check in. There wasn't actually a line but it felt like it, and not only did it feel like it, it felt as if it stretched all the way to Siberia and back again. It also took ages to check in, although to judge by the keys hanging on the rack the place was practically empty. Another Russian trick. They deliberately keep their hotels 99 per cent empty for tourists they know will never come. In the end, in order to save time and make the most of what few hours I might have had left, I managed to check out before I had even checked in.

My cell, I mean room, was, when I finally got to it, nowhere near as bad as the Sheraton's. It was pure Soviet Russia 1930. The fittings were Stalin. Plain walls. Chipped tiles. All the rusty pipes showing, à la Lord Rogers. Light bulbs that weren't there. Fans that didn't move. Taps that didn't work. Drains that didn't drain. Electricity that was more off than on. For which we must be truly thankful. If the Soviets had not been such perfectionists, maybe the whole thing wouldn't have crumbled away into its own dust.

The furniture was also Stalin. Cheap plastic chairs. Cheap plastic table. Thick heavy sofa. Flat board for a bed. And all the wildlife any mortal man can stand. Except here the wildlife was not just wild it was huge. Twice I woke up during the night, peered nervously over the top of my delightfully black-, brown- and What-the-hell-caused-that?-stained sheet to find the furniture being shifted around the room. In the morning you wouldn't believe the problems I had trying to get my shoes back. That's not all. Here the wildlife not only killed each other, they merrily dragged the dead bodies across the middle of the floor to some hideaway in the walls, leaving a pretty trail of blood and guts behind them, and there they munched away day and night. At one stage the noise was so bad I had to force myself to watch French television to block out the sound.

The bathroom was Beria. Russia I know. The -stans I know.

Even Cuba I know. But the thrills of a Soviet bathroom is an experience to be treasured for ever. Like your brother-in-law offering to buy you a round of drinks. Just offering. Not buying. The shower tray was the size of a horse trough – but perhaps the whole place was built by the Cossacks for the Cossacks and their horses, in which case I apologise. The toilet when it flushed, flushed so violently that everything went all over the floor. And I mean everything. But all was not agony. The toilet paper was considerably softer than the toilet paper even in today's Russia. It was as thick only as a sheet of plywood and about as smooth.

I'm not saying it's the worst place I've ever stayed in, it's just that the cockroaches would waddle into the room, take one look at it and immediately roll over on their backs and die. Not that I'm complaining. It did at least have a ceiling through which I saw my five stars (although I suppose in this case it was five tsars). It was also I think one of the few hotel rooms I've been in anywhere in the world that didn't have a Gideon Bible. Which either means that it's not a hotel and it really is a concentration camp, that the Gideons stick to warm countries or that they think anyone who goes there is beyond help, let alone redemption.

There was only one thing to do: push all the hairy-looking electric wires and plugs back in the wall – wouldn't want a passing cockroach to injure itself, would we? – and head for the bar. The walls I could tap for microphones later. If they were still standing.

The bar was maybe a touch Philby. Wide open. Spread out. Smoky. Chunky chairs and sofas neatly squared up all over the place. Like the Common Room of a cheap public school. In the furthest corner from the door I recognised a government minister from Burkina Faso knocking back the whiskies and smoking away like a trooper. In another corner – I might have been mistaken – but I swear there was Sidy Badji, the heavily bearded military leader of those freedom-loving people who desire nothing but the true independence of the Casamance from Senegal. In other words, terrorists. As for Sidy Badji, he was the man, I suppose, ultimately responsible for my having to fly to Bissau instead of driving across his beloved Casamance.

Was it a coincidence? Were they trying to get negotiations going? Was Mr Badji embarrassed that I had had to fly to Bissau and not drive there as I had originally planned? Was he plucking up courage to apologise? Or were they putting together another cannabis-for-guns deal? Those who know about this kind of thing tell me cannabis from Casamance is among the best in the world. The fact they've been able to trade it across the border into Guinea has enabled them to finance their operations and keep the war going for so long.

There was only one thing to do: escape. I went outside to get a cab. All the cabs had disappeared. Now, in any developing country the thing I normally do whenever there are no cabs around is to persuade the driver of one of the millions of big, white United Nations four-wheelers that are always standing around gathering dust to do a bit of moonlighting. A quick handshake, a word of praise for Kofi Annan's turning of the UN into an African organisation and a petit you know what and we're away. This time there weren't even any UN cars around. They and their drivers had disappeared. The only lift I could get into town was in the hotel's fish wagon which was going not to the big port but the small local port to pick up fresh fish for the night. The driver, a tall, thin Mauritanian, turned out to be the grandson of the first independent President of Mauritania, Mokhtar Ould Daddah. As soon as he realised that I wasn't French and I wasn't American he insisted I sat in the front of the truck with him and not in the back with all the Ugh.

The traditional port was pure Conrad. A primitive shaky pier.

People everywhere. Rough, dodgy-looking fishing boats slopping around in the mud. The President's grandson leapt from boat to boat, never putting a foot wrong, which is more than could be said for his grandfather. Showing all the dexterity of the professional politician, he ended up by buying practically everything on board the boat owned by the local chief inspector of police. Ah Africa, Africa, Africa.

Not that the poor, hard-working fishermen are above a trick or two. Far from being jolly, bouncy, loyal and three-times liars like Saint Peter, they are apparently the biggest bunch of crooks on earth, which perhaps puts another spin on why Christ chose them and not merchant bankers and accountants upon which to build his Church.

Over a couple of beers in a shack on the edge of the port, a government fisheries officer who was actually from Burkina Faso told me that fishermen anywhere in the world will lie and cheat their way out of everything.

When he first started, he said, he used to feel sorry for the poor fishermen: hardly anything to wear, out fishing day and night, risking their lives, always fighting the local dealers and merchants to get a fair price for their fish. No more.

'I used to buy new nets for them out of my money. They agreed to pay me back, a little every week, from the sale of their fish. No one paid me back. When I went to the harbour to see them, they stay out at sea. When I go home, they come in. I go to visit their homes. Their families say they are not there. Everything. I lose everything,' he told me.

Over another beer another fisheries officer, who had worked in Benin, told me a similar story.

'The local fishermen, they come to me. They say they want engines for their boats but they are poor. They have no money. I get money from the government. I buy them engines. They promise to pay the money back from the extra fish they catch. But they don't pay back. They say they don't catch extra fish.

'One day we have big storm. The fishermen come to me. They say they have lost all their money. The water comes and washes away their houses and all the money they keep in their houses in plastic bags. One fisherman he says he lose as much as US$10,000. Another fisherman has all his money on the ground to dry. But everybody in village tries to get it. He has big problem. But still they not pay me back money for engines.'

The President's grandson drove me back to the hotel. Flapping around in the back of the truck was a whole shoal of odd-looking fish that might have been edible or might not; something that looked like a cross between a cobra and a stingray and a whole mountain of chunky, white-skinned fish known the length of French Africa as capitaine.

That evening I had a great time. The bar was full of people drinking and smoking away to their hearts' content. The minister from Burkina Faso had his jacket off and his feet up on the table and was chatting away like mad. The man with the beard was plying him with no end of whiskies and cigarettes. After a couple of beers I felt everything going to my head and retreated to the restaurant, which brought me up cold straight away. It was not just pure Social Realism but pure Social Realism in action. Through the door and you're immediately greeted not by a happy, smiling, have-a-nice-day, retired lap dancer as you are in the States, but by an officious prison officer with a heavy scar across her face, pointing at a greasy cabinet where uncooked specimens of the meals on offer are gently sweating away. Having been at the port and seen the fish landed, bought and thrown in the back of the van, I chose one of the less sweaty and more robust specimens on offer. The cost of my tiny portion: CFA8000. About the same price the President's grandson paid for the whole thing. Who says hotels have a hard time struggling to make ends meet?

Next I was asked, 'Beer?'

'Beer,' I nodded and made my way across the almost empty Soviet-style dining room with its big empty table in the centre waiting to be decorated with food that will never arrive. I collapsed at a table in the furthest corner. More than ever I felt that this was the time to keep an eye on the door. Except I could hardly see it for the wildlife criss-crossing this way and that across the room: on the floor, in the air, hanging upside down from the ceiling.

I waited an age for the meal to arrive. In fact, I waited so long I reckon the trainees in the kitchen went back to the port, threw the fish in, waited until the magistrate's back was turned then fished it out again. By the time it arrived I'd drunk so much of their local, slightly apple-tasting Pampa beer that I couldn't catch the darn thing. It kept wriggling around all over the plate.

Just as I was finishing, two waiters descended suddenly on my table. The first to give me a paper napkin, which he did oh-so-slowly and oh-so-carefully with the napkin poised between a tiny fork and a greasy spoon. The other, again oh-so-slowly and oh-so-carefully, as if he were about to dismantle an unexploded bomb, removed the two or three fish bones I had piled neatly on the edge of my plate and placed them delicately in the centre of another, larger plate before carrying them off triumphantly to the kitchen no doubt to form the basis of tomorrow's soup of the day.

The following morning everything was completely different. It was so totally unSoviet that I couldn't believe it. I wasn't woken up by a knock on the door at three o'clock or the sound of jackboots, searchlights and dogs sniffing around all over the place. I decided not only to risk breakfast but to risk the laundry as well. I sent off a shirt and my old, much stained linen jacket. I also managed to grab one of the UN 4×4s parked outside. The driver was from Senegal, which made it even easier.

Instead of the usual tour we decided to do the civil war tour: look at the state of the various ministries and other buildings and try to guess which war destroyed them: the war against the Portuguese from 1961 to 1973; the Civil War of June–July 1998 when Senegalese troops crossed the border to come to the aid of the government and hurled bombs and missiles at Bissalanca airport, at the surrounding area occupied by the rebels and all over the capital itself, killing hundreds of innocent people in the process; the Civil War of May 1999 when fierce fighting in Bissau shattered a six-month truce, troops loyal to the president surrendered, the president fled and rebels again took over; the Civil War of November 2000 when a former junta leader, ignoring the wishes of the new democratically elected president, declared himself head of the army and one half of the armed forces started fighting the other.

But one swing around the roundabout in the centre of town and we decided against the whole idea. Everything was derelict. Everything looked as though it had been destroyed. First, the PAIGC (African Party for the Independence of Guinea-Bissau and Cape-Verdo) headquarters – the party that fought the copybook war of liberation. Today it doesn't look as though it could organise a boot sale let alone a war of liberation. It's crumbling to pieces. The Ministry of Foreign Affairs. I can tell you that it at least sums up Guinea-Bissau's position in world affairs. The Ministry of the Economy and Finance. More than graphically illustrates the state of the economy. About the only buildings that looked in good working order were the Ministry of Justice, the Portuguese Embassy and the Coca-Cola bottling plant.

Some say the President's House was also in good nick. But that was because it was hardly ever used for what it was designed for: building a better life for the people of Guinea-Bissau. Instead things have continually got worse and worse. Not only have the poor Guineans got poorer and poorer, they have watched the whole place crumble around their ears.

Since the mid-1980s politicians have hardly been able to agree on who the cheque should be made out to. You name it, they've had it. Violence. Civil war. Corruption. Admittedly they had elections in 1999 but it was no dream process. Neither is the present President, Kumba Yala, a dream democrat. The Constitution says that the judiciary is free of political interference. Oh yes. Will somebody please tell the President. Early in 2001 the deputy president of the Supreme Court announces that the court intends to pursue the President for 'menaces, slander and meddling in judicial affairs'. On 10 September 2001 the President dismisses three Supreme Court judges including the deputy president. Not content with that he also dismisses the Attorney General and appoints in his place a former prime minister who happens to be connected to him by family ties. As if that's not suspicious enough, what happens when the privately owned Radio Pidjiquiti reports the story? The newly appointed Attorney General himself and two armed soldiers raid the studios, threaten to arrest the journalist involved and demand the tapes of the news programme.

It doesn't stop there. Two other journalists reveal that senior government officials have between them bought at least 127 houses in Portugal and sent huge sums of money abroad. Another journalist reveals the luxurious lifestyle of the President's wife. Offices are stormed. The journalists concerned are arrested without official warrants and held not by the police but by the security services.

Then there is the coup that never was – planned no doubt in the President's House that most definitely is. Suddenly the radio denounces 'a conspiracy to destroy our democracy and kill the Head of State'. Troops are reported to be on the move. The ringleaders are arrested. The government urges everyone to stand by the President and promises swift action against those who oppose him.

Yet . . . Where were the conspirators? Where were the troops? Where were the ringleaders? Opposition leaders demanded proof. Did the President supply the proof? No way. Instead he threatened to suspend parliament for ten years unless they stopped asking silly questions. If he were Tony Blair, of course, he would just ignore it altogether, let it wither away of its own accord and insist that everybody move on. But that's what comes of not being a true democrat.

The old part of town, the genuinely old part of town, however, was a revelation. It was Portugal in Africa. All fancy houses, balconies and railings. UNESCO should declare the whole area a World Heritage Site immediately. Whether you think the Portuguese were the worst colonisers of all is another matter. Although I must say from what I've seen, heard and read, I think they were, perhaps run close by the Belgians. On the plus side they brought to Africa the basics such as corn, manioc, tobacco, oil palm and bananas; technical words such as 'palaver', 'fetish' and, of course, 'dash', without which Africa could not begin to exist today.

On the minus side they were responsible for the roughest, cruelest form of colonialism imaginable.

Free speech and any other civil liberties were unheard-of. So was education. Everything was run from Lisbon. The press was censored. Secret police all over the place. Africans, if they had a job, had an employment book that had to be signed by their employer every day. If the employer didn't sign it and they were picked up by the authorities their heads were shaved and they were thrown in gaol or shipped out to the middle of nowhere. If they didn't have a job, they worked for the government six months a year. Special Chefe do Postos rounded up groups of men at random and shipped them off to work on the plantations virtually as slaves. The more the Chefe do Postos could round up and the better the quality of their victims, the more money they made. If any victims ran away or broke any of the rules laid down by their employer they were beaten with a *baramatola*, a ping-pong bat with holes in it carefully designed to cause maximum pain but the minimum evidence of a beating. For serious offences the victim was simply shackled, shipped to the middle of nowhere and dumped. Whether he survived or not nobody cared.

But the buildings, the style, the designs the Portuguese left behind are as worth preserving as many of the historical sites cluttering up the world today. (While they're at it UNESCO should also take a look at the old Portuguese trucks and armoured cars rotting away into the dust. They must be worth preserving as the symbol of something or other.)

As for the rest of the place, it's Africa twenty years ago. Maybe thirty years ago. Rough tracks. Rubbish. Filthy hovels. Pigs wandering around wallowing in the mud. Batteries chained and padlocked to vans and trucks. Graffiti over whatever walls are standing, including one referring to the Beatles that, my Portuguese not being what it might, I could not quite understand and that nobody seemed to be prepared to translate for me. The offices I visited looked much the same apart from the occasional splash of faded colour provided by recycled Che Guevara posters.

Having seen the traditional port, I took a look at the official port. You can see why everybody wonders what happened to the US$500,000 the Taiwanese gave them to modernise the place. The local markets are as busy as any you come across in Africa: a million people. Tiny Guineans. Tall, thin Senegalese and Mauritanians. Busy Chinese. Casual Lebanese. Flowing robes. Traditional costumes. T-shirts. A marked lack of T-shirts. Kids of every size, shape and colour you can imagine. In the huge, sprawling central market I came across Christian, a young, tough-looking guy from Zimbabwe. Zimbabwe! What was he doing here running a market stall in Guinea-Bissau?

'I wanted to get away from Mugabe. Everybody wants to get away from Mugabe,' he told me. 'I wanted to go to Austria. But I was stuck in Moscow. A friend said to me, "Come to Guinea-Bissau." Here I am.'

Was he making money?

'I am surviving,' he almost smiled. 'It's better than Zimbabwe. But it's not good.'

He had high hopes, however. The drugs companies had finally agreed to ship low-cost AIDS drugs to Africa.

'You're going to sell them to local people suffering from AIDS?' I wondered.

He laughed, wiped his face with his hands and pointed his finger at me.

'You very funny man,' he grinned. 'Poor African people have no money for even cheap AIDS drugs. I am selling them to my brother in Holland. He sells them to people in Europe with money. We make lots of money.'

'So how do you get the drugs?' Forever the practical man, that's me.

'How do I get the drugs?' By now he is practically rolling around the centre of Bissau with laughter. 'I have another brother. He works at airport. He drives the buses. We get drugs when they arrive at airport. Good, yes?'

About the only uplifting experience I had in the whole place was the sight of the Bra military camp and its display of rusty old cannons. It was so overgrown with grass it didn't look as though it could withstand an attack by lawnmowers let alone tanks – provided, of course, the sand didn't gum up the engines like it usually does.

One evening towards the end of my trip when I had finally discovered that man can live by bread alone, I realised that not only was the hotel a genuine Soviet hotel – it was built by the Russians as a super-VIP guest house – but that it still operated like a genuine Soviet hotel. After three days I still hadn't had my shirt and my linen jacket back from the laundry.

'I don't know why you're complaining about your shirt when you haven't got your jacket back either,' the babushka in charge of the laundry told me.

Not that I was worried. Throughout my stay, whenever it was time to pay or I had to sign a bill, instead of giving my room number, which was 666, I turned the wooden key ring upside down and showed 999, even though it would have been quite obvious to even the most junior Soviet under-secretary of state that there were nowhere near that many rooms in the hotel, nobody queried it.

Long live the five-star hotels of Africa.

Conakry

My brothers and fellow international trade unionists. It is a great honour for you to invite me to give the first annual John Prescott Memorial Lecture on Great Trade Unionists of our Time.

It is an even greater honour for you to listen to me speak on the theme: Leading with the Left – Punching Your Way to Freedom.

In the words of the great John Prescott himself as he stood waiting for one of his two Jaguars to transport him just 100 yards from his humble five-star luxury hotel to the New Labour conference centre where he was to play a major role as a listener to the thoughts of President Blair, 'The average in proportion of great trade union leaders from all world countries must, should and has been in the future increasing on a country by country basis and we are showing leadership though it actually reduced recently and the commitment therefore to get the kind of resources necessary to deal with this ecology environment are in the region of which everyone is aware of the figure in monetary terms to deal with how we can marshal this kind of proportional proposal so that we can get the order of priority to deal with this leadership in a leadership environment.'

Nothing could be clearer than that, could it?

My subject today, therefore, is one of the great trade unionists of our time, who rose from being yet another humble, shy, unassuming trade union leader to become president of one of the richest countries in the world, brother His Excellency Sékou Touré of Guinea. So called because if he was in any negotiation and the bloated capitalists offered five pounds he would always demand a guinea. But don't be misled. The great Sékou Touré was no cheap politician. He cost his country a fortune.

Opponents say that he behaved as any responsible trade unionist would in a position of power. In a completely straightforward, honest, direct and unbiased manner he dodged all his responsibilities and completely destroyed the social, economic and political fabric of his country. He also, they claim, set back the development of his country by fifty years.

Supporters say that he kept all the promises he made. They found them after his death, in his own handwriting, on a screwed-up piece of paper at the bottom of his wastepaper basket. No one, however, can deny that he got the country moving. Everyone capable of moving, moved. To next-door Guinea-Bissau. To Senegal. To Mali. To Côte d'Ivoire. To Liberia and Sierra Leone. The less fortunate found their way to France.

What today should be one of the richest, fastest-growing and most dynamic countries in Africa, if not the world, is instead still bouncing along at the bottom of the heap. Some say that being French it was because he stayed Toulon. Others say that whether he stayed in Toulon or not it was the people who had everything Toulouse because of him.

As a result his successor, Colonel Lansana Conti, who is definitely not a great trade union leader, is desperately struggling to get the country back on its knees. He is doing his best to develop the country's enormous natural resources: gold, diamonds, bauxite – they have the world's largest supply – copper, iron, manganese and so on.

He is also desperately trying to persuade tourists to come visit a country that for years was way, way off the beaten track, even though it's got everything to offer. Fabulous scenery. Forests. Mountains. Waterfalls. Especially during the rainy season. Friendly – sometimes too friendly – people. Good food. And music. Guinea sets the standard for music throughout west Africa. Listen to any cassette. Go into any bar or club. Two out of three times the music will be from Guinea.

As for other visitors, they have no problems. The country is practically overrun with refugees. Most official estimates, in fact, claim that with over four hundred thousand refugees already in the country, one in ten of the population is a refugee, the highest proportion of refugees in any country in the world. They've come from Sierra Leone. From Liberia. And also from Guinea-Bissau. Wander around Kindia, about three hours' drive north of the capital, Conakry. In the old days people used to flood here to see the famous Bridal Falls, which I thought referred to something other than a fairly miserable-looking waterfall. Now they flood here to get away from the fighting in Sierra Leone. It's the same story in Yagouya, Kissidougou and Gueckedou.

Worse still, the rebels fighting the government in Sierra Leone have followed the refugees. The British hoped that by sending troops to back up the Sierra Leone government they would help them put a stop to the rebellion. Which they have. In Sierra Leone. Now the problem is affecting Guinea as well. Hardly a day goes past without them attacking and looting villages along the border, kidnapping recruits and getting their hands on as many of Guinea's precious diamonds as possible.

Backing the Sierra Leone rebels are soldiers from Liberia who are acting either officially, unofficially or both. Officially, the view is that Liberia believes the rebels in Sierra Leone have a case and – in the spirit of brotherly love – wants to do everything it can to help them bring down an unfair, unjust and corrupt government. Officially and unofficially, the view is that they'll do whatever the hell Charles Taylor decides he wants to do. In the meantime innocent villagers along the border are being attacked, robbed and killed, and the flood of refugees, already in their hundreds of thousands, gets bigger by the day.

The refugees from Liberia, however, are more likely to be found in and around Conakry than in camps along the border. They tend to be either political refugees trying to hide from Charles Taylor and his henchmen or businessmen who have fallen foul of the system. The refugees from Guinea-Bissau tend to be military refugees: senior officers and commanders who backed the wrong side in one of many military coups or attempted coups.

In the UK a favourite game is Spot the Illegal Immigrant. In Guinea, with so many refugees in the country, their favourite game is Try to Spot the Real Refugee from the Fake or More Likely Military Refugee in Disguise. Either military refugee trying to escape or military chasing the military refugee trying to escape. Some say you can easily identify them by their confidence, their swagger and their bulging wallets. I'm no genius, but go for the guys in the bars and clubs and restaurants who are ordering filet de boeuf and the best French wines. You won't go far wrong.

Given the state of the Guinean economy and the number of refugees in the country, domino theorists have for some time predicted that Guinea would be the next to fall. Not so. They seem to be hanging on probably because of the amount of business generated by the refugees.

But I am getting ahead of myself, as John Prescott said on the second day of the New Labour Party conference when he found it was quicker to walk to the conference hall than take one of his two ministerial Jags.

Once upon a time and a half our brother Sékou Touré was a legend. He was the most famous Communist, the most famous trade union leader in French Africa. He was up there with the poet philosopher Léopold Senghor, who led Senegal to independence, and with the good doctor Houphouet

Boigny, who did the same in Côte d'Ivoire. The difference was they were establishment. They were almost more French than the French. Senghor was a member of the Académie Française. Houphouet was a minister in the French government. But Sékou Touré was a trade unionist through and through, a founder member of the Democratic Party of Guinea and a man of the people. Once before going to Guinea Conakry, I had had half a mind to study his political philosophy to better acquaint myself with the country and its history. As it turned out that was all I needed: half a mind. It was so simple it was unbelievable.

'Zee daffodils. If zay is out, everyone is out,' he would say.

Sékou Touré's first victory came in 1956 when he led the French-African trade unions in their fight to break away from the French trade unions and set up their own self-serving, grossly inefficient, overstaffed, hugely overpaid organisation. Flushed with success he then turned his fire on the big one: Le Général himself. Throughout Africa everybody was clamouring for independence. De Gaulle wanted to play the usual French game and instead of giving all the French colonies their independence he wanted to establish a 'community'. Sékou Touré wanted nothing short of independence. Full. Complete. Total. All those in favour, vote now.

'Freedom in poverty,' he declared with the fervour of an old-time trade unionist, 'is better than prosperity in chains.'

Sékou Touré won. Guinea became the first French colony to gain its independence. Full. Complete. Total. All those in favour, vote now. De Gaulle acted as any democratically elected French President would have acted in the circumstances. He ordered the French out. *Immédiatement*. Not only that but he told them to destroy everything before they left. The files. The papers. The documents. The telephones. All the military equipment. Full. Complete. Total. In diplomatic circles this was known as a Guinea fowl.

Sékou Touré turned naturally to the Russians. Oh, those heady days when we all knew who were our friends and who were our enemies. Immediately, using tried and tested Russian employment policies, he cut the length of the unemployment queues. He made everybody stand closer together. But his affair with the Russians didn't last. Next he turned to the Chinese. The whole country was turned into one vast Chinese takeaway. The Chinese took away the Guineans' freedom to go into business, to work for themselves and to make their own money. Instead everything had to be run by the state. Everybody had to attend revolutionary meeting after revolutionary meeting after revolutionary meeting. He banned the teaching of French. He introduced censorship.

'If we regard artistic and cultural activities as a means of education, and if we intend to use them as the means of our revolutionary thinking, we must ruthlessly reject from our artistic and cultural expression everything that does not contribute to the dissemination of revolutionary thinking or foster the reinforcement of revolutionary action. The control over our artistic and cultural production will be effected by a censorship committee, which will authorise the publication and distribution of works found to be in keeping with the orientation and aims of our revolution,' he wrote in his book *Africa on the Move*. Which, as I have said, it undoubtedly did. Within days of publication all those who hadn't moved already left Guinea for Paris. Those who couldn't were promptly moved to prison or one kind of imprisonment or another. To compensate he introduced shorter hours. Instead of sixty minutes to the hour, he made it thirty minutes. The result: nobody did any work. The whole country collapsed even more. But it wasn't his fault. He did everything he could to them—I mean, for them. In order to give his people what he knew they wanted he was chained to his desk. Which was only fair. So many of his colleagues were also chained to their desks or whatever was handy.

Like any true liberal, he also saw conspiracies and enemies both to the right and to the right of him. He accused practically everybody of plotting against him: the French, *naturellement*, the Americans, the Russians, the Chinese, the Germans and, for some reason, the Rhodesians. He even turned against his own tribe, the Fulani. The tribal chief was arrested and thrown in prison, where he was starved to death. The great champion of workers' rights then turned against his own workers. The place became a police state. People were arrested and shot without trial, on one occasion as many as seventy-one in a single go. Torture was commonplace. The whole place was a nightmare. Full. Complete. Total. All the time, however, he maintained he was a democrat. People could say what they liked about him. What they couldn't say was what they didn't like about him.

The break came with the market women. Sékou Touré decided that instead of what little farm produce there was being sold to them in future it would go to a string of state-run distribution centres. The market women, most of whom were built like tanks, went for his throat, which was not what he had expected. They broke into police stations. They attacked the police. They waged war on the politicians. In three provinces they killed the governors. Sékou Touré backed down.

He also did a U-turn. A full 360-degree U-turn. Instead of being the great enemy of France, he now became its greatest friend. The President, now Giscard d'Estaing (and known following a visit to President Bokassa in the Central Africa Republic, throughout French Africa as a true diamond), was invited to drop by for a *petite quelquechose*. Sékou Touré himself then started visiting other African leaders as if to make amends, and to warn them, whatever they did, to stay away from market women.

His thesis finally hit his antithesis when he died in 1984 and he was once again a hero. Heads of state flocked to his funeral. Some said it was to make certain he was dead. They had no sooner got home and out of their black suits than the military moved in, overthrew the government, released all the political prisoners and promised to undo the total mess that Sékou Touré had created. The result is that today the country is twenty to twenty-five years behind his manifesto.

The capital, Conakry, is enough to make you wonder at the lengths, not to mention inconvenience, people are prepared to go to help the local wildlife. Instead of collecting up all the food, all the rubbish, all the yuk that is no longer needed, thus depriving the local wildlife of many a happy hunting and breeding ground, they deliberately allow it to pile higher and higher. Not just in one spot. But all over the city. The place is littered with so many broken campaign promises, it is the dirtiest, smelliest and filthiest city in west Africa. Worse even than Lagos, which is saying something. Not that one believes in negative implications let alone historical materialism, but on a Smelly City Index – Dakar, fish; Luanda, gunpowder; and Lagos, Fattachachajaha (which is the noise you make when you smell something in Lagos) – I'd give it five. Not stars. Pegs. Because that's how many you'll need clamped on your nose to keep the smell out. All over the place you can also see their dedication to the masses – masses of rubbish, masses of yuk and masses of I-hope-that's-not-what-I-think-it-is. But all is not in vain. Their efforts have been more than rewarded. Wherever you look you can see the local wildlife benefiting from the fruits of their labour. Or rather the fruits of their New Labour.

For historical determination – or, rather, struggling to rejoin the world, I'll also give them five. Stars this time. Not pegs. All over the place you can see at long last the first signs of real capitalist degeneration. In other words, progress. Not much. But it's there. All the old dinosaurs from the days of Sékou Touré still exist but they're being either shut down, cleaned up, given a lick of paint or brought back into operation again.

Although – talk about supply and demand – it will still be many years before there is a bath plug in every bath, let alone running water for 99 per cent of the poor proletariat.

The Hôtel de l'Indépendance is still there, with its fifty-odd identical Moorish-style self-contained chalets. It was specially built by Sékou Touré for the 1984 meeting of the Organisation of African Unity, which, in accordance with the law of revolutionary inevitability, never took place, because rather than stand up and say he fell for the whole stupid idea and coughed up the readies in advance, he died shortly before it opened. Some say it was when he finally got the bill: it was less than the commission he was demanding for agreeing to build it in the first place. People then wondered what to do with it. I always thought it should have been turned into an OAU Theme Park for African Presidents. Nothing could better illustrate what not to do. The different chalets could have been devoted to different themes: Why not to suspend elections; Why not to build up the army; Why not to put your best friend and most trusted adviser in charge of interior affairs and security; Why not to use luxury hotels as presidential offices because it always leads to an army mutiny. That kind of thing. The new President, General Lansana Conte, however, decided to use it as his presidential office. What happened? The army mutinied.

The Hôtel de l'Unité is still there. This was the massive Chinese-built People's Palace – except that very few of the people were allowed in it. Only Sékou Touré's buddies, hangers-on and all the usual Party hacks. Today it's as hollow and as empty as all the slogans they used to parrot. I wandered around it, no problem. The only danger came not from being stopped by security guards but by being hit by bits of the ceiling that were falling off.

There is also still one glorious reminder of the Soviet days. Parked in the middle of the main road into town from the airport is a real-life snowplough. The Guineans say it's for moving rubbish. But they can't fool me.

The town itself is busy, dank and damp. In fact, speaking as a completely non-twisted, non-cynical, dialectical materialist, I would say it looked about ready to take off. The hotels are full. The bars are busy. Even Le Nelson Night Club is throbbing especially as, I understand, they turn a blind eye to practically everything. In the Hotel Camayenne I met a little fat Belgian who was making a fortune selling all kinds of diamond mining, assessing and cutting equipment. The more upmarket bourgeois Mariador Palace was full of obviously more important and more serious exploiters of the proletariat, all lounging around, falling asleep, scratching themselves and doing multimillion dollar deals buying and selling diamond mines.

Everywhere else there are market stalls and markets. Even in the very centre of town there are often so many petit bourgeoisie and market stalls on the pavement you have to walk in the street.

The biggest market of all, the Medina, is so jam-packed with people that not even the most persistent *agent de redistribution* could get his hand in your pocket to lift your wallet. The reason: war.

As I tried to shuffle from stall to stall I came across a group of serious-looking Sierra Leonians. They saw me wandering around and thought, God help me, that I was Lebanese and therefore in their eyes and in the eyes of most Africans that I was their man. Their leader, who had a deep, festering gash running the whole length of his right cheek, told me they were from Tongo, one of the rebel-held areas. Until the UN got involved they used to meet their Lebanese contacts in Freetown. When things began to get hot and Britain sent troops to Sierra Leone to beef up the army, they simply upped and moved to Conakry. The Lebanese had problems following them. They thought they were being shadowed. Every time, therefore, they sent somebody different.

'The market is good place to meet,' Scarface whispered in my ear. 'Everybody is here. Everybody is doing everything.'

'Market is very safe,' added one of his sidekicks, who looked more like a bodyguard with attitude than a dealer. 'Everybody knows a stranger. We see stranger we disappear.'

How much business did they normally do?

'Diamonds, this much.' Scarface poured a pile of tiny bits of glass from a black bag into his hand. 'This much US$50,000.'

'So what does a million dollars look like?'

He pushed back the rubbish in the ground and drew a circle in the sand with his foot.

'This much,' he said.

In Europe, in Asia, in the US, of course, the diamonds would be worth so much more. For all the agony and heartache and risks, the poor African miners and fixers – like the cocaine growers and fixers in South America – get next to nothing, which is probably just as well. If they got what they should for their diamonds, Africa would be knee-deep in nuclear weapons by now. But what they do get is enough at least to keep them knee-deep in conventional weapons: anti-tank weapons, surface-to-air missiles, rocket-propelled grenades complete with launchers, guns and cartridges. Most of them delivered under cover of darkness in huge Ukrainian-built Antonov 124s to places like Ouagadougou, capital of friendly-to-all Burkina Faso, or the more respectable Abidjan in the Ivory Coast. From there they disappear.

Again and again, the Western governments, with the support of the worldwide diamond industry, have tried to ban what they call blood or conflict diamonds: diamonds – again like cocaine in South America – sold outside the system to finance the weapons shipments. They talk about audits, codes of conduct, legal sanctions. All I can say is, Come to Conakry. Take a walk around the Medina, see for yourself how effective it is. I've also been to the world trading centre for diamonds, three anonymous-looking streets opposite the central railway station in Antwerp: Hovenierstraat, Schupstraat and Rijfstraat. I didn't notice them any less busy than usual.

Whether my new-found friends thought I was their Lebanese contact or not, or maybe even a United Nations inspector on the snoop, I couldn't tell you. All I know is they never left my side.

'Lebanese,' Scarface kept saying. 'He is like snake in grass. Swish. Swish. Swish. You can't see him. But he is there.'

As we wandered from stall to cardboard box to piles of rubbish on the ground, they gave me the low-down on diamond smuggling.

'Lebanese good,' they kept saying.

They also told me they had contact with Canadians working with government soldiers in Sierra Leone.

'They know what to do,' they grinned.

'The British?' I asked.

They laughed. Mr Bodyguard revealed four huge white teeth with what appeared to be blood congealed all around them. It was anyone's guess what the other guy looked like.

We stopped to speak to one stallholder who was completely bald except for a thick black brillo-pad patch on top of his head that looked as though it had been cut into the shape of a crumpled peaked cap. He told me he also did regular business with traders from Ghana, Côte d'Ivoire and Senegal, Niger and Mali as well.

'We have the products. We have good prices. They come,' he grinned.

I gave him the usual African greeting. How many children have you got?

'Fifteen or sixteen. Maybe twenty. I don't know.'

'But surely . . .'

He told me he travelled around all the time. He had five or

six wives in different countries. Sierra Leone. Liberia. Ghana. Mali.

'It's difficult,' he said, 'to remember.' He wiped his face with his two big hands. 'They're just children.'

We picked our way through the rubbish and slush and I-hope-that's-not-what-I-think-it-is-either to a roadside bar. Behind it was a huge poster that said, Welcome to London, which gave me quite a start. London turned out to be a cigarette.

I ordered a beer. So did the stallholder. I got the barman to take the top off the bottle for me and slugged it down. Not the Father of Africa. He insisted on a glass and five cubes of ice. He swirled the cubes round and round the glass. He then wanted the barman to add some water to the glass until it covered the ice cubes. He then swirled the cubes round the glass three times, sipped the water carefully, swirled the water round again three times to the left and three times to the right. Finally he turned and emptied the whole lot on the ground. Finally he poured the bottle of cheap beer into the glass. My God, do the French have a lot to answer for.

We were joined by a group of fellow travellers, some Senegalese who were so tall they had snow on top of their heads. They told me that they regularly travelled three or four days in filthy jungle taxis to get to the market and three or four days back loaded down with all their goods.

A surprisingly small sparrow of a Senegalese, who looked like Gandhi might have looked if he had stayed in Africa and stuck to the black suits, told me he was from Rufisque, which I've visited many times. He was there to buy clothes, perfumes and to change money.

'Business is good,' he grinned. 'Very good.'

He used to be a teacher. He learnt English from visiting Canadian aid workers. But he gave up teaching because he didn't make enough money. Now he spent three weeks a month at Dakar airport, chatting up the tourists, helping them fill in their Immigration forms, finding them taxis and whatever else they wanted. The fourth week he comes to Conakry.

'It's not respectable,' he told me. 'But I make more money than being a teacher. Now my family can eat. The children can go to school. We have new clothes.'

How much more money?

'Twice? Three times? Four times?' He began laughing. 'Much. Much more. And it is in my hand. Now. Not like being a teacher when we have to wait, wait, wait.'

Then suddenly I was on my own. No Sierra Leonians. No Scarface. No Bodyguard. No nobody. Just me, an empty bottle, the barman and the poster, Welcome to London. Maybe their real contact turned up. Maybe a United Nations inspector was on the snoop. Maybe because it was their turn to buy a drink. I made my way back through the rubbish, back through the stalls, back through the mass of people. This time nobody smiled, swore, said a word or even acknowledged my existence. It was like being a socialist at a New Labour conference.

But enough of the past. It is time to move on. My conclusion, therefore, brothers and fellow international trade unionists, is that brother His Excellency Sékou Touré laid the foundations. From the thesis and antithesis has come the synthesis. Life may not now be soft, but neither is it as hard as it used to be. As the great John Prescott himself would have said, 'They have nothing to lose but their jeans.'

Praia

Forget Seattle. Forget Genoa. Forget even Doha. It's boring. No fun. No excitement. And the fuss they make about having a drink. The place for all those super-super-top-level international conferences like the World Trade Organisation and the G8, or even peace conferences between the warlords in Afghanistan, is Cape Verde.

It's a million miles from anywhere . . . well, it's around 600 kilometres off the west coast of Africa to be precise. Except it feels like 600 million kilometres from anywhere. It's the kind of place that if the whole world blew itself to pieces would continue jogging along on its own quiet way, at its own pace. In fact, it probably wouldn't notice the world had blown itself to pieces.

It's pleasant, or if you're lucky, very pleasant. No aggro. No hassle. Not like being at home at all. Stay there a month. There's no way it would set your trousers on fire.

It's dry. (Forget the Sahara.) Some say it's the driest place in Africa, if not the world. It rains only once or twice a year. Even then it's just a quick burst, not like, say, Manchester or Bergen, Norway or any of the other great rainforests of the world where again it rains only once or twice a year. For six months non-stop.

And there is plenty for the overworked, hard-pressed international conference delegate to do on Cape Verde away from the prying eyes of the press and the poor people who elected them in the first place.

There is diving, windsurfing, deep-sea fishing, game-fishing, hiking, climbing volcanoes or even just soaking up the sun. Nonetheless, Ryszard Kapuscinski, the famous Polish-born journalist and self-styled expert on Africa, keeps referring to 'the hell of the Cape Verde Islands'. Which proves how much journalists and self-styled experts know.

Six hundred kilometres off the coast of Senegal it may be, but Cape Verde is not African. It's Portuguese. The people look Portuguese or, at least, like descendants of the Portuguese. The houses with their verandas and fancy railings are Portuguese. The streets with their plazas and cobblestones are Portuguese. I've never known any country in the world to have so many cobblestones. The food and drink are Portuguese. You can live the life of luxury and order bottle after bottle of Mateus Rosé in Cape Verde.

The amazing thing is until 1456 the place was wholly deserted. It was completely uninhabited until the Portuguese discovered it or as a guidebook I bought in Praia, the capital, says, 'Portuguese semen first arrived in Cape Verde in 1456.' Either way – or maybe both ways – you've got to admit, it's strange. Usually wherever you go in the world there is always a Lebanese there to welcome you and sell you something.

The Portuguese were so shocked by the fact that they were the first to set foot on the place, and the fact that there was nobody there for them to murder, attack and mercilessly enslave as they did throughout the rest of Africa, that it took them six years before they even bothered to make a return trip. But when they did, they stayed for good.

They built their first town, Ribeira Grande, in their own image and likeness. Then to feel at home they shipped in slaves from all along the west African coast to plant and run their plantations and their vineyards, which is they say one reason why there is no rain. They chopped down all the trees to make way for the plantations. No trees: no rain. Have another glass of Mateus Rosé. Others blame the goats. After the Portuguese chopped the trees down, the goats munched up all the undergrowth. The trees didn't have a chance to throw off even a few shoots before they were gone again.

Cape Verde has also got the one thing that will force any conference to a rapid conclusion: Portuguese music. Threaten anyone – delegates to a World Trade Organisation conference, members of G8, even representatives of the European Union – with three choruses of their jolly, jolly *batuque*, which is like a cross between a high school song and a boy scout jamboree jingle that somehow bores its way into your head and starts – God help me. I can hear them even now – taking over your whole life and you'll agree to anything. Admitting China to the WTO in sixteen weeks not sixteen years. Throwing ever more money down the drain in Russia. I reckon it would even make Tony Blair sign up for the euro with or without Gordon Brown. Failing that there's the *morna*, which is not only miserable, it positively makes you feel like committing suicide just to get away from it. Usually they play it late at night, after a heavy session when . . . when . . . when . . . No. No. I'll sign now. Anything but the music. Anything.

What the Cape Verdeans should do is turn Praia into a sun-drenched offshore diplomatic haven, safe from the world. I'm sure the United Nations would cough up the readies. It would be cheaper than rebuilding Seattle or Genoa or whichever city pulls the short straw for the next big international conference.

Kofi Annan would like the idea: African helping African; the opportunity to inject huge resources into the continent; the creation of millions of jobs; the chance for Africa to be seen centre stage playing a mediating role between world powers, helping to make the world a safer place; blah blah blah. You know the story.

They've got plenty of international experience. Before the UN, the WTO, G8 or the EU was even a set of initials, Cape Verde set itself up as the world's first offshore trading centre. Admittedly it was an offshore slave-trading centre, but one international offshore trading centre is very much like another. With America coming into the market and demanding more and more slaves, they then also turned themselves into an international distribution and financial centre. Slaves could be shipped out from Africa by the Europeans to Cape Verde. What the Americans wanted, they took. The surplus went to Europe. Cape Verde being in the middle of nowhere meant there were no problems with the authorities, no problems with rules and regulations, no problems about where the money went. Later they turned themselves into a major halfway supply depot for the big transatlantic liners and cargo ships.

They know what it's all about. They know about running things. They may look laid-back, casual, eager for the next beer. But they're smart. They've provided some of the best African politicians around. For a number of years they've also been, officially and unofficially, running a number of nearby countries not a million miles from Guinea or Guinea-Bissau.

They know how to entertain foreign visitors. They speak all the important languages: English, Creole, French Creole, English French Creole, African Creole, African English French Creole. They're well practised. In between buying and selling slaves, the Portuguese set to work. They dedicated themselves to doing what they felt only they could do: increase the population. From one man and a goat four hundred years ago, the population today is over four hundred thousand and one very exhausted goat.

They know how to work. They were hit again and again and again by drought, and every century, even up to the twentieth, literally hundreds of thousands died. To escape many jumped ship and headed for the States where they landed jobs on whaling ships out of New England. Others went to other Portuguese colonies throughout Africa. Some made it big time. Others, especially those who went to São Tomé, the one-time Portuguese colony off the coast of Nigeria, were treated almost like slaves. Of those who stayed, most had it rough and very, very thirsty. The privileged few hit the jackpot. They went to school. Cape Verde was the first Portuguese colony to establish a college for higher education. More education, however, meant one thing: they wanted independence. Cape Verde on its own and later together with Guinea-Bissau (under Cape Verde leadership, of course) began the fight for independence that was finally won in 1975.

On the main island of São Tiago, Praia, which is home to practically half the population, is like a huge fort overlooking the sea. In the old days, apparently, you could hardly walk along the streets for people smashed out of their minds on *grogo*, raw alcohol distilled from mashed sugar cane. Today it's clean, quiet, safe. Around the Esplanada, the town square, things get a bit hectic. Beware the women with handbags. They're the unofficial money changers. They are always guaranteed to make you a good offer. The real money, however, is in Prainha, which stands on a low cliff overlooking the sea. Not that there seems to be much obvious money. It's more Tunbridge Wells than, say, Cheltenham or Chester.

Outside Praia things are pretty basic, even in some cases just about medieval – and I don't just mean those cobblestones. The whole island is little other than steep slopes, sugar cane, bananas, derelict and near-derelict cottages, goats tied up to trees, pigs rooting around in the dirt, donkeys standing contentedly in the shade, chickens scratching in the dust, rusty old Bedford vans, prehistoric Land Rovers, friendly old men, sitting in the sun, chatting away about the old days and, of course, as there are wherever you go in the world, miserable old women, bent double with huge piles of sticks or sugar cane, moaning and complaining and yelling and swearing at everything and everyone in sight. There are also lots of dykes and ditches and water-retaining walls. And trees. They've started to plant trees again, even an acacia specially developed for them. But this time they're doing it properly. The goats are kept well away.

Cidade Velha is the 'old city', the first town built by the Portuguese. But the way they go on about it you'd have thought it was the Parthenon, the Colosseum and the latest wobbly Richard Rogers bridge all rolled into one. In fact, it's pretty much the same as any other Cidade Velha built by the Portuguese. Except this one seemed to be low on the Mateus Rosé bottles and big on cobblestones.

Far more fun is the bar on the beach down below. Many's the evening I sat there with the locals, drinking and chatting away in whatever language I thought they were speaking, as great red streaks and flashes of light suddenly appeared, as the air grew slowly cold and colder and a thick, heavy all-enveloping darkness surrounded me.

Other evenings I watched the sun go down.

St George – the town is not one of my favourite St Georges. It's not worth killing a chicken let alone a dragon for. At the end of a precarious track – those cobblestones again – it's a tiny huddle of old buildings, some of which look as though they could have been home to St George's great-great-great-grandfather. At one end is what they call a botanical garden, although to me it looked more organic than botanic. At the other, a pig factory. Outside was a tiny open-air bar. Which somehow or other I didn't fancy, but you can bet your life the pork scratchings are fresh.

Assomado is more the real thing. It's a proper town, overgrown with scrub, full of half-built or maybe unbuilt houses and masses of people. The plaza and the church look as though they could have been home to any number of slave traders. I went into one bar called, strangely, Bar One Love. 'What Is This Thing Called Love?' indeed.

I avoided Ribiera Grande. It's where, in 1585, Sir Francis Drake and his band of merry men arrived and – in typically British fashion – did their best to destroy the place in reprisal for the killing of just one of his men.

Tarrafal at the far end of the island looks as if it were already home to people who have just upped and disappeared. Imagine a beautiful little bay. One or two boats bobbing up and down in the water. Broiling hot sunshine. Dogs lying in the shade. Almost nobody around. Looking down on one side of the bay, an open-air bar and restaurant where for next-to-nothing you can wash down bowl after bowl of the local throw-everything-in-it catchup soup with bottle after bottle of Mateus Rosé and practise your Creole on the waitresses.

'*Mneena. Castabon.*'

Castabon? Wasn't he the miserable old vicar in *Middlemarch*?

'*Meena. Oh-joo. Boo-oh-joo-eh-ben-ee-toh.*'

Further down, closer to the bay, is a small, fancy hotel with all the more upmarket delights. I sat out on the upstairs balcony. It was fabulous. It was quiet. The sun was hot. The only people in the place were an elderly married French couple. I could tell they were married. The wife, who looked as though she had never wanted for anything in her obviously overlong life, was doing everything she could to totally ignore her overworked, downtrodden, more than tolerant husband. As for the town itself, it's everything Cidade Velha wasn't. Warm, friendly, dusty, perhaps a bit dirty. Fabulous.

Apart from São Tiago, the biggest and most densely populated island, there are nine others that make up Cape Verde, stretched out over 250 miles of Atlantic. The locals call them crumbs, because, they say, they were left on God's hands after

He had finished creating the world. Very funny Cape Verdean joke.

Six of them, the windward islands (Ilhas do Barlavento), are to the north. São Antão is the wettest of the lot. It rains so much that people have forgotten what it is to be dry.

São Vicente, home to the second largest city, Mindelo, is the fun island. It's the place to go for parties, carnivals, musical raves and everything hardworking, exhausted sailors do over 600 kilometres away from anywhere. It's not exactly Rio – not unless you've got a couple of pints of grogo inside you – but it's the nearest you'll get stuck 600 kilometres out off the west coast of Africa. It was labelled 'the gravel heap' by the British when during the nineteenth century they used it as a pit stop for their coaling operations up and down the north and south Atlantic. Almost every Cape Verdean you meet is eager to tell you that one or other of their great-great-etc.-grandparents was British (which must be a tribute to the hardworking, exhausted British businessman over 600 kilometres from anywhere); that their name was Randall or North or Griffiths; and that they are one-eighth, one-sixteenth or one-somethingth British, which would scare the hell out of our tolerant, sympathetic British government. If they find out, they'll have immigration officials over here checking them out.

São Nicolau is a softer, gentler version of São Antão: softer rain, gentler showers. The same appalling double pneumonia. Sal is like Mars: all dry red rock, salt and 10 per cent extra for free. Boavista is as flat with the occasional sand dune blown grain by grain across – would you believe – the 600 kilometres of Atlantic from the Sahara. Santa Luzia is uninhabited, unless, of course, somebody goes and stays there.

The remaining four islands are all to the south or leeward (ilhas do Sotavento) if you happen to be related to any of the hard-working, exhausted sailors.

Next door to São Tiago, Maio is flat, quiet to the point of

being dead. Fogo boasts the active and smoking volcano Mount Fogo, which has coffee and vines growing on the black lava inside the giant crater.

In spite of no end of encouragement – even begging letters from home – I never got to Brava, the old whaling port, which is probably just as well. They say that once you drink its strange, vinegary spring water you'll never ever leave, which would be a crying shame. Not for me but for the world.

For, having sampled the delights, I am convinced that it is now my duty to persuade our leaders that the world will be a safer place if instead of making war they pop over to Cape Verde and talk about it. In other words plead a Praia engagement.

Victoria

I saw a little bird high in the sky above,
A lonely bird making for a destination unknown.
Little bird, where are you heading for?
Where are your friends?
What are you doing up in the sky so high?
There were flowers blossoming around me
As I sat alone on a garden bench;
I could hear my heart beating within me.
What am I looking for?
Where are my friends?
Will I ever see that little bird again
In the sky so high . . .?

Not many people send me poems. Not many African presidents send me poems. But James Richard Marie Mancham, the first President of the Seychelles, did.

I first met him in a small terraced house backing on to the Thames in Putney, south London. He had been the playboy President. Always wearing his trademark Hawaiian shirts. Always driving around in fancy sports cars. And always surrounded by more than enough silicone-enhanced eye-candy for one man.

He had just been overthrown by his loyal deputy, the hard-line Marxist, Comrade Albert René, while he was attending the

Commonwealth Conference in London. So quiet, so low-key and so successful was the coup that the first Mancham knew about it was when – typical Jimmy – he turned up at the Playboy Club for some quiet post-conference relaxation and discovered that his credit cards were no longer valid.

He was looking for things to do. More than anything he was desperate to make money. Which surprised me. I've met enough African presidents in my time to line a Swiss bank. Not one of them gave me the impression that they were in the slightest worried about such a mundane thing as money. That had been taken care of years ago. Mancham, it seemed, was the exception. He was working as a consultant for some fancy concern based in north Wales. Which, again, didn't seem right for a—or rather for an ex-playboy President of a scattering of paradise islands in the middle of the Indian Ocean. He was also trying to act the fixer for one of the big German brewers. He was trying to line up introductions for them in Africa. They would then take care of everything else. And everybody would live happily ever after. But not in north Wales.

He wanted me to help him. With contacts. With introductions. With anything that would make money. My advice, however, was the opposite: forget the money. You are the legitimate leader of the Seychelles. You have been illegally deposed. Campaign for your reinstatement. First, among African leaders. They would be bound to support you because they do not want to be overthrown themselves and end up working as consultants in north Wales. Second, with the French. They ran the Seychelles until the British moved in, but it still came within their orbit. The last thing the French could afford was to be seen not to be supporting French-inclined heads of state. Third, other world leaders. Again the north Wales argument. That and the fact that none of them would want to be seen to be supporting the illegal overthrow of a government.

We met. We talked. We drank. In Putney. In hotels. In trains to and from various parts of the country. I also spent a long time with his personal assistant, Paul Chow, who was a bit like a junior Oddjob. We did the circuit. We lobbied. We met MPs. We hung around the House of Commons.

I got notes thanking me for my 'esteemed' letters. One day they were on Airominor Ltd stationery. The next day, from JRM International. The day after, International Promotion, Marketing & Development Ltd. I got invites to tea, coffee, lunch, even dinner.

One day Mancham, who had been the Seychelles' first Prime Minister before becoming their first President, not to mention their first ex-President, was for getting his throne back. We had it all worked out. Don't just campaign to be reinstated, I said. That looks like you're power mad. You just want your job back. Instead campaign to be reinstated so that as the legitimate head of state you can ask the people to choose whom they want as president instead of having one imposed on them.

The next day he was for making money. He was hotfooting it yet again to north Wales. He was off to Germany. He was off to Africa hawking German breweries to whomever would talk to him.

In the end, he ignored all my advice – which proves I was right – and went for the money. We drifted apart. Paul Chow drifted away with him. Which was a shame because you have to say Mancham was a better President than Comrade René.

Under Mancham, the Seychelles was paradise. Happy-go-lucky. Non-stop partying. Nothing but pop stars, film stars, models, Arab princes. It was *Playboy* meets *Vogue*. Ice-cold champagne. Stirred not shaken. He had plans to turn it into an even bigger and more exciting playground for the super-rich. Exclusive beach developments. Casinos. Everything your everyday, home-loving millionaire could wish for. And probably more. He also wanted the Seychelles not to be independent but dependent on France, like the Channel Islands, Réunion, Polynesia or virtually any department of France.

Under Comrade René the Seychelles continued to be a paradise. A socialist paradise. Russian advisers. North Korean troops. Five-year plans. Rules. Regulations. Forms. There are even forms for farmers to register all their female coco-de-mer palm trees. Now I ask you. Is that crazy? Or is that crazy?

Tourist brochures all over the world insist you enjoy yourself. Not in the Seychelles, which it insists is 'one of the crossroads of travel'.

'Fishing is not permitted indiscriminately . . . Spear-fishing is banned everywhere . . . Big game fishing in the deeper waters is a specialised pleasure outside the range of most people's skills and pockets . . . Surfing is restricted to only a few places on the coasts . . . The yacht club of Victoria is often willing to admit visitors,' is the come-hither approach adopted by one visitors' guide I had thrust upon me.

It gets worse. Or better, depending on your non-socialist point of view.

'A light-weight raincoat is a useful standby even in the drier half of the year,' it says mysteriously.

But best of all is the What to Wear section: 'Clothes are generally informal. Men usually wear shorts during the day but change to less casual wear in the evening.'

In the old days the Seychelles, 1000 miles off the east coast of Africa and covering a grand total of just 107 square miles, was known as a five-star destination with three-star hotels. Now, outside the hotels, it's a three-star socialist destination. In some cases even less. Things are so desperate that they've been forced to borrow money from their arch-competitors, the people they said were doing it all wrong: the hugely successful capitalist-loving Mauritians.

President René should 'give up the disparaging remarks about the Mauritian economy', declared the local newspaper,

Regar, when the news broke. 'At least it produces the money to lend rather than being continuously in need of borrowing.'

What odds on them getting any government advertising?

The Vice-President, James Michel, who is Minister for Finance as well, should also give up promising, No more loans. The government has all the money it needs. Within just a year he had borrowed money not only from the much despised Mauritians, but over US$100 million from the Germans, Japanese, French, Arabs and goodness knows who else.

Yet for all the money they keep borrowing they never seem to have any. I've been there when the hotel stocks of wine have been the same as their stocks of beer: zero. Because of their socialist policies they keep running out of foreign exchange. Once it was so bad that the government itself had to go out and charter a shipload of booze from South Africa. A good move on the part of the government? Helping hotels. Ensuring the dwindling number of holidaymakers still determined to come to the Seychelles don't go thirsty? Oh no. This is the Socialist Republic of Comrade René don't forget. The government would sell the booze to the hotels only if they also bought imported cigarettes that had been in store for so long they'd gone stale.

Cars, however, don't seem to be a problem. Foreign exchange or no foreign exchange, there always seems to be no end of fancy Daihatsus and Subarus being unloaded at the New Port, parked on the quayside and then quickly driven off to warehouses on the Providence Industrial Estate. The names of half the importers seemed to be the same as those of half the ministers in the government. Interesting, as they say.

Who says governments are no good at business? Take the way the Seychelles welcomes tourists bringing desperately needed foreign exchange. Arrive at most holiday destinations and you are greeted with a garland of flowers, a large rum and a big wet kiss from your tour guide. I say wet because invariably his moustache gets in the way. Arrive at Anse aux Pins airport and you're greeted with nothing but rules and regulations. You must have a return ticket. You must have valid travel documents. You must have enough money to pay for your stay. You must have 'evidence of acceptability' at your next destination.

'Evidence of acceptability. But how can I have evidence of acceptability?' I asked the immigration officer pawing the stack of forms I'd thumped down on his desk. 'I'm going back home to my wife.'

Which is not what you tell Comrade Immigration Officers in the Socialist Republic of the Seychelles. I was taken out of line, marched to a shabby office with fingernail scratchings all over the walls, the odd splash of red, er, paint and an unhealthy smell. It was only by following age-old Soviet traditions and promising beer all round that I was able to leave without having to pay what they kept referring to as 'a substantial sum' as a guarantee of my good behaviour on their squalid little island.

Oh yes, and there were no benches or tables available for filling in immigration forms at the airport. You want to use one of their special exclusive counters? That'll cost you US$5. Cash. But hanging around the airport isn't really a problem. So much luggage goes missing that at least by the time you've finished rolling around the floor trying to fill in all their forms it just might have turned up.

I'm not saying a word.

About the only people who are able to move around the place without being in any way hindered by rules and regulations – let alone forced to stretch out on the floor to fill in the forms – are escaped convicts. They seem to be able to break out of their prison on Long Island, grab a prison boat and make for the mainland whenever they like. Most popular time of the year for breakouts is Christmas and the New Year. Prisoners in the Seychelles see no reason why, just because they happen to be in prison, they shouldn't spend it with their family and friends like everybody else. Personally, I prefer the opposite. At the moment I'm trying to rent the cells that they leave empty. But you'd never believe the forms they sent me to fill in.

Once out of the airport it doesn't take long to realise that like all socialist republics where all men are equal the Seychelles is a safe haven for drug dealers, money-launderers, fraudsters and every kind of crook you can imagine. Just US$10 million in a Seychelles bank and you've got yourself a Seychelles passport, Seychelles citizenship and – if you squeeze the right flesh – even Seychelles diplomatic status, which means not only that your luggage, whether it arrives or not, can never be searched anywhere in the world, it also means there's not a police force in the world that can touch you. Cheap at the price, I would have thought.

You also have to be very careful who you don't see talking to whom. Come across a mysterious meeting on an empty road near the US Tracking Station between a top policeman and a top official in charge of foreign exchange and it could be your last. Some say it's the French influence. Some say it's down to the Seychelles' being halfway between Africa and Asia. Some say they were born that way: Seychelles is where the old pirates used to bury their treasure. The whole island is built on stolen goods.

But for the workers it's as unequal as ever. Wander around the capital, Victoria, and paradise it is not. First of all it's tiny. Half a dozen streets, a couple of shacks, a car park, a bus terminal, a Victorian Big Ben-lookalike clock tower, one cinema and one set of traffic lights. Red. Not so red. Not so not so red. That's it. Toytown comes to the Indian Ocean. Clause Four in the sunshine. Rip up your unread copy of *Das Kapital*. Lay all the pages side by side and that would be the end of Victoria.

True to form the shops are empty: the shelves are empty; stacks of empty boxes are scattered all over the floor. Not a tin of Ma Ling, shredded pork and vegetable preserve, a Seychellois delicacy, in sight. And the prices. Buy a pair of cheap plastic shoes and – if they have them – you'll need your own loan from Mauritius to pay for them.

Revolution Avenue looks more than dated. It's scruffy. It's dirty. It doesn't look as though it's been swept since 1917. There's nothing about it to make you rejoice at the overthrow of the sunburned bourgeoisie.

Market Street is hardly a tribute to market forces. It's more a tribute to the lack thereof. To stop shops charging what were called 'exorbitant' prices, Comrade René established a price-control unit to control, among other things, the price of white goods: fridges and gas cookers and so on. What happened? Shops, which couldn't make any money charging the prices set by the price-control unit, stopped importing them altogether. Result: everybody loses. Customers. Shopkeepers. The government because it loses its tax rake-off. The only winner is Comrade René. Who is always right.

The post office is pure Kaliningrad circa 1960. All dark barriers. Low ceilings. Low lighting. Long queues. Lowest possible standards of service.

Offices, especially government offices, are piles of papers. Rubber stamps. Dust. At least so I was told. I had a meeting at the Government's Unity House. I never made it. I didn't have the right letter of invitation. I didn't have the correct permission. I didn't have an official pass. Company offices I stayed clear of after Cable and Wireless's top Seychellois, Cyril Bonnelame, told the local press, 'I keep growing within myself.' If that's what's happening to local businessmen, I thought it safer to have nothing to do with them. Well, you never know, do you?

Maybe because there are so few people not doing anything, traffic is practically non-existent. A few cars. A couple of trucks. The odd taxi. As for the police station . . . the fact that they're building a new Anglican cathedral right next door to it doesn't fool anyone. All it means is they don't have to take the bodies far to give them a decent funeral. Not that the police are inefficient. Two German tourists I met who were sitting in the street enjoying a tin of Ma Ling outside the police station told me that when their hotel room was burgled two policemen promptly arrived to investigate – in a hired car. They didn't have a car of their own. The police force couldn't afford it. What's more, even though it was pitch black, in the middle of the night, they didn't have a torch between them. The police . . . you know the story.

In fact the whole place is a bit like East Berlin before the wall came down. Calm. Quiet. Civilised. Orderly. Regulated. Not a word, not a foot out of place, unless you happen to be wandering along the road at Anse Forbans in South Mahé, the largest island in the Seychelles, when suddenly you turn a corner and there marching along the side of the road is a bunch of soldiers firing wildly into the air – or, worse still, lazing around Port Launay when they start, for no reason at all, trying to bomb the place to kingdom come.

People, however, are not starving. But they're not exactly putting on weight either. Two tins of Ma Ling a day, three on Sundays, what do you expect? They can also go months on end without onions. On the other hand, say Comrade René's supporters, they have free schooling, a sound infrastructure, free healthcare (unless you turn up at Victoria Hospital for your regular kidney dialysis treatment and are told there is no medicine left. In which case you go home and keep your fingers crossed).

About the only thing they lack is practically everything they need. Including onions. Because not only are they, thanks to Comrade René, almost always desperate for foreign exchange, they are also crippled by an exchange rate as high as a stack of Comrade René's unsuccessful policies; as well as being at the mercy of their Soviet-style Seychelles Marketing Board run by none other than – guess who? – Comrade René, which has an ironclad monopoly on what it calls 'staple goods', such as Lucozade.

So expensive is everything that those who can, find it cheaper to buy a US$350 same-day return ticket to the hated and reviled Mauritius, 1250 miles away, and do their shopping there.

As for the hotels, in Mauritius they're like a wet dream; in the Seychelles they're a nightmare. You think I'm exaggerating. Listen to what their very own visitors' guide says: 'Hotel buildings blend harmoniously into the landscape . . . Local people had no experience of working in the catering trade and had to be trained quickly to become cooks, waiters and chambermaids . . . The food is generally good . . . The Barrel Restaurant in Victoria has a high reputation for its onion soup!'

Wowee. Onions.

The first hotel I tried to check into just outside Victoria, which did not in any way at all blend harmoniously into the landscape, wanted to know so much information about my bank accounts, my credit cards and personal guarantees that I gave up. Which was just as well: on the way out I discovered they were charging US$40–50 for an ordinary bottle of wine and anything up to US$10 for a bottle of the stuff fish swim and do all kinds of things in.

The next place I tried, a guest house overlooking the city, wanted to know exactly the same and more, but agreed to fill in the forms for me, whether the information they gave was correct or not – I agreed to stay. The following morning I regretted it. It was the only time in my life that I had to go into a hotel kitchen and actually beg for my breakfast. Then I couldn't sit where I wanted to sit in the completely deserted restaurant. All the other guests had obviously died of Ma Ling poisoning or starvation long ago. I sat where I was told to sit but that still wasn't the end of it. I wasn't allowed to move the cup and saucer from the far left-hand corner of the table closer to my right drinking arm. The plate of, er, charcoal had to stay right in front of me even though every time I breathed it was like breathing in coal dust. I managed to use the knife and fork only when nobody was looking. Coffee. I didn't have any. I didn't fancy risking going in the kitchen again to make it myself.

If that's not more than enough fun, fun, fun for the day there's then the thrill of wondering, first, whether they've got any booze or not to while away the boredom – answer: only beer. South African. Warm – and, second, how many tins of Ma Ling they will slop out for dinner. Answer: too many.

The way I found to relieve the tension was to play Who Owns the Hotel? Every hotel I stayed in – as well as many I didn't – I always tried to find out who owned it. Sometimes I was told COSPROH, the government-owned hotel holding company. Sometimes mysterious-sounding private companies. Sometimes even more mysterious private individuals. On a number of occasions I was told all three. Which is very reassuring. If I ever decide to sue them for serving nothing but Ma Ling three times a day, seven days a week with no beer and no wine I'll collect three lots of compensation.

In one small hotel, owned by nobody in particular and far away from the luxury hotels, the pristine beaches, the Seychelles' so-called rich, natural environment, its unique coco-de-mer palm trees, its sea and land turtles – it has more than anywhere else in the world – and its Saint Anne National Marine Park, I came across a group of Kenyans. They were doing the thing Kenyans do second best:

- Moan about Nairobi. It's now so dangerous it's known as Nairobbery.
- Complain about their long-running President, His Excellency, Daniel Toroitich Arap Moi, KANU National

> Chairman, Commander-in-Chief of the Armed Forces, and how he has virtually destroyed the country; how Kenya was once economically on a par with Portugal, Malaysia and Hong Kong and is now falling to pieces; how people are now 20 per cent poorer than they were when he came to power; how the tea crop is rotting at collection centres such as Nyanko, Getungurumu, Kebiego and Nyakwana for the want of decent roads that would allow trucks to take it to the tea factories for processing; how a 500-gram loaf of bread now officially weighs 400 grams but costs exactly the same; how judges were 'creatures of the President' who were appointed on the basis of their loyalty to the ruling Kanu Party and nothing else; how a sketch plan of the scene of the murder of a well-known Nairobi businessman, Lawrence Magondu, had been drawn by police a year before he met his death; and how Moi was backing Uganda's President Museveni.

Moi finished with, they turned to the Big Men, how various politicians had set up their own petroleum companies; how they order the Kenya National Oil Company to sell them oil cheap, give them 365 days' credit while they insist their own customers pay high prices and get no credit whatsoever; how the Central Bank of Kenya just happened to pay out US$2 billion to unidentified sources and for undisclosed goods or services; how 1600 acres of public land in Trans Nzoia allocated for the poor and the landless ended up being owned by a collection of chiefs, councillors, KANU Party officials and even senior police officers; how Kenyatta National Hospital had dodged all the official tendering procedures and bought US$1 million worth of what they called 'nuclear medical equipment' direct from the manufacturer; and, of course, most important of all, the latest goings-on at the Buffalo Bill bar at the Heron Court Hotel in Nairobi. I mean Nairobbery.

In desperation I thought I'd try some of the other eighty-seven islands scattered over 400,000 square kilometres of Indian Ocean just south of the equator that make up Comrade René's Socialist Republic of the Seychelles. The government publicity machine claims that island-hopping is 'one of the many pleasures to be experienced on a holiday to the Seychelles'. Locals say they only hop from one island to another desperately searching for a drink and some decent food.

'Islanders', says the government, 'welcome those who come to share in their peace and tranquillity but [*nota bene* the hectoring tone of the Socialist Republic] they expect co-operation in the preservation of their sheltered world in the sun.'

Peace and tranquillity? say the locals. The place is a police state. I'm no local but I came across people who told me they had been stopped and searched by the police in car parks; how their taxi driver had been searched in front of them at the Beau Vallon Hotel. One woman told me that her four-year-old daughter had even been strip-searched for foreign currency.

But when I tried to island-hop Air Seychelles had run out of planes. One had been sold. One was being repaired. Nobody knew what was happening to the other three, when they were likely to arrive, when they were likely to take off, and if there were any chance they would ever return.

Talking to other people at the airport trying to escape, I mean island-hop, I wasn't too worried. First, because I discovered that most of the islands I wanted to hop to were not in fact really Seychelles islands. They were islands owned by somebody else. Darros, for example, is owned by Prince Shuram Pahlavi, nephew of the late Shah of Iran. Cousine is owned by Fred Keely, some big-shot South African millionaire. Grande Socur is owned by the French, Frégate by the Germans and Thérèse by the Russians. Marianne, for some reason, is owned by Guinness PLC.

The other problem was that the only good hotels and restaurants worth visiting were all Thai- and Indonesian-style hotels and restaurants. So what's the point? I might as well book into the Blue Elephant in Fulham. It would probably be just as good – if not better – and cost me a darn sight less.

Back in Victoria, over a spicy octopus curry and coconut milk, I was told that Mancham was back in town. He'd patched up his spat with Comrade René. Word was that in this land of calm, quiet and peacefulness Comrade René had agreed to give him – nudge, nudge – US$1 million a year to pay for the round-the-clock security due to any former president of the peace-loving Seychelles.

I was also told the only sure-fire sign that Comrade René is about to call a quick election is not when untold luxuries such as biscuits and boxes of cheese spread suddenly appear in the shops, but when our security-conscious poetry-writing friend, the ex-playboy president, Jimmy Mancham, suddenly bursts into action and starts vigorously campaigning to lose the election.

As for Paul Chow, he's still around. He's now Secretary-General of Jimmy Mancham's party. So establishment is he now that nobody mentions the coup he tried to organise to overthrow Comrade René; how Colonel 'Mad Mike' Hoare turned up at the airport with a bunch of fellow mercenaries disguised as members of the Ancient Order of Frothblowers; how their cover was blown almost as soon as they stepped off the plane; and how they fled back to South Africa in a hijacked Mauritian plane.

Unfortunately for me, leaving the country was not so easy. I forget how many times I had to unpack my luggage so that Comrade René's greasy-fingered thugs could search, re-search and search again: clothes, books, the insides of my spare pair of shoes just in case I was trying to smuggle US$10 out of the country. Ordeal over, I thought I was free. Then a certain Cecilia Cupidou insisted that I was carrying weapons of mass destruction: safety pins. They could, she said, be used to hijack a plane.

'Hijack a plane?' I replied as quietly as I could. 'How could they be used to hijack a plane?'

'By pushing them into the pilot's hand,' she replied, as if I were the complete fool.

'But how can I push them into the pilot's hand?' I began . . .

'It is possible,' she barked back at me.

I looked at the other security officers for some kind of support. Nothing. They were all in on this nonsense together.

'OK,' I said, trying to be accommodating. 'Remind me. When was the last time a plane was hijacked with a safety pin?'

Oooooooh. The frozen look. That big stare.

'OK,' I said. 'Take the safety pins. But can you assure me that on the plane there will not be one single safety pin? None of the air hostesses will have safety pins. None of the crew will be wearing badges clipped on with a pin. None of the women. None of the children. None of the babies . . .'

You should have seen the look on Cecilia's face.

'Well, it's only fair,' I continued. 'If my safety pins are dangerous everybody else's safety pins must also be dangerous. So if you're taking mine you must take . . .'

Cecilia by now was carefully placing the safety pins into a plastic bag.

'Hey, hey,' I went on. 'You can't just take them. I want a receipt. I want to be able to tell people I was carrying safety pins that could hijack an airliner.'

And I got one too. Signed by Control Officer Cecilia herself.

While all this nonsense was going on – you guessed it – one clearly top-dog Seychellois after another was ambling through the VIP channel unhindered, undisturbed and unsearched.

Where was I sitting on the plane? Next to this woman with a baby practically dripping with safety pins. Who served the drinks? Air hostesses with not just name badges but I-can-speak-these-languages badges as well.

It's no wonder the tourists are not going to the Seychelles like they used to. There's a limit to the amount of hassle people can take. Even when that happy-go-lucky traveller General Gordon came here in the late 1880s he could put up with the place for only so long. After that he made for Khartoum – and look at how they treated him there.

'In most countries the airport is just a utility but this one has a special significance,' says my favourite visitors' guide. 'It has put the Seychelles on the map.'

You bet your giant coco-de-mer it has.

'Pas en bon letan Sesel.'

You're welcome to it.

Oh yes. Why did I have those safety pins in my luggage? Because my cuff-links were confiscated by security on the way in. Don't ask me why.

I saw a little bird high in the sky above,
A lonely bird making for a destination unknown.
Little bird, where are you heading for?

Not the bloody Seychelles, I can tell you.

Nouakchott

I love the place. But I can't for the life of me think why anyone would want to invest in Africa.

Take Mauritania, for example. It's nothing but the three *S*s: sand, sand and yet more sand. It's got over 400,000 square miles of the stuff. Enough to cover the whole of the United States with plenty to spare. And many's the time I've wished they would cover the United States and have none to spare. It stretches from the Atlantic across to the border with Mali. From Rosso on the banks of the River Senegal in the south right up to, depending on whom you speak to, either the border with Morocco or the border with the Western Sahara, which to many people is one and the same thing. The only decent land of any value is the 10–25-kilometre strip along the bank of the Senegal, which from what I can remember is full of old boars.

As if that's not enough to put up with, it's hot. Up to 150° Fahrenheit in summer. It's so hot I've seen people in oases strip off, soak their clothes in bitterly cold water from the rocks and get dressed again just to keep cool. Then when their clothes are dry do it all over again. At night it's cold. And in winter it's not just cold, it's so cold that the sudden change of temperature can split solid rocks clean apart.

Then there's the wind. Forget your dainty little red and white Yasser Arafat headcloth – the winds, which can last for three, six, nine days at a time, can slash through them in no time at all. Even the traditional, heavy blue Tuareg wraparound headdress with its tiny slits for the eyes is often no protection. Get caught going east, a bitterly cold wind howling in your face, and your nose is streaming as if you've got triple pneumonia, your throat is like parchment, and you're so dry that you could just about steel yourself to take a few sips of your wife's beloved high-energy, ginkgo biloba-flavoured carrot juice. Open your eyes and the sand can blind you. Open your mouth and you can suffocate. To survive the Arabs used to bathe their eyes in a mixture of condensed milk and water. In the middle of the desert to quench their thirst they would even slit open a vein in their camel to drink its blood if not its urine. Today they can't even afford to do that.

Mauritania is one of the poorest countries in the world. Annual income per head of population is two egg-timers and a sheet of sandpaper. Years ago it was even worse. They had nothing at all. The whole country was a country of nomads. Now it's a country of nomads trying not to be nomads and struggling to learn the delights of settling down, having a boring nine-to-five job and coming back to the wife and kids every evening. There is also no booze. No distilleries. No breweries. No off-licences. Unless, of course, you know where to look. Mauritania is one of the oldest and strictest Islamic countries in the world. Less than two hundred years after Islam had established itself in Egypt, it was already eight hundred years old in Mauritania. It's no wonder that it was here that Saddam Hussein shunted off his wife and family during the Gulf War. On the other hand it was once the proud home to both Aoudaghost, the capital of the ancient kingdom of the Sanhadja Berbers, and Koumbi Saleh, the capital of the equally ancient kingdom of Ghana, one of the three great ancient Sudanese empires of medieval Africa. But it does have one priceless asset: 700 kilometres of coastline, not to mention one of the richest fishing grounds in the world. At least, in principle, it has one of the richest fishing grounds in the world. It still has to fight off the Chinese, the Koreans, the Dutch, the Spanish and whomever can afford a factory ship that hoovers up whatever it can straight off the seabed, processes it and takes it direct to whomever pays the highest prices. Admittedly the Chinese and the others pay the Mauritanians for the privilege. The factory ships, however, are in and out like the English cricket team before the Mauritanians know about them, let alone try to charge them. At least Mauritania is in the unique position of being the only country in the world with a trade surplus with Japan, their largest official customer for fish.

The poor desert-bound nomadic Mauritanians, however, have to make do with their ordinary fishing boats, traditional wooden canoes and the occasional passing dolphin. Along the coast around Nouamghar, home of the fast-declining Imragen people – last count there were just two hundred and fifty of them and still falling – whenever they spot a school of fish, instead of rushing to their boats and grabbing their nets like other fishermen the world over, they run home, grab their sticks then race back to the sea and start beating the waves for all they're worth. At first I thought some repressed sociopath in the Anglo-Mauritanian Society had told them they had to get their own back on the sea for refusing to obey King Canute. Instead it was all to do with dolphins. The dolphins hear the noise of the beating and turn and head for shore. This drives the fish towards land and the waiting nets. I tried to find a local Imragen to tell me if it was true or not, but I couldn't find one. Next time I go there there probably won't be any left.

Fishing is, therefore, high on their list for attracting foreign investment. So too are all the back-up services: processing, freezing, packaging and dispatching to world markets, and all the necessary services and infrastructure for the support sector.

Apart from fish, their number one export earner, there's iron ore, their number two. They've got over five hundred years' worth of the stuff. As if that's not enough for a poor country to be getting on with, they've also got gold, copper, gypsum, phosphates and extensive oil and gas reserves, and then there's the roaring trade they're doing providing a safe backdoor route for refugees from all over into Morocco and across the Strait of Gibraltar into Europe. On top of that, they're rationalising like mad. For example, they've just drastically restructured their national airline. Air Mauritanie cut staff by 30 per cent and brought the work force down to 243, which has provoked an uproar. Many people claim it is barely enough to operate and service their single Fokker-28 aircraft.

Says the World Bank, 'Mauritania needs as many investors as possible, as quickly as possible.'

But how to invest?

First, there's the minor problems of finding out whom to talk to, whether you can trust them, what the rules are, whether they're negotiable, how to handle the money, can it be done direct, must it go via the minister's cousin, how secure are the government's guarantees, if they promise you a tax holiday do they mean it, what happens if there's a change of government let alone a change of minister, can you honestly rely on the minister's brother to recruit the right staff and run the company the way you want him to run it, and how may times do you have to pay for the tax inspector's daughters to go shopping in Paris? Next there are all the other complications, like getting an airline ticket. A slew-eyed clunker I knew years ago in the Midlands was fooled by his local Chamber of Commerce export adviser, who was obviously chasing some extra Brownie points with the DTI or an OBE (whichever is the lesser), to look at the possibility of establishing a pallet-packing plant in Nouakchott. The thinking was OK. In theory. A growing fishing industry. The need to pack, move and distribute around the world. Fast. Piling boxes on top of one another takes time both stacking and unstacking, creates breakages, damages the product, costs money. Pile everything on pallets to begin with and you solve a lot of the problems. Less wasted time. Fewer breakages. Less damage to the product. Fewer losses. Somehow or other – don't ask me how – he got all the background together. Somehow he made sense of it. Somehow he decided it was a viable project. He decided to go take a look. Then came the problem of simply getting there.

I met him quite by chance in a scruffy room downstairs in the Mauritanian Embassy opposite the Gendarmerie Nationale in Dakar, the increasingly seedy capital of Senegal. We exchanged the usual pleasantries. How's life? How's business? Still unhappy? Then we sympathised with each other's predicament. He'd tried to get a visa in London. No Embassy. No Consulate. No luck.

We'd both tried to book airline tickets in London. We'd both found it impossible. For some reason Air Afrique had stopped flying there. Air France was taking bookings, then not taking bookings, then cancelling everything in sight. Both our travel agents had told us to fly to Dakar and to try to book a local flight from there. Which we both did. We'd both been to the tiny Air Mauritanie office in the Place de l'Indépendance and we'd both been told, No visa, no ticket.

We didn't have visas, we both explained to them, because getting visas to Mauritania in London was impossible. No Embassy. No Consulate. No luck. Mr Palletboard tried to get one from the Embassy in Paris. Three times he'd been there. Twice it had been closed. The third time the Vice-Consul was at lunch and not expected back for two weeks. One of the fixers who always hang around African embassies anywhere in the world told him to try at the Mauritanian Embassy in Dakar, Senegal. From there he could catch a flight back up to Nouakchott. My story was similar. Apart from the Paris bit. I learned a long time ago that the last place to find any African diplomat in Paris is in his office. There are so many other affairs of state and otherwise to attend to. Years of dragging myself around Africa had taught me that the nearer you can get to the decision maker the better, the more you can shake his hand the better still. It doesn't necessarily guarantee anything at all. It just makes you feel better when still nothing happens.

Now we both sat on the scruffy, sweating sofas in the Mauritanian Embassy in Senegal and did what everybody does well in Africa: wait. We waited as people ambled in with single pieces of paper, took long lingering looks around the room and ambled out even more casually with the same pieces of paper. We waited as a filthy-looking old man in an even filthier-looking boubou came in and sat down on the floor in a corner and began to do strange things to his feet that I wouldn't even think of doing in private. We waited as a smart-looking young man in a suit came in, promptly sat down on the sofa next to me, opened his briefcase, took out a booklet and started saying his prayers out loud. We waited one hour. We waited two hours. We waited two and almost a half hours. The Vice-Consul, an impossibly tall, thin man, ambled out of his office and announced that he was leaving for the day. We would have to come back tomorrow.

'Tomorrow,' I muttered with all the deference I could summon up. 'At what time?'

'Tomorrow,' he said crisply and was gone.

Tomorrow we were back there at nine o'clock. The Vice-Consul had not arrived. He was expected at ten-thirty. The Vice-Vice-Consul, however, was there. Four of us again shuffled into our temporary prison: the pallet man, me, the foot-picker, the prayer-book man.

Around ten o'clock, the Vice-Vice-Consul, a little man in a blue boubou, announced that we would need forms and that the forms would have to be completed; one photograph would have to be attached to each form; the forms, photographs and passports would have to be checked by the Vice-Vice-Consul;

the forms, photographs and passports would then be submitted to the Vice-Consul for approval and signature. We could then collect our passports and visas in about three years' time. Express service was one year.

Now, what would you do if you were the Vice-Vice-Consul? You'd do the whole thing in one go. Not this Vice-Vice-Consul. We had to queue up, all four of us, first to get the forms, then to submit the forms and photographs for checking, except that when it came to submitting the forms for checking the Vice-Vice-Consul now insisted on two photographs each. I had about twenty hidden away in my wallet so I was safe. The poor pallet maker – oh, such innocence – had only one photo because that's what the regulations said. Away he rushed to try to find in the middle of Dakar somewhere not only a photo booth but one that worked. The rest of us, the foot-picker, the prayer-book man and me, queued up again to have our forms and photographs double-checked. Except, of course, the form wanted to know when we were arriving in Mauritania, where we were staying and when we were leaving. But we didn't know when we were arriving, where we were staying and when we were leaving because – the usual African catch-*vingt-deux* – we couldn't get our airline tickets or book our hotels until we had our visas.

'Necessary.' The Vice-Vice-Consul stubbed his finger all over my form.

'Not possible,' I began, 'because—'

'The regulations,' he barked.

'But—'

'Essential . . .'

'No ticket.'

'Proof.'

Back to Air Mauritania. They're not interested.

'No visa. No ticket,' says the bimbroglio with the fantasy hair.

I solve the problem by risking my life, racing across the

Place de l'Indépendance and going into Senegal Tours. I ask Madame Miche – short for Michelle – for a quote for a tour of the wonderful, marvellous, delightful country of Mauritania. She prints it out for me. I take it back to the Embassy. I wait. I queue up again. I see the Vice-Vice-Consul.

'There you are,' I say. 'My ticket.'

He grabs the bit of paper, doesn't look at it and pushes it under a mass of papers spilling all over his desk.

'Regulations,' he says. 'Wait.'

The pallet maker turns up. We do our best not to break down and cry on each other's shoulders. He queues up to see the Vice-Vice-Consul. The Vice-Vice-Consul is now no longer interested in a second photograph. Neither does he want him to get an air ticket.

'Wait,' he tells him.

We wait.

Forms and photos completed, submitted and checked, was the Vice-Consul now ready to lift the Imperial arm and scribble his so important scribble all over . . .? Was he hell. The Vice-Vice-Consul announced that His Imperial Majesty, the Lord and Master of the Universe, the Vice-Consul would not be coming to the Embassy today because he was not feeling well.

Off we tramp, praising the efficiency and dedication and determination of the great nation of Mauritania to do all it can to attract foreign investors to its great country.

Back again the following morning we all were. Back again to queue up to have the forms checked, to have the photos checked, to pay for our long-hoped-for but hardly expected visas.

'How long are you staying?' the Vice-Vice-Consul asks me.

'A week,' I say.

'CFA70,000,' he says.

Around US$100.

'CFA70,000,' I choke. 'There's nothing in Mauritania worth more than CFA70,000. What's the cheapest price you have for a visa?'

'CFA28,000,' he says. 'For three days.'

It was still expensive, but – and this was obvious even to me – not as expensive as CFA70,000. But I paid the money. Did I get my visa? Are you kidding? We still had to wait another hour for the forms to be taken upstairs to the Vice-Consul to sign, for them to be brought down again, for them to be put in order, for us to queue up and for us to receive our passports and visas.

The result: instead of going to Mauritania when we should have done – when, that is, all the meetings with the Ministry were arranged for – we went four days late. Instead of arriving on a Monday, we arrived on a Friday, when the whole place shuts down for prayers. Instead of discussing plans to invest millions in back-up services for their fishing industry, we sat for hours on end in alcohol-free bars, watching for hours on end as the barmen pressed oranges with their skins on overheated juice makers but oh-so-carefully peel each apple before doing the same with them.

For fun we tried to guess the contents of their alcohol-free cocktails, which for some reason were always listed in English. My favourite – oh all right, my least detested – was an Incorruptible. I kept asking every alcohol-free barman I came across if such a thing was popular throughout Mauritania, whether it was favoured by members of the government, what would happen to you if you didn't like it?

There's a limit to alcohol-free cocktails just as there is to alcohol-free barmen. After my third set of teeth had dropped out, I felt I couldn't take any more. I decided on the city tour.

First things first. The centre of Nouakchott is not, as they say, built from packing cases left over from aid delivered to the port. One aid worker, who looked and sounded as if he spoke

Polari before he spoke English, I can remember telling me it wasn't even a city.

'What is it then, if it is not a city?' I asked him.

'It's one vast refugee camp. Nothing else. In fact, some refugee camps have better facilities than Nouakchott,' he said. 'The men leave to find work. They go to Senegal. Some then go on to Paris. A few. Very few. Most stay in Senegal. But they never come back. They try and send money to their families. But it never lasts. They need the money to feed themselves. Even if they send money, it probably never arrives – the postmen are just as poor and have their families to feed. It's an impossible situation.'

Nouakchott is, in fact, a nice, almost cosy little town with long, broad, sweeping avenues; some spectacular modern buildings that could almost be rejects from Brasilia; plenty of smart-looking villas in their own compounds; and masses of open space – for markets, for animals, for parking, for short cuts and, of course, for nothing at all. The traffic is Sunday-afternoon French traffic. There's lots of it. But it's manageable. They shoot across crossroads without looking. They overtake on the inside. They drive as fast as they can. But somehow you don't feel as though you could lose more than perhaps two lives driving around town.

If you're looking for a bit of retail therapy, forget Maceys de la Nouakchott. It's marginally more interesting than Maceys de la New York, but there's still no drinks department. The central market – like all central markets throughout Africa and the Middle East – is packed, dusty, broiling hot and crammed with shoppers and stalls selling Osama bin Laden T-shirts, Osama bin Laden matchbooks, Osama bin Laden wanted posters, even phony US$5 million bills – the amount the US promised to pay anyone providing any information leading to his arrest. Dead or alive.

I met a lot of people keen to tell me how much they loved,

honoured and adored the Americans because following September 11 they had achieved what no Arab had ever achieved in history: they had united the whole of the Arab world in a single force behind a common philosophy, an agreed set of objectives and an overwhelming determination to succeed.

'We shall win. We shall win,' they kept telling me.

A very thoughtful young man – he was either a student or a would-be suicide bomber – told me he could understand people's feelings. Against a background of social upheaval throughout the Muslim world people were leaving the villages and heading for the towns; towns and cities were bursting at the seams; family traditions and values were breaking down; more and more people, young and old, faced years without work; and all the time, day after day, on television they saw Israel ignoring the demands of the United Nations, ignoring US pleas for peace and ignoring the world's condemnation for using excessive force while they continued to kick hell out of the Palestinians.

Another guy came up to me as I was crossing the road. He told me he was a teacher in Algeria. He was so overcome that he wanted to show me what I think was the traditional Algerian handshake of peace, but my taxi arrived when my arm was only halfway up my back so we had to break it off. The attempt. Not my arm.

Consequently I missed what at least half the population consider the most important part of the market: a whole block of fancy shops built, run and owned by women because they said they were fed up with men, the way they ran the show, they felt they could do better. Blah, blah, blah.

I couldn't help but notice that – as befits one of the strictest Islamic nations in the world – Nouakchott had more than its unfair share of mosques, all of them dominated by the big two: one built and paid for by the Saudis; the other by Morocco (not, I'm sure, that it had anything to do with the fact the Mauritanians walked away from Western Sahara and handed it to them on a plate. Such sordid deals are unknown in the Arab world).

Call me suspicious, but my Saddameter makes me wonder if Nouakchott could be the secret hideaway for, shh, the tall thin guy with the straggly beard, long white gown, Kalashnikov over one shoulder, dialysis machine over the other, who can disappear into a crowd so easily the Americans cannot find him.

Think about it. The government is about as Muslim as they come. Saddam sent his family here for safety during the Gulf War. The country is the size of the United States, if not larger. It's desert. There are plenty of places to hide. If somebody comes looking, it's not difficult to spot them. People can fly in and out unhindered. There is already a good system in operation for shipping illegal immigrants up to Morocco and Europe. Finally, the clincher. Who's going to go looking in Mauritania when the whole world thinks he's still in Afghanistan or across the border in Pakistan?

No? Just you wait and see.

In fact because I didn't particularly want to bump into the gentleman concerned, I decided to check out the port, which is way out of town across a whole wasteland of scrub and desert and mud-built shacks. It's not huge containers, huge cranes and huge fork-lifts: it's fishing the way it used to be. Huge, crashing waves. Huge numbers of tiny stretched rowing boats. Huge mountains of fish piled on the beach. All round are men, donkeys, women buying and selling, cooking and eating, some scooping up great mouthfuls, others ravaging around in the sand for the odd scrap of bread. The big guys are in battered cars and trucks and vans. And, as befits a fisherman, I mean battered. It's a wonder that many of them are at least still in what looks like a thousand pieces let alone able to move. The rest have donkeys and carts or nothing at all.

But whether you're in the centre of town or out at the port, the people are as varied and as colourful as you would expect. First, there are my favourites, the blue men of the desert, the Tuaregs with their blue robes and deep, parched, burned faces, and the Harratins, the former slaves and workers who some say make up 40 or maybe 50 per cent of the population and generally hold the place together. Then there are the black Africans, who comprise around one-third of the population, and the Toucouleus, the Soninké, the Nemectis from Nema down in the south-east, the Fulani with their upside-down cone-shaped hats and, of course, the Wolofs. Finally the smallest group of all, who look as though they dominate everything: the very smooth, very sophisticated light-skinned Moroccans in their collars and ties and suits. They are obviously determined to continue the process started by Sultan Ahmad al-Mansur when he set out to conquer the Sahel in 1588, and they not only dominate the whole kebab but are clearly set on handing the whole thing back to Morocco. If they're not, they're certainly doing a very convincing job of pretending they are.

With the exception of the new rulers – the Moroccans that is – most people are in Nouakchott not because they want to be city dwellers but because of the drought that stretched from the early 1970s to the early 1980s. It more than decimated their herds. It destroyed what little rural economy there was. It also destroyed their traditional way of life: wandering backwards and forwards across the desert armed with spears and old flintlocks hunting lions, gazelles and antelopes. From just twenty thousand people in 1960, Nouakchott is now bursting with over three hundred and fifty thousand people.

But even though they have been beaten by the desert, the desert has not given up. It is still pursuing them. In the mornings, the first thing everybody does is sweep the sand from the doorways and clear the streets. Leave it just one day and the desert will gain the upper hand.

You need stand still only for a few minutes on the edge of any town or village or even cluster of houses anywhere in the country to see the meaning of desertification – and how impossible it is to find a solution.

On the edge of town there is a thin patch of grass and scrub land. The occasional tree. A small bush. Lapping the edge of the grass is the desert. It has already advanced a few feet in the last few months. Some tufts of grass still manage to survive. But not for long. Now along comes a boy, thin as a matchstick with about a dozen goats, most of them pure white, one brown and another a curious black-and-white mix, a bit like a piebald. The family need the goats for milk and for meat. But they must be fed. The boy knows that if he allows the goats to eat the grass, it will mean that the desert advances a little bit further.

'I know. They tell us at school. The man from the government tells us. But what can I do? Where can I feed the goats?' he told me. 'They must eat. If they don't eat we don't eat.'

What can you say?

An old woman wanders along the grass picking up pieces of wood, a branch here, some twigs there. She goes up to one of the trees. One of the branches is within easy reach. She breaks the branch off. Again she is helping the desert.

'But we need the wood for a fire. We must eat,' she says.

You can't say anything.

The goats are busy tearing up the grass on the edge of the sand. It is coming up in great tufts. They have learned to go for the grass by the sand because it's loose and comes up in great bunches. If you're allowed out to graze for only a few minutes every day, you might as well make the most of it. You stand there and watch. Within five minutes they've torn up a good couple of square feet of grass. The desert has won a few more inches. Multiply that all over the Sahel and you know why the desert is winning *and* why there's little anybody can do about it.

'Sure we have conferences and seminars and working groups and strategy documents and everything else you can think of. That's tackling the problem. The one thing we can't do is tackle the solution,' one government official told me. 'For the fact is – there is no solution.'

'But there must be. You can't let it go on and do nothing.'

'What can we do?'

'Something. There must be something.'

'Sure. Turn the clock back and undo all the mistakes that we've made over the last twenty to thirty years. We survived – not very well – but we survived up to about twenty, thirty years ago. Then everything started to go wrong.'

'What went wrong? What was the problem?'

'Foreigners. Outsiders. People coming in and telling us how we should run our country. That's what went wrong.'

'But how?'

'Look. For thousands of years people lived in the Sahara. Maybe not well. But they lived and they survived. Today they are dying.'

'Why?'

'Why? Because foreigners came in and told us we were doing it all wrong. Look, for generations people lived in the desert and on the edge of the desert. In the rainy season they took their herds to the north. In the dry season they came south for the grass. They planted crops. They ate the crops. The animals ate the stubble and, at the same time, fertilised the soil. Then they moved on to a new area and left the ground fallow to rest for a year before coming back again. Everything was fine. Then came independence. What happened? Foreign aid. But not money we could spend the way we wanted to spend it. No. We could only have the money if we spent it the way foreigners told us how to spend it. And, of course, they got it all wrong.'

'How?'

'First, they insisted we planted new types of crops, crops which grew faster and bigger than our old crops. What happened? People no longer had to plant such large areas and, because the crops grew faster, they no longer left the ground fallow long enough to recuperate. Which weakened the soil, and the weak soil could not withstand the onslaught of the desert. Second, they persuaded our governments that it was dangerous to have so many nomads wandering about the country outside government control. A nation within a nation. A separate people. A law unto themselves. That kind of thing. Just after independence the governments were obsessed with security. Immediately they saw the danger. They started controlling the movement of the nomads: you can't do this, you can't do that. They even built houses for them and made them live there. The nomads were nomads no more.'

'But why was that bad?'

'Because if the nomads stop moving, their animals stop moving as well. Which means you've then got problems feeding the animals – and even worse problems if you haven't got the crops or the decent land to grow the crops.'

'So then what did they do wrong?'

'They dug wells. Thousands of them.'

'But why was that wrong?'

'Because wells attract animals. That's why they were built. But our problem was that we had too many animals, not enough good soil and almost no crops. So what happened?' he asked himself. 'Disaster. The animals, so many animals came to the wells. They ate all the vegetation, everything, around the wells. They stripped all the vegetation away. The topsoil was exposed and blown away by the wind. The result: more desert, more hungry animals and, of course, hungry and angry nomads. Before they were free to move from place to place, looking for food. They might not have had security. But they weren't hungry. Now they have a house they don't want – and no food.'

'So what are you going to do about it?'

He shook his head.

'I don't know,' he said, 'I don't know.'

'What's the answer?' I asked. 'Or is there no answer?'

'I don't know,' he said. The scale of the human devastation was getting to him.

'You must. It's your job. Why else are you here? If you didn't think there was hope you would get a job in a bank.'

'You're right,' he said. 'There is a solution. But I don't think it will work.'

'Why ever not?'

'Because of the sheer size of the problem. Look,' he said brightening a little. 'We're fighting the Sahara. Nobody ever fights the Sahara and wins. It's impossible. You take one step forward. The desert pushes you back ten steps. How can you fight that? You can't.'

The following morning I went out with him to see what he meant. He looked as if he'd overslept on the non-alcoholic cocktails. He had on a black suit, white shirt, a black tie tied around his neck like a cravat and over his shoulders a long brown woollen coat.

We climbed on to the dunes surrounding Nouakchott. There they had begun to plant trees in square blocks in a desperate attempt to stem the sand. In Niger I had seen similar experiments that in some cases had actually worked. The barrier of trees had held back the desert and increased yields of the protected crops as well. Here, nothing had happened. The sand had swallowed the trees almost as soon as they had been planted. If not sooner. We stood looking at the pathetic blocks of trees.

'Now do you see what I mean?' he said.

I could see exactly what he meant.

It's no wonder many Mauritanians give up and head south to Senegal hoping to find their fortune in Dakar. Those that return, return with less than they took with them. Dakar is a different world and there is a completely different attitude there. They are baffled, out of place and even more desperate. Talk to the Senegalese and they will tell you about the Mauritanians starving to death in the back streets of Dakar or hanging themselves in huts and sheds. The cruel empty wastes of the Sahara are more hospitable to some people than so-called twenty-first-century civilisation of the Dakar variety.

But you can't blame them. They might be one of the oldest peoples on earth but they've had a capital city for just around forty years. When the Almoravids, the Muslims who ruled Spain as well as the whole of north-west Africa, ran the place they as good as left them alone. After the Almoravids came the Arabs, but they hardly made any more impact. In fact, the poor Mauritanians were still so nomadic they probably didn't realise what was happening – or not happening, as the case may be. Next came the Europeans. In their mad scramble for Africa they just about ignored the place.

Anything wrong with Mauritania is, therefore, wholly and totally their own fault. Unlike the rest of Africa, they have no one to blame but themselves. I hate myself for saying this, but in all honesty they can't even really blame the French. The Treaty of Paris in 1814 gave the French only the right to explore the place, which they didn't really take up. They had much richer and juicier pickings elsewhere. It took them about a hundred years before they turned it into a colony, which shows you how interested they were in the place. Then it was only somewhere to station their troops in case they were needed elsewhere.

It was in 1960, when the Mauritanians finally got rid of the French who were never really there in the first place, that they started building a capital and a country. Not that they've got very far. There are hardly any roads. To get from Nouakchott to the economic capital, Nouadhibou, and the big iron ore mines at Zouerate 300 kilometres to the north, the choice is camel, four-wheeler or plane. I'm sure camel is the fastest. Not that the mines are just a hole in the ground. They're big stuff. Sales are US$200 million. Profits are US$15 million. The workforce is over four thousand. It's all very organised, very efficient, very successful. Yet try to get there . . . The whole place, I reckon, is run by the brother of the Vice-Consul at the Embassy in Dakar.

It's the same – but worse – when trying to get to the diamond mines near Chinguetti, the once lost seventh holy city of Islam. But it's worth it. Not because of the desert, which to me was pretty run-of-the-mill. Not that I'm an expert on deserts . . . I've only crossed the Sahara two and a half times; shuffled backwards and forwards across the Namib and the Kalahari; trundled across the Gobi in a broken-down Russian jeep; plunged into the Rub al-Khali; and been in no end of shopping malls in the States. Up to the Adrar plateau it was pretty much nothing but a mixture of sand and rock. Some people claim it's like Colorado in the US although I couldn't see it. Beyond the Adrar plateau, however, it's more *Beau Geste* meets *Lawrence of Arabia*.

Forget the diamonds. I was interested in Chinguetti because apart from being the once lost seventh holy city of Islam it is also they say the slave capital of Africa. Officially, of course, slavery or *haratine* was banned in 1981. But because of the lack of roads, the news has yet to reach Chinguetti. When it does, the whole town will be covered in sand, so it probably won't make any difference anyway.

We'd passed Akjoujt where I got my first lesson in killing a sheep from a wizened old man dressed in a long, flowing, spotless white darraa. He looked like Floyd's elder brother.

First catch your sheep. Hold it on the ground. With one hand hold the sheep's mouth tightly shut. Push knife into upper part of the neck. Slice down to throat. Avoid blood, which spouts out like thick fountain. Watch out for legs, which thrash around wildly for a second then – a tiny cough – nothing. Even after it's dead, the legs will still twitch with nervous spasms and even kick out for a short while.

Then come the flies. They will suddenly descend on everything: the blood in the sand, the half-severed neck. Take no notice. Skin it immediately starting down inside the hind legs, cut out its stomach and its guts. Cook immediately.

Sink three bottles of claret in the process.

The sheep out of the way, we were making for Adrar when the driver pulled off the road into a cluster of tents and red clay shacks almost buried in sand.

I expected to see a camel train setting off across the desert. In the old days they used to send out caravans of up to thirty-two thousand camels laden with salt. Nowadays it's more likely to be thirty-two, if that. Instead we stumbled across a group of Swedes, who – judging by the ones I've come across – are usually slaves to one passion or another. In this case, their passion was slaves.

They were going from tent to tent and from house to house, asking if the occupants had any slaves to sell. The good citizens of the patch of dust were insulted. The smart guys immediately said, 'Yes,' and sold them their sons and daughters and all the first, second and third cousins they could find, pocketed the money and headed for Nouakchott, the first plane to Paris and the Champs-Elysées, the Moulin Rouge and all the other tourist spots. The happy socialist-minded Swedes with gold chains around their ankles climbed into their air-conditioned Land Cruisers and drove away happy that they had set the world to rights.

The slaves or at least the genuine slaves they had bought and then immediately abandoned were distraught. Before they might have been slaves, but they had security. Now they were free, they were on their own, they had nothing and nobody wanted them. The so-called slaves returned to their shacks and the loving embrace of their families.

I've seen the same thing in Mali, in the Gulf, in Pakistan, in Burma or rather Myanmar. One-eyed do-gooders read trashy novels like *Jonathan Corncob*, which has your pretty little black slave coming up with the immortal line: 'If massa want ee chamberpot, ee will puttee ee's hand out of bed, if ee want me he will puttee out ee foot.' They drop out of the sky. Think they know everything and rush around buying everyone they are told is a slave. Then climb into their air-conditioned Land Cruisers leaving the poor ex-slaves to get on with it. The whole thing is a nonsense.

Of course slavery is wrong. But so is going around buying slaves, taking fancy smug self-satisfied photographs of yourself, and then letting them find their own way in the world. Ex-slaves need help, advice, assistance, someone to help them build up their confidence and adjust to their new liberated world. Just like a downtrodden long-married man coming through a divorce and realising that a straight 50–50 split down the middle means the wife ends up with the six-bedroom house, the two cars and the holiday apartment in Ibiza, and he ends up living in a one-room flat above a greengrocers in Seaford. It doesn't happen overnight. It takes time. Many slaves who've been bought by would-be do-gooders – official, unofficial and 'Let's do it. It'll make a change from sponsoring a penguin' – have, in fact, gone back to their old way of life because it means security, a roof over their heads, something to eat, the companionship of their fellow slaves.

Look at the facts. First, the Buy a Slave campaigners never know whether they are actually buying a real slave or whether they are being conned.

Second, if the slave *is* real, they don't know what type of slave they are buying: an apprentice, a housemaid, a trainee, a deputy under-manager. For generations many poor Africans have been either willingly or unwillingly selling their children to middlemen: because they want to; because they don't have the food to feed them; because they want them to have better lives. There are no end of reasons.

The middlemen have then been selling them to rich and not-so-rich families wherever they can find them, usually in the slightly more developed areas of Africa. Where people have money to buy. Where families are trying to educate their own children instead of making them do the dirty work. Where controls are nix. Where, if there's a problem, people can be bought off.

Some say that's slavery. Others say it's domestic service, a form of apprenticeship, flexibility of labour, the only hope Africa will ever have of training and educating its people.

Some say the slaves have lost their freedom. But many poor African families desperate to know where their next meals are coming from would give anything for the guaranteed two-meals-a-day security of being a slave.

Some say the slaves are slaves for life. Others say the slaves are in fact the ones with the skills, the learning, the abilities, the trades. They are the ones who are actually supporting their masters and their place in the world. Most drive donkeys and camels. Some drive cars. I met a slave once who was a qualified airline pilot and flew his master around all over the world.

Third, the do-gooders don't know whether the slave is actually capable of handling their sudden freedom. Some can. But I would guess that most would go to pieces without help.

Fourth, the do-gooders have no control over the money they have paid for the slave, how it's going to be spent, whether it will be spent on buying more and better slaves either to be kept or resold at a profit in the future. It also creates problems with the slave-owners if, in fact, they are genuine slave-owners. Many's the time both real slave-owners and pretend slave-owners have, after a bit of the usual hassle, sold their real or so-called slaves to the do-gooders. The real slave-owner then takes the money he's received and promptly goes and buys a whole new batch of bigger and better slaves and thus prolongs the whole business. The pretend slave-owner either splits or does not split his money with his pretend slaves and then makes off to set up another pretend deal.

After the Swedish do-gooders had disappeared in their cloud of air-conditioned dust my driver took me into one of the shacks to meet one of the village elders. There, over glass after glass of *z'rig* – camel's milk – he showed me how the parents did the best they possibly could for their baby daughters. By clamping their feet in what looked like a giant pair of nutcrackers. The nutcrackers are slammed down on the kid's feet and they open their mouths and scream, and when they do food is pushed down their throats. In a country in which a woman is no good unless she has plenty of flesh on her, it is believed that the nutcrackers will quickly fatten her up and help her to find a husband. The quicker she finds a husband, the quicker the parents make a return on their investment. Not that they were totally primitive. They also showed me the latest Mauritanian technology: a metal stove. In most of Africa you throw your wood on the ground and set light to it and cook. But with a stove, you set light to the wood and cook on the stove.

'It is very good,' the old lady kept telling me. 'Very good. I like it.'

The way some ginkgo-biloba frenzy would boast of having kilim rugs all over her pelvic floor.

'Why?'

'Because I don't have to do so much work. It is much better.'

'Why don't you have to do so much? I don't understand.'

'Before I put the wood on the ground. I light my fire. The wood burns very quickly. The next morning I have to go out and collect more wood. With this stove, the wood burns slowly. Now I only have to collect wood every four or five days. It is much better.'

She told me that in the past she often had to walk five or six miles a day looking for wood and, of course, the more she and everybody else scoured the countryside for wood, the further she had to go.

'It is hard. And I have my baby to carry as well,' she said.

The stove, I said, must have been a godsend or rather an Allahsend.

'It is lovely. My baby was getting heavier. I had to walk further every day and' – she smiled – 'I am getting an old lady. The stove is lovely.'

I asked her what she now did with all the spare time she had.

'There is always work to do,' she said. 'Always too much work. Maybe one day I sell my baby. Big fat baby. Make lots of money from people with big car.'

In the fancy hotel in Chinguetti, which looked as though it was full of off-duty Foreign Legionnaire slobberheads, I met an Austrian engineer who was making lots of money. Thanks to President Waldheim. When Waldheim was elected President of Austria, the West went bananas.

'Best thing that ever happened to me,' said Fritz. 'Immediately the Arabs knew our President was anti-Jewish they call me. They want to do business. I sign so many contracts in Algeria, in Libya, in South Africa, in Iraq, here in Mauritania. I make so much money. I hope we have another President like Waldheim. He is very good for business.'

As for my poor friend in the pallet business, rather than

investing in Mauritania, he decided to invest in Japan instead. The whole deal was signed, sealed and delivered in an afternoon. The karaoke afterwards took much, much longer.

Banjul

Why, I don't know. But for some reason or other Gambia is forever associated in the popular mind with that little three-letter word: the. It's not Gambia, but The Gambia. Like The Congo. The Czech Republic. The Netherlands. The Ukraine. The Punjab and, of course, The Once United Kingdom. Although why it even exists as the country at all is the nonsense. It's the smallest the country in the Africa. It's 500 kilometres the long and at most 25 kilometres the wide. It runs the practically the length of the River Gambia. It has over ten major the ethnic groups, among them the Mandinkas, the descendants of the Mali kings and the chiefs; the Wolofs, the tall, thin guys who run the Senegal, the next-door the country; and the Fulanis, the farmers and the herdsmen. Total population: around seven hundred and fifty thousand. It has nothing but scrub, grass and peanuts. It is completely surrounded by Senegal. It is also about 95 per cent Muslim, but nobody talks about that.

Forget all those stories about all women of a certain age going there for one thing and one thing only: somewhere nice to shop. To shop for whatever they want. Which invariably turns out to be another three-letter word. Of course, when I say *all* women, I naturally don't include English women. Heaven forbid. All they're interested in doing when they go to the Gambia – or anywhere in the world, come to think of it – is feeding the stray cats.

The first hotel I stayed in, or rather the first beach hotel I ever stayed in, in The Gambia, you could hardly move for menopausal women leaping about all over the place chasing all the stray cats they could find.

'Come here, Blackie. Eat this lovely, lovely food I've bought for you.'

If they couldn't find any, they would make up cats. They would pretend they were locked in cupboards and shriek their blue-rinsed heads off until they weren't released.

'Brownie. Quick, drink your milk. Pinkie's coming.'

And if two or more old ditzes saw the same cat you could see the Botox bursting out of their ears in their frenzy to grab hold of the flea-ridden old thing.

'That one I call Omar because he's the sheriff. Keeps the others in order.'

Aaaaaagh. That was enough for me. I moved out. Straight away. Immediately. That instant. The next hotel was not much better. All cheap tiles, cheap furniture, paper-thin towels, temperamental showers, electricity that was more off than it was on. The whole place looked as though it had been furnished from a boot sale held somewhere near the back of the station in Stoke on Trent. The only good thing about it? There were no cats. The night before I got there had been their weekly curry evening, which may or may not have had something to do with it.

Forget all those stories about the Gambians being shy, quiet, innocent, at the mercy of any cruising battleaxe covered in goo from a burst silicone implant. They're a smart, clever, double-dealing, say-one-thing-do-another bunch of crooks, which, of course, is something they learned from the British.

Up until 1807 we believed in slavery. In 1807 we not only changed our minds, we believed – even without the aid of President Blair – that everybody else should as well. The Gambia was the place from which to stop others doing what we had been doing for centuries. The mouth of the River Gambia was the place for us to position our boats to police the seas and stop everybody. But, being British, we were typically mean about the whole thing. Instead of building a big port, a big city and all the necessary infrastructure to enforce this world-changing moral initiative, we threw up a couple of wooden huts, laid out a few streets, called the centre of the patch MacCarthy Square and ran the whole thing from Sierra Leone, about 1000 miles away.

The result? In spite of the immense sacrifices made by that great Distributor of Stamps for Westmorland and part of Cumberland, William and his sister, Dorothy, to free the slaves – they gave up sugar on their morning porridge. Instead they had a dollop of honey – we didn't actually do much about the slave trade. We also did precious little for The Gambia. By the 1960s, when we deigned to grant them their independence, they still had only one school, one hospital and about 1 square foot of paved roadway in the whole country.

To me, however, The Gambia means one thing and one thing only: the great unexplained mystery of modern Africa. Gold. Where's it gone? There is supposed to be over six tons of the yellow stuff hidden in containers in various parts of the country. That's over US$100 million worth. Maybe US$200 million worth. If Bush stays on as President and continues doing what he's doing, it won't be long before it's worth US$1000 million. Either way, there might even be enough of the stuff to buy a couple of first-class tickets on British Airways at today's prices.

Talk to the slew-eyed jackets in the bars and clubs in Kinshasa, the desperately run-down capital of Zaire. They will tell you – if you can hear them over the strains of Papa Wemba that are so loud they practically melt your eardrums – that they know where it is. It's just a question of making one or two arrangements.

Talk to the Gambians who are all over the African Development Bank, the Economic Community of West Africa, the ECOWAS Fund, EcoBank, the United Nations Economic Commission for Africa – and any other set of initials you can think of. They will tell you they know someone who knows where it is.

Whisper in the ear of certain Swiss bankers in that coffee shop in Zurich by the station. They will tell you they are awaiting instructions from one of their clients.

No matter who you talk to, the explanations are all about as reliable as a Jeffrey Archer alibi.

Just before that grand-daddy of all kleptomaniacs, Mobutu Sese Seko, was overthrown as President of Zaire, the plan was that his son Kongolo would ship out Papa's personal collection of solid gold bars by containerload by containerload by containerload. Through the usual channels. All covered by false papers and documents. Every one sent via different people and different companies to different destinations.

The idea was that they would all be held in various secret locations. The gold would then be shipped out from the containers in 100-kilogram consignments to various addresses in Zurich. Trouble is, Mobutu was overthrown much earlier and much more quickly than he imagined. Everything had to be speeded up. The result was the usual total African chaos. Today – surprise, surprise – nobody knows. Where exactly the containers were shipped from. How they were shipped. Where they were shipped to.

Although, my dear Watson, I have my ideas.

Who wasn't involved? It wasn't the old President of The Gambia, Sir Dauda Jawara, who was President at the time of independence and had led the country since then. To many people, the fact he was a vet was somehow reassuring. To me it was yet another sign of Britain's attitude to The Gambia. I mean, how come under the French, the first President of Côte d'Ivoire was a doctor, the first President of Senegal was a poet, but the first President of Britain's The Gambia was a vet? There wasn't even a junior night nurse they could find to do the job. Not that when it came to it Britain didn't have second thoughts about handing over to a vet. They asked for a second opinion. The United Nations sent in a team, handed out a couple of horse pills, said a merger with Senegal wasn't on the cards and instead prescribed a federation.

Britain took note – as we always do – of any second opinion and did the opposite. We gave The Gambia their independence. The vet took over. There he stayed until The royal wedding, when he was in London checking out the corgis. Back home a handful of military staged a coup. After twenty-one years in power he was overthrown.

Under the terms of a mutual defence pact with Senegal, however, Jawara called on Senegal to get rid of the military, which they did. But the vet was senegalled when the Senegalese troops decided to stay behind, which definitely wasn't part of the defence pact. Jawara, however, swallowed a couple of bales of hay to give him strength, caved in and agreed to the creation of what was called Senegambia – a bit like the result of trying to breed zebras from horses – and was returned to power.

The British, of course, did nothing even though it was our fault in the first place. If it hadn't been for The royal wedding, Jawara wouldn't have been in London, the military would not have staged their coup, the Senegalese would not have moved in, they would not have stayed, and The Gambia would not have been swallowed up by this thing called Senegambia. I'm not saying he was Africa's answer to Mr Herriott. All I'm saying is he's not the kind of guy to lift six containers of gold. In any case, last time I heard of him he was still living in that house near Gatwick airport surrounded by loads of trees. Now, I ask you, would anybody with six containers of gold stashed away somewhere want to live anywhere near Gatwick airport, trees or no trees?

I also doubt whether any of the old ministers who were overthrown together with Jawara either in 1981 or for the second and final time in 1994 lifted it either. After the second and final coup against Jawara, one Gambian minister after another would tramp through London, check their safe deposit boxes, and confidently wait to be showered with introductions, a fancy job, a big house, limo and all the usual. A number of them got my name, came banging on my door and blamed me when nothing happened.

I met the old finance minister a number of times in mysterious mews houses in Belgravia. He seemed shell-shocked by what had happened. How could it? In peaceful The Gambia. Completely out of the blue. If any of them had US$100 million stashed away they wouldn't have bothered to get off the plane in London. They would have made direct for the fun, fun, fun.

Which can only mean that it must have been the military who staged the coup in the first place. In fact, the more you look at what happened the more mysterious it becomes.

First, the military said they overthrew the President in 1994 because they had not been paid. Nonsense. You don't overthrow a president if you're not paid. If every African army overthrew every African president when they weren't paid there wouldn't be a president left in Africa.

Second, how come an American warship, the USS *La Moure County*, just happened to be in port when the President was overthrown when it could quite happily have been preparing to invade yet another defenceless country? So that when the coup came the President was able to wander across from the President's House to the warship and be off and away to his home in Gatwick, if not exactly to peace and quiet. All terribly civilised. All terribly un-American. The theories abound.

Arch-loyalists and those sucking up to the new military

regime led by Lt Yaya Jammeh claim it was pure coincidence. Oh yes. Like the soldiers only wanted the President out of the way because he was holding up their pay. African conspiracists say it was the Senegalese. Senegal already completely surrounded The Gambia. They wanted the President out of the way. But trained as they are in the black arts of French diplomacy, they didn't want to do it themselves. They gave the wink to the French. The French gave a nudge to the Americans. *Voilà*. As for the Americans, judging by their track record of subtle diplomacy throughout the world, they didn't know what in the hell they were doing. They just blundered into the whole thing the way they normally do. They probably thought they were preparing to invade Iraq although I suppose we should be grateful they didn't kill anyone.

Third, a president is overthrown, a government is ousted. How come there were no street demonstrations, no banners, no marches, no nothing to greet the new regime? When the military blocked Denton Bridge, they effectively blocked the only way in to and the only way out of the capital, Banjul, which is virtually an island – it's the tip of a peninsula at the mouth of the River Gambia – everybody just sat tight. Nobody tried to break through. When they heard machine-gun fire from the headquarters of the Police Tactical Support Group nobody went to investigate. They thought it was the Americans doing their usual thing. When Radio Gambia went off the air no crowds gathered outside the parliament building. Nobody said a word.

Fourth, when the announcement finally came not on the official Radio Gambia but on an independent station, Radio 1FM, that the armed forces had taken over and a new government had been installed, there was no rejoicing in the streets, no demonstrations of support, not even *organised* demonstrations of support. Everybody just seemed to carry on as if nothing had happened. Now, that's not normal is it? Especially in Africa.

What happened I reckon was that the military heard a rumour about the gold being moved. Then they completely misread the signs the way the military usually do. They thought that the President was going to make off with it as the military would think any African president would. That he'd done a deal with the States. That they had sent a US Navy ship to collect him and the gold on the basis that a US Navy ship was probably a tad more reliable than your ordinary commercial ship. They decided to move in, grab the gold and make off for the high-spots.

But it was all a ghastly mistake – like marrying a wife who's not blonde, beautiful or rich. They ended up with no gold, no blonde, no happy ever after, which explains why they took so long to announce the coup, to announce the leaders of the new government, to announce their policies *and* why there were no demonstrations, no making whoopee, no dancing in the streets. But – again like the military anywhere in the world, when they get it wrong, they get it wrong – they said nothing, dug in and prepared for a long siege. They also, of course, now had a country to run.

By all accounts, however, they seem to have confounded everyone. They not only survived, they also seem to be doing as good a job as if not better than Jawara.

My old friend the finance minister was impressed. Especially when they invited him back to rejoin the government. A recognition of his true standing, professionalism and integrity, he claimed. The obvious way for a new gang on the block to suck up to the World Bank, the IMF and all the other financial institutions a new gang has to suck up to, I thought. But I didn't say a word.

The new government also plastered the country with better-quality billboards with catchy slogans such as 'For Continuity', 'For Stability and Sustained Development', and the more stirring 'The Gambian People Congratulate His Excellency Jammeh Yaya for his . . .', etc.

In fact, when after a few years in power they put themselves up for election against Jawara, they won – even though he had holed up in Dakar with a shipload of rice waiting for his people to summon him back. His plan was to return in triumph and distribute the rice to a grateful people. Except that they obviously weren't that grateful. Jawara promptly sold the rice and headed back to Britain, no doubt to bone up on the latest techniques for putting dumb animals out of their misery.

All this means the gold must still be hidden in various containers in various parts of the country. But where? Purely in the interests of modern African historical research, I've scoured the country looking for it.

First I thought: gold. Sese Seko Mobutu. They would have hidden it miles from anywhere, in a deserted part of the country, far from people and the risk of it being accidentally discovered. I decided to search the beach resorts where there's mile after mile of empty, deserted beach. Deserted because the women are busy shopping for whatever it is they're looking for at that particular moment.

From Kolou to Kotu to Fajara to Bakau I travelled in my search for clues. Most of the resorts seemed to be perfect for the British: cheap, downmarket and plenty to complain about. No wonder Mungo Park, a Scottish country surgeon (which he called 'at best but a laborious employment'), chose The Gambia from which to set out on his big expedition to discover the source of the Niger accompanied by only a black servant, a boy and two asses. Trouble is it went to his head: he kept all his notes in his hat.

At one resort near Kotu I met a white-bread Roedean has-been who kept shaking her booty at me and going on and on the way they do about child reductions. Which, I said, sounded like one hell of a good idea. But the way she freaked out I don't think she agreed with me.

No gold there.

The restaurants had a novel approach. They seemed to be busy competing to see which one could serve the best buffet. About the only one I fancied was the way upmarket Coconut Residence. But that was more Caribbean than African.

No gold at any of them.

I had a hunch it could be hidden in the Palma Rima, which was the secret hideaway for General Ansumane Mané, the Gambian military chief who was head of the army in Guinea-Bissau and who staged his own *coup d'état* there in 1998. He had been suspended for smuggling arms to the Senegalese separatist movement, Mouvement des Forces Démocratiques de Casamance, which was struggling for its independence from Senegal. He was also said to turn a blind eye to the arms sales and drug smuggling being carried on between the army and the MFDC. His favourite bungalow was 3B, to which he used to disappear when the temperature got too hot. But it was as empty as the bank account of an African government. Any African government.

I thought of Juffure, made famous by Alex Haley in his worldwide blockbuster *Roots*, about how his great-great-great-great-great-grandfather Kunta Kinte was captured and, God help him, transported as a slave not just to the US but to Maryland of all places. Years ago I might have said, Yes. Everybody went there. But not since Haley just about admitted that like most great autobiographers he had made most of it up.

The other thing that puts people off going there – apart from the fact it's a long alcohol-free drive from the beaches – are the stories about the Juffure people themselves moaning and complaining to all and sundry that they hoped one day *Roots* would make them all as rich as Haley; that Haley promised them the world but actually handed over only US$1600; and that the widow of the man who told Haley the whole Kunta Kinte story now sits old and toothless outside a corrugated-iron shack in a dirt courtyard surrounded by begging letters from people who claim they were moved by the worldwide books, films and television series about her family's history.

Sorry. If you had over US$100 million to bury, you wouldn't bury it there. Neither would Mobutu or any of his henchmen. They wouldn't go within a million miles of the place.

How about Serrekunda, the second-largest town? No way. It's still pretty basic. In any case, every other businessman seems to be Lebanese. If there was any gold in town they would sniff it out immediately and have it distributed around the world by lunchtime.

Which means, of course, My dear Watson . . . Banjul, the capital. It's virtually an island. The only way in and out is over that Denton Bridge. So you've got security. A quick word to the chief of police (who's got such a wonderful cockney accent that he could get a stand-in role in *EastEnders* any day if he is ever ditched by a grateful military) and down come the barricades. Nobody can get in or out.

The Atlantic Hotel, the big hotel in the centre of town, is full of bright red overweight lobsters, most of them English, most of them complaining about having to wait thirty seconds for a drink, and all of them complaining about the price, which is enough to scare away any prowlers.

Banjul would also sound right to Mobutu – both as a Zairois and a kleptomaniac. Lagos. Lomé. Cotoneau. Accra. They all sound dangerous. To pull off the biggest heist in history, stash everything away in the capital of The Gambia, the name of which is derived from the Spanish '*cambio*' meaning 'exchange'. That would be the biggest Banjul in Mobutu's crown.

Trouble is, I reckon, Gaddafi's on to it. Why else are most of the taxi drivers in Banjul Libyans? They are not taxi drivers. They are a cover. They're double agents. They're working for Gaddafi.

But where in Banjul?

Not Independence Drive. Mobutu didn't believe in independence. He didn't believe in anything but money and the need to grab as much of it as he could. Not MacCarthy Park. To Mobutu that would have sounded too American, and it was the Americans in the World Bank and the IMF who were forever hounding him and trying to find out what he had done with their money. Not Albert Market. He didn't believe in markets. He always insisted on dictating his terms, doing what he wanted, stealing as much as he wanted. Of course, Wellington Street. Zaire was Belgian. Mobutu knew his Belgian history. Waterloo. Napoleon and all that. The number? 1815. What else?

Whatever you do, don't tell Gaddafi or I'm

Nuku'alofa

Fat. I thought the Americans were fat or, rather, nutritional over-achievers. Then I discovered Tongans. They're huge ginormous lumps of blubber, the size of the Empire State Building, about as wide as the Grand Canyon. They're so too big for this world they give elephant growth hormones a bad name.

Normally wherever I go in the world I fit in. Not in Tonga. I stand out. Because I'm so small, so petit, so svelte. And I'm, well, not exactly small, petit or svelte.

When the Tongans eat, which they do all the time, they eat. You are invited out for a quick snack. You are expected to glomp your way through Everest after Everest of roast pig, lobster, oysters, clams, octopus, breadfruit, sweet potato, taro cooked in coconut cream. All washed down with six bottles of beer. And that's just the first course.

Second course. More roast pig. More lobster. More oysters. More clams. More octopus. More breadfruit. More sweet potato. More taro cooked in coconut cream. And another six bottles of beer.

Third course. More . . . More . . . More . . . More . . . More . . . More . . . More . . . More . . . And another six bottles of beer.

Not only are you expected to pack it all away like a twelve-month-pregnant elephant, you've also got to observe impeccable Tongan table manners. No elbows on the table even when you're straining to delicately balance a 47-ounce chunk of roast pig on the end of your fork. No knife and fork scattered casually all over the table. They must always be returned to your plate even when you've swollen up to three times your usual size, your stomach is the size of your mother-in-law and your chair is shattering to pieces under you. By the end of the meal you feel like a knuckle-dragging gorilla.

I'm not saying the Tongans know how to barrel it away. All I'm saying is that if Tonga gave up eating for a week, I reckon they could feed Africa for a year. The average Tongan shovels down over 12,500 kilojoules a day, about 25 per cent more than your hamburger-stuffing, back-to-front-baseball-cap-wearing American, 50 per cent more than your European and about a thousand times more than the poor, desperate African even dreams of having in a week.

And when they drink, they drink. I'll deny it if you quote me, but I've been in some drinking sessions in my life. But a Tongan drinking session! I was lucky to escape with my liver. At least I think I did. I hope I did. One evening in the Billfish bar facing the harbour in the capital, Nuku'alofa, I was with a group of Tongans who slugged back around fifty bottles of beer. Each. They then got up and drove home. Me. I got as far as eight or nine. That was it. I couldn't take any more. Not that I was under the affluence of incahol. It was the sheer quantity that got me. Or rather my poor, overworked bladder.

The women, it hardly needs to be said, are far more sensible. They go out and only drink one bottle, maybe one and a half bottles. Of gin. There was one woman with us who had everything a man could wish for: big muscles. A beard. Moustache. Hairy legs. Huge pot-belly. I saw her drink two bottles of gin. Then she also got up and drove home. Although, God knows, whose home.

I staggered back to my B+B, clambered into my bed and – not that I was as think as you drunk I was – I suddenly felt the room swimming around me. It was only the following morning I discovered why. I was sleeping on a water bed, the only one in the country. All the others had burst. They couldn't take the weight of the Tongans.

And so it goes on. There are no lifts in Tonga. They couldn't take the weight. Well, that's not true. There is one. But it's in the only international hotel in the place, so it's not for Tongans, it's for foreigners.

There are no buildings over two storeys high. Again the same reason. Weight. Cost of reinforced construction. It's cheaper to build out than up.

Offices. They're more like cattle pens: the amount of money they have to spend on such huge areas – ten times what they must spend in Japan – leaves precious little for decoration.

Weddings. When two Tongans get married, they are so fat they have to use adjoining churches.

Funerals. In this country it takes six men to carry a coffin. In Tonga they have to use fork-lift trucks. Around six.

In fact, Tongans are so fat they can't wear ordinary clothes. The only thing they can do to protect their enormous proportions while they wait for Anne Widdecombe's old clothes to hit the charity shops is literally to wrap a mat around their more than ample girths: a *pa'atetele*, a rough and ready mat, practically falling to pieces, which they wear for funerals; a *ta'ovala*, which they wear for more elegant, happy events such as christenings, parties, weddings. Well, maybe not weddings.

Of course, they give you all the baloney. The mats, whether they're for happy events or for weddings, are made from the finest mulberry bark, cut into strips, pounded like hell, soaked for hours on end, hung up, left to dry, turned into paper then delicately woven into intricate, traditional patterns, each with a wealth of meaning.

Some say it's all history and tradition. When the first settlers arrived in the early 1700s (when the island was about 500 ft higher than it is today), they realised they'd forgotten their black ties and dinner jackets – whoosh, they cut up their matted sails, wrapped them around their throbbing loins and were ready to party.

Others say it's because of the King, His Heaviness Taufa'ahau Tupou IV, who dominates the country in every sense of the word. Eighty-six years old. Six foot six inches tall. Thirty-three stone. Size 20 shoes. Arthritic. A bad back. If he roly-polys out of nowhere wearing a silk shirt, the traditional Tongan skirt and two watches, they have to immediately rush to the other end of the room to balance the building to stop it from collapsing to one side and, whoosh, whip their mats off, sit down on them and pay their respects.

The Tongans, of course, claim it's protocol, decorum, their sense of respect for royalty and all that it stands for. But then they would say that wouldn't they? It was only when the airlines discovered that they were doing the same thing whenever they saw the King board a plane that they decided that whenever His Heaviness flies anywhere, not only did they have to ditch half the passengers they also had to hide him behind sheets and screens and special dividers if there was to be any chance of the plane taking off.

But at the end of the day, a mat is still a mat is still a mat.

In fact, it's probably because of the size of the mat industry in Tonga that there's been no serious attempt to persuade the country to go on a diet. Just think: one hundred thousand people each wearing 100 yards of matting, most of them all at the same time, is big business; whereas one hundred thousand people wearing skinny Armanis and next-to-nothing Versaces equals collapse of mat industry.

Most Tongans, don't forget, see nothing wrong with being fat and spending their lives choking down angiotensin-converting enzyme inhibitors to try to ward off heart attacks. It is, they say, their heritage, their culture, their ancestry. But it's not so. They started thin. They came originally from sushi- and rice-eating south-east Asia. About two thousand, maybe three thousand years ago. A bunch of them, tired of fighting for the last lump of sweet and sour, jumped in their vast double-hulled canoes to find out whether the sea was bluer on the other side of the horizon.

We think the Greeks, the Romans, the Vikings, even the Irish in their little coracles were great seamen. They were nothing compared to these weedy, rice-eating little guys.

Around AD 500–700 the Polynesians reached Hawaii, New Zealand and the Easter Islands, landing on and settling every tiny island, atoll and lump of rock they passed on their way. Some archaeologists maintain that among the earliest Polynesians setting sail for the wide blue yonder were one of the lost tribes of Israel, so called because they had got lost somewhere between Java and Golders Green, headed for Melanesia and ended up in Tonga. Which is why, they maintain, their pre-Christian religion is very much Do not kill, Love thy neighbour, and Pass the chicken soup, you schmuck.

Those left behind at each stop cultivated and domesticated everything they came across. The others ventured on until they had the whole slice of the globe covered. Then they too settled down. But as each settlement grew, so too did the arguments and rows between them. First there were skirmishes. Then short-lived battles. Then outright war. The winners stayed near the coast. The losers moved further inland, desperate to get away from their in-laws, I mean enemies. Each built their statues to their gods either as thanks or for deliverance or to give archaeologists reasons to travel the world, argue and write books. The difference with the guys who landed in Tonga is that they had nothing to argue about, nothing to fight about, no reasons to build huge castles and fortresses. All they could think of was lying in the sun, eating and getting fat.

Not everyone, of course, agrees: although the weight of the evidence is overwhelmingly against them, they say the Tongans are naturally thin. It's just that the government failed to put any health warnings on the buckets of food they push down their throats every day.

His Heaviness has done his best to advocate the thin way of life. Or, rather, thinner. To look at his majestic proportions now, it is difficult to believe that in his youth he was an outstanding sportsman, a member of Sydney University's rugby and rowing teams and the Tongan schoolboy pole vault champion. Of course, the pole was a telegraph pole and the bar about 10 inches off the ground, but if you're the son of the King that doesn't make any difference.

Today, when he's not indulging his little passion, brass bands – he loves nothing better than to be woken up by one playing outside his room every morning. He also loves his organ. Although how he can see it, goodness only knows. He also loves playing the guitar, the Greek bouzouki, and driving around in his reinforced stretch Cadillac, which looks as though it could double up as an elephant transporter. Or rather a double elephant transporter – he's on his bike. Twice a week he turns out in baggy shorts, T-shirt and baseball cap to cycle fifteen laps round the palace grounds in full view of the public.

Some people have suggested that he should cycle fifteen laps round one of his citizens, but his doctors feel that would be too great a distance for him to cover. He is after all eighty-six years old. Outside experts have also tried to help him. One research organisation after another has produced weighty evidence to prove that the Tongans are not only probably the fattest people on earth – now you know why Tonga is in the southern hemisphere as opposed to the northern – but that they are more at risk from being fat than anybody else on earth. About 40 per cent of the men are seriously overweight. Clinically obese, to use the correct medical phrase. For women, it's more like 60 per cent. For fat people between twenty-four and thirty-five it's not so bad: they are only twelve times more likely to die prematurely than thin people. Women who are fat when they are young and get fatter as they get older are seventy times more likely to develop diabetes than thin women. Then there are all those other exciting things to look forward to: high blood pressure, heart attacks, hypertension, gall-bladder blowouts, cancer, increased construction costs, the desperate shortage of fork-lift trucks for funerals, weighing machines in banks – it's true. Go into a bank to cash your cheque in order to buy more food and more booze. There's a weighing machine there so you can check your weight.

'Phew. I'm still only 29 stone. I'll cash two cheques.'

The World Health Organisation has even weighed in with what they call a special obesity prevention and control programme. Eat less fat, they say. Reduce portion sizes. Take 7500 steps a day.

But the biggest influence of all seems to be, inevitably, television and cinema. In other parts of the world it is blamed for turning young and old alike into couch potatoes. Not so in Tonga. In Tonga they just love any kind of potato.

Today girls, who in the past would be so desperate to be fat they would be stuffing sack after sack of animal feed down their throats, see one Hollywood movie after another and instead of big is beautiful, thin is. Even Miss World, so loved by feminists around the world, is having its effect. Backsides and bosoms the size of double-decker buses are out. Just about every girl wants to be so thin she hardly casts a shadow.

My first contact with Tonga was – as it was for everybody under seventy-four and a half – Queen Salote. I can remember when practically the whole street packed into our tiny, ornament-loaded living room to watch the coronation on our brand-new television set with its flickering black-and-white screen. The Queen. The coronation itself. The Horse Guards. The crowds. Nobody was interested. Everybody kept on about the big, fat, laughing Queen of Tonga who sat drenched in the back of her open carriage, in the pouring rain, smiling and laughing and waving at everyone in sight.

'Who's that with the Queen of Tonga?' some courtier whispered to Noel Coward.

'Her lunch,' he said.

A million years later I was working in Togo. Again I was pestered with Tonga.

'You mean Tonga. You're working in Tonga.'

If I had a bottle of Dom Pérignon for every time anyone said that to me, I'd be a happy man.

'No. Togo. West Africa. Different part of the world altogether.'

'Where the Queen came from. At the coronation. I remember.'

'No. That's . . . Oh, what the hell. I'll have a large one.'

The Post Office. DHL. FedEx. The rest of them. They also get it wrong. In fact, if I had two bottles of Dom Pérignon for every time my post went to Tonga instead of Togo I wouldn't be able to remember a thing. In the end, I had no choice. I had to go there to pick it up. Where was it when I got there? You got it. In Tokyo. Why? Because when it got to Tonga it could be delivered the old-fashioned way only: by attaching it to a rocket and firing it from the old supply ship, *Tofua*, to as near as they could get to the shore. In the end they decided it wasn't worth the effort. Either the mail missed the beach and fell into the sea or it reached the beach and was burned by the flames of the rocket. They sent everything to Tokyo instead.

Not that there was any other reason to go to Tonga which comprises 170 islands, only forty-five of which are inhabited. Originally, of course, there were 237. The others sank under the weight of the Tongans. Today the surviving 170 are divided into three main island groups: Tongatapu, which means, 'My God, their average weight is about 30 stone'. Ata, which means, 'Just as well they don't have any shoes. They'd never be able to bend down and do up the laces', and Teleki Tonga Tokelau, which means, in the famous words of the talking weighing machine, 'Only one at a time please'. Total population: one hundred thousand, although reduce that down to normal person size and it's about three hundred thousand.

Tongans are so huge, so fat, so blubbery that perhaps it explains why they have never been conquered, never been colonised. Perhaps they are so huge, so fat, so blubbery that nobody was able to see whether the place was *worth* conquering or colonising.

From what I was able to see of it, the capital, Nuku'alofa is definitely not worth trying to conquer. It's so downmarket and scruffy. Although in it *could* be the most beautiful place on the planet: smothered with colourful wooden bungalows, coconut trees, poinsettias, hibiscus, bougainvillea, breadfruit trees and no end of frangipanis. Except nobody seems to be interested.

The king's whitewashed wooden palace, which I managed to catch a glimpse of, looked like it could have been an offcut from the end of Brighton Pier, except that the supports would never have been able to carry the weight. It also looked remarkably flimsy for a monarch of such majestic proportions. Why? Because the official residence of the proud monarch of the Tongans is not Tongan at all. It's from New Zealand. The whole thing was designed and built in New Zealand and shipped across by boat. About the only truly Tongan thing in the place apart from the great man himself are the four *fangu-fangu* – nose flutes to you and me – which are used to waken the king every morning. As for the ducks and geese waddling around the lawn, there are doubts about their parentage as well. But that's not unusual. There are doubts about the parentage of just about everything in Tonga.

If that didn't make you howl with laughter, this will. Next to the palace is an inconspicuous shack called Niukasa. Niukasa? Tongan, my hinnies, for 'Newcastle'. Built by a local – and seriously demented – heavy who not only liked going to Europe just to visit Newcastle, but decided that he wanted to come back to a home that reminded him of Newcastle. Judging by the look of it – small, pleasant, clean, quiet, civilised – I would say he must have stayed in a different Newcastle to the one I stay in whenever I'm forced north of Watford.

Down the road is the Queen Salote Memorial Hall, which I also didn't see, but which apparently looks like a garden chair once sat upon by the good Queen herself. It was built as a symbol of the love and respect of her devoted servants, the loyal people of Tonga. Work started shortly after she died in 1965. The loyal people of Tonga then promptly ran out of money. Work came to a stop almost as soon as it started. It was completed only when the loyal, loving government of Tonga came up with the readies some thirty years later – with, that is, the aid of the Chinese.

The parliament building, which I did catch a glimpse of, shows you what His Heaviness thinks of parliament. It looks like a garden shed. What's more, I can't see how all the members of parliament could possibly get in there at the same time. I also can't see how, if they did, it could take the weight. But that's probably one of His Heaviness's little jokes.

Most British high commissioners lording it up in the capitals of the world like nothing better than to look down on the people they are supposed to be lording it over. The British High Commissioner's Residence in Tonga is no exception. So determined were the British to look down on the Tongans, who are not exactly the smallest people in the world, that they had the whole High Commissioner's Residence in all its colonial splendour jacked up 9 feet off the ground and then gently lowered in post-colonial isolation on to a string of 6-foot concrete posts. They said it was to stop the termites from eating the place alive, but you know how far you can believe the Foreign Office.

For all their aloofness, the British are well and truly immersed in Tongan affairs. While I was there, His Excellency the British High Commissioner was trumpeting the major role the British were playing in Tonga's fight against drugs. They had just donated $2278 for bumper stickers with 'advising words about problems of drugs'. Wowee, $2278 dollars. That's going to make a hell of an impact. The High Commissioner probably spends more than that getting his grass cut. No. Not that grass. The grass in front of his imposing mansion.

The Australian High Commission had its own problems. The whole building was flown in from Australia complete with packs of Fosters. They called it Mirrabooka (Southern Cross), which was a bit of an understatement. The High Commissioner was bloody angry. She'd no sooner moved in than the place was flooded. Then came the big question: how to stop the flooding? Try to repair the metal-framed-and-constructed-in-Australia-to-the-latest-Australian-technology building or build a sea wall. They went for the sea wall. The Australians did, however, decide to put on a hurricane-proof roof. Presumably in case the High Commissioner ever blew her top again.

Just as Samoa has its famous Aggie Grey's hotel; the Cook Islands, Trader Jack's; and the Solomon Islands, the even more famous Gizo Hotel; so Tonga could have had its own famous hotel. It would have been Bella Riechelmann's near legendary Beach House had it not been knocked down and the land on Vunu Road and Fongoloa Road not been sold to the Chinese for a new embassy. Well, I say legendary. In the old days when Tongans' average weight was only 27.5 stone and seventeen pints was about average for a night out, Bella Riechelmann's Beach House, which was more a flop sweat than a hotel, was famous for the size of its cockroaches.

'Cockroaches, smockroaches,' La Bella used to scream at any passing South Pacific island salt who plucked up courage to complain as he saw his plate of good, wholesome home cooking disappearing out the door. 'It means the food is good.'

It was also the perfect place to meet people. A large rambling South Sea colonial mansion or a boring mid-Victorian lookalike – depending on whether or not you'd hit fifteen bottles for the night – it had only eight bedrooms. All twins. No singles. Doubling up was compulsory, which may or may not explain why even today Tonga is still desperately low on conventional hotel accommodation. Even the 'upmarket' Dateline Hotel, the only conventional hotel on the island, was a long time coming, and it still doesn't look as though it's finished. In 1954 they said it was going to be a small tropical-style hotel for twenty-eight guests. Then like everything in Tonga it grew and grew. In 1957 it was going to have twenty-four rooms. Come 1964 it was going to have fifty-five rooms. Finally it opened in 1966 just in time for the King's coronation. Today it has seventy-eight rooms, the only lift in the whole country and a snack bar which serves the soggiest food I've ever had in my life. Every time a Tongan jumps in the swimming pool alongside, it's like being in the middle of a tropical storm.

The Yacht Club, however, *is* legendary. It's the last male-only bastion in the South Pacific. Not because they hold anything against women as such – or would want to – it's just that the building couldn't take it. It's already in a pretty precarious condition: one Ladies' Night Buffet Dance and that would be the end of it, especially if they got round to the tautolunga. The tautolunga is their strange national dance and is supposed to recall ancient tales and legends of love which the dancer – glistening in coconut oil, flowers on her wrists, in her hair and around her ankles, waving her pandanus leaf fan all over the place – has to perform with her knees continually clammed tight together.

The new Visitors' Bureau was fantastic. And it was so typically Tongan. It incorporates so much of the island's natural resources – 5589 feet of the finest Tongan tamanu and tangato from the island of Eua, four large koka posts each measuring

3.05 metres long, 1200 metres of young bamboo, over 1000 square metres of woven paonga matting, over 30 metres of brown and black plaited coconut husk fibres to bind the whole thing together – that there is nothing left for the visitors to visit.

Outside Nuku'alofa I did manage to catch a glimpse of the blowholes at Houma. They were up the spout. They were even more pathetic than the ones in Savaii, Samoa.

I saw the Stonehenge-like three-stone structure they call Ha'amonga. Each upright is about 17 feet high and weighs about 20 ton. The crosspiece on top is about 19 feet wide and weighs about 4 ton. His Heaviness says it's an ancient Tongan clock. Some tiny notch on top, which nobody but him has ever noticed before, points directly to the sun on 21 June and 21 December, the shortest and longest days of the year. My theory? It's an ancient Tongan weighing machine. If you can't get through the 19-foot gap between the two upright stones, you've got to go on a diet.

I also saw in the far, far distance the Crown Prince's hang-out, which looks like a giant aircraft hangar. But not his old London taxi, nor his Second World War plane. Some people criticise him for being a bit of a Prince Charles. He is fifty-four, unmarried, forever looking for things to do. Not so. He has a keen military mind. He used to be at Sandhurst. He's also got undoubted leadership skills. He once formed a band called the Straight Bananas.

But I didn't see the offices at the peace-loving Tonga College Boys' School. They were burned down by the peace-loving boys at the Methodist Church School because they beat them at rugby. At least it took their minds off eating for a few minutes.

I did, however, see the sacred flying foxes of Kolovai, on the shores of Maria Bay. By day they hang around upside down in the trees in the centre of the village. By night they're eating their hearts out in every banana plantation on the island.

'So how sacred are they?' I asked one gastric grunt who looked as though his tracheotomy valve was on the blink as he barrelled along the road through the middle of Kolovai.

'Very,' he said.

'So, if you see them eating your banana crops, can you kill them?'

'Yes,' he said. 'Providing it's at night-time. But during the day when they are resting, no.'

On the way back to Nuku'alofa, close to yet another one of Captain Cook's famous landing places, I bumped into a funeral.

In Fiji the best part of the funeral used to be when everybody had had their fill of food and booze and they then strangled the wife so that she could keep her husband company in the next world. Or that used to be the custom. Nowadays most blokes don't want their wives to accompany them into the next world. They've had enough of them in this.

In Tonga, the best part naturally is the food. They decorate the house inside and out with so much black and purple that it looks like a Black Magic wedding cake. They call in the caterers. They bring in lorryload after lorryload after lorryload of booze. So much that it makes a traditional Irish wake look like an Alcoholics Anonymous tea party. They prepare mountains of food. They death-chomp away days and nights to their bursting stomachs' content. You get the impression that they're desperate to get the burial over and done with as quickly as possible because it gets in the way of the eating and drinking.

Almost hidden behind a huge plate of what looked like mammoth steaks I came across an old man about the size of the Millennium Dome. Except he looked anything but empty. He told me he was 105 years old. The secret of old age, he said, was coconut shells. He only ever had anything provided it was barbecued on red-hot coconut shells and, of course, washed down with ten or twenty bottles of beer a day.

Were the mammoth steaks he was stuffing himself with barbecued on red-hot coconut shells?

'No.' He shoved three more down his throat. 'But at 105, I think I can take a chance.'

Trouble is in Tonga while there's no dispute about the size of a mammoth steak, nobody can tell you what the time is, let alone what year it is. One hundred and five years in Tonga might well be seventy-three years somewhere else or even 125.

The problem is the dateline. When did I go there? I couldn't tell you. Not because of the usual. At the time I was severely limiting myself to just twenty bottles of beer a day. Not because I'm suffering the early signs of Alzheimer's, although I will admit that I do now spend my time meeting nobody but new friends. But because I was crossing, recrossing and crossing again the international dateline, the international time zone, the international everything else, and so often that I landed there two days after I'd left prior to my arrival yesterday after tomorrow on a day that never existed. If you see what I mean.

As if that's not bad enough they keep playing games with the clock. In order to beat Kiribati and New Zealand's Chatham Islands into the new millennium, His Heaviness jumped the clocks to fourteen hours ahead of GMT. Now they can't remember whether they are still fourteen hours ahead, whether the clocks have been put back, if so to what, or if they were never put forward or backwards at all. The result is that one bar says something different from another. One bank closes while another opens. Taxis turn up to collect you two hours late for trips you never meant taking until yesterday anyhow.

The other problem is that when you get back to civilisation you can't prove you've ever been to Tonga in the first place. Even though you've still got the bills to prove it.

It was, therefore, for me at least, the one place in the world to try again to plough through Proust's so-called great *A la recherche du temps perdu*, in which Proust's snotty little cupcake of a narrator remembers everything from popping out of the womb, having a glass of champagne with the nurses, admiring his own afterbirth and banging his head on the back of the pram the first time he went on one of those blasted walks to—oh hell, I can't remember what's on page 300,757.

Now I know I know nothing, but according to my French–English dictionary '*temps*' means 'weather', 'time' is '*heure*' so surely the title should be *Remembrance of Weather Past*, which would tie in neatly with the first three million and a half pages, which seem to be about nothing but Combray and the weather: whether they should walk this way or whether they should walk that way. In the end Proust has his precious Madeleine and eats it. He walks both ways.

On the other hand the time difference does have its advantages. If you keep meaning to move your millions into a safe tax haven or you're just looking for somewhere your wife or her teenage lover can't get their hands on your hard-earned money, Tonga might be the solution. Because of its position on the dateline you can actually wait until you get hammered by the Inland Revenue or whoever and then open up your offshore account there the previous yesterday before tomorrow. All honest. All legit. All above board. Nobody can touch you. You're safe. More importantly, so is your money. Your worries are over. You can catch the next flight to Tonga on a plane that leaves tomorrow which in two days' time will be yesterday, land yourself a young Tongan maiden who has big muscles, a moustache, hairy legs and a huge pot-belly, eat all the food you can handle, all the beer your poor stomach can take, and get fat, Fat, FAT.

Avarua

Take what looks like a lump of cold potato covered in green mould. Sprinkle all over with people who look like a cross between Delia Smith and Anthony Worrell Thompson, and talk halfway between Jamie Oliver and the lovely Nigella. Throw in a couple of handfuls of New Zealand tourists clutching airtight polythene bags containing their packets of Rice Krispies, marinate in a lukewarm mixture of fresh lime juice, coconut milk and Keith Floyd's spit. Serve with a dollop of old colonial paternalism. That's Raratonga, the big cheese of the Cook Islands or, as the local Maoris call it, The Land of the Bright Heavens.

In fact, Captain Cook stayed only for a couple of days. First in 1773 when he spotted the tiny Manu'ae atoll. For a Yorkshireman it was obviously too much like home. It's also a miracle there weren't any mutinies there either. I mean, can you imagine sailing halfway round the world to be greeted by chickens wandering around all over the place, women the size of both of the Two Fat Ladies and only one decent bar, Trader Jack's? Well, I say decent bar, it's more your typical imitation South Pacific hang-out where your typical rough, tough South Pacific swarthy, burned to the colour of an overdone Gratin de pêches Marjorie, swaggers up to the bar and demands a straight, no-nonsense mineral water. With bubbles. And for his friend, who looks a bit like Somerset Maugham in a crisp white

T-shirt, a cup of coffee. With lots of milk. Which, as far as I'm concerned, gives a whole new meaning to kiwi fruit. And – talk about typically British – they stop serving lunch after two o'clock.

Arrive by plane and you'll Roux the day you decided to dump Torquay for the Cook Islands. You stagger off a ten-hour flight from Los Angeles to be greeted at the airport by an idiot-friendly, plucking awful George Formby clone, complete with his damn ukulele. As if that's not bad enough, he seizes on poor unfortunates and drags them up to join him for a jolly, happy-campers sing-song.

As soon as I heard him, I tried to get straight back on the plane. Even though it was going on to New Zealand. The security guards wouldn't let me. Not because I didn't have a ticket. But because I objected when they – I'm not kidding – insisted on searching my glasses. The constant ukulele playing had obviously sent them stark, staring mad. There can be no other explanation.

The good Captain Cook was back again – not on Raratonga, the main island, but on Mangaia – on 29 March 1777, when he was greeted by heavily tattooed yahoos with knives dangling from their ears. Soon convinced he'd made a mistake, he didn't bother stopping. Today Mangaia, which is the most southerly of the islands, is little more than taro swamps, from which they produce the deadly taro cards and no end of caves.

Strictly speaking, the islands shouldn't be called the Cook Islands at all. The good Captain stumbled across only the odd – very odd – two small potatoes out of fifteen of them, some about the size of Delia's boiled eggs, spread across an area the size of Clarissa Dickson Wright's waistline. Raratonga, which is about one-third the size of the Isle of Wight, was first discovered by Captain Philip Goodenough in the HMS *Cumberland Sausage* in 1814. So, on the basis that he discovered the biggest of the lot, I suppose the whole chicken stew should be called not the Cook Islands but the Goodenough Islands. Not that the marketing people would agree. 'Come to the Goodenough Islands' is hardly going to have the swimming, snorkelling, fish-scaring, coral-destroying, seabed-littering fraternity pouring in in their millions. On the other hand, it would be different from all the other big holiday advertising campaigns: it would be telling the truth.

Take a Cook's tour of Raratonga, which is nine-parts jungle-clad craggy volcanic peaks with romantic-sounding names like Wigmore's Waterfall, and one-part coral beaches, almost surrounded by a protective reef. It's no big deal. You can see all the ingredients in an hour largely because – thank God – there are not many Rhodes on the island. In fact, there is really only one, which goes on and on and on, largely because it forms a complete circuit of the island. The only good thing about it is the complete circuit is only 32 kilometres so you can be there and back in less time than it takes to fix a Rosette de boeuf Grand Hôtel. I went round it twice. Once clockwise. And then anticlockwise to see if it would be more exciting coming at the good enough hotels, the good enough villas and the good enough Quality Budget Accommodation signs from the other direction. It wasn't.

The only exciting thing on the whole trip, whichever way I went, was the sign at the bus station in the capital, Avarua. It not only announced the times the buses were leaving on their clockwise and anti-clockwise tours, it also included a helpful little diagram indicating which way was which.

See what I mean about Captain Cook thinking he was back in Yorkshire. Or maybe that was for the New Zealand tourists. Even Jamie Oliver knows the right way to whisk an egg.

In fact, come to think of it, the whole island has a good enough feel about it. From the buses that keep you waiting hours on end when you arrive at the airport; the hotel rooms with their thick white-painted wicker chairs; the taxis with their broken windows and non-existent air-conditioning; to the Friday-night highlight, 'steak followed by bus tour'. The British disease all over again. Spend as little as possible. Minimum maintenance. And don't even think about reinvestment until whatever it is, is broken beyond repair. Then there are all the signs that say No Tipping. It may be the official line, but try explaining that to Tata behind the bar at the Edgewater. You'll end up by getting only what you pay for.

The locals, who delight in such romantic South Pacific Island names as Arbuthnot, Boggs, Newbigging, Pratt and Trott – maybe Captain Cook and his merry band of chefs did find something of interest after all . . . – are slow, dull, plodding, maybe a touch, well, Yorkshire. They have none of the sparkle, the *joie de vivre* of the other islands. Unless, of course, it's the change of diet. Years ago they were happy-go-lucky cannibals who so loved their fellow man they ate him whenever they got the chance, especially missionaries who always tended to be (Marco Pierre) White men and whom they regarded as an essential part of any balanced diet.

Not that they weren't civilised. They would never dream of talking with someone in their mouth. The only way for any visitor to survive was to lose interest in the tribal chief before he lost interest in them. If he didn't, it was, as one ancient Cook Island recipe says, 'insert spear at the fundament. Run through the body appearing again at the neck. Singe body slowly over a fire in order that the entire cuticle and all the hair may be removed. Next take out intestines. Wash in sea water. Wrap in singed banana leaves. Cook with body in oven over red-hot basaltic stones until crisp.'

Then it was each man for himself – or rather each man for somebody else. The best bit was the thigh, which was supposed to taste salty. After that, everything else. The intestines wrapped in their singed banana leaves being reserved for the cooks. By the time they were finished, according to the recipe book, 'nothing would be left but the nails and the bones'.

Sometimes they would cook one of their own children. One chief, Taoro, even cooked his only child as a special treat for all his friends. So thanks a lot Abraham. Killing your son was no big deal.

Girls, however, were never eaten. Instead they were fattened up; sometimes even locked up and force-fed so that they could be as fat as possible. Neither were grown women ever eaten. Because, it is said, the chiefs feared that – desperate as they were to get their teeth into them – they would be far too tough and gristly.

'Is the meat as tender as a woman's heart?' was said to be one of Taora's constant questions to his chefs.

Those were the days when you could talk to chefs and, what's more, chefs deigned to talk to the customers who were paying their exorbitant bills.

'Yes,' the chefs would say.

'In that case,' Taora would reply, 'I'll have the fish.' Or rather, 'N a case, I ae e is' – the local language had only thirteen letters which no doubt also accounts for the fact none of the local chefs ever got as much as a single 'Micein' star.

Missionaries, however, were in a class of their own. Because of the amount of clothing they wore, they were known locally as *papa'a*, 'four layers of clothing', although how exactly the locals knew the missionaries wore four layers of clothing I never found out. From practically the first moment they arrived in the Cook Islands, especially those from the London Missionary Society, they seemed to gel. Like a good ris de veaux aux feuilles mixed with some fresh young spinach and left to simmer for half an hour.

Except that things didn't always work out the way the chiefs would have wanted.

'OK,' said Taora one day when, according to ancient Cook

Islands legend, he was faced with three missionaries. An Englishman, a Frenchman and an Irishman. 'We're going to put you in a pot, cook you like mignons de chevreuil à la purée de persil washes whitest and eat you. Then we're going to use your skin to build a canoe. But seeing as Delia is on the telly tonight, I'm going to let you choose how to die.'

'The gun,' said the Englishman. They gave him a gun. He shot himself.

'Ze sword,' said the Frenchman. They gave him a sword. He fell on it.

'A fork,' said the Irishman.

'A fork?' said Taora.

'A fork,' said the Irishman.

They gave him a fork. He started dancing around, stabbing himself, blood spurting all over the place.

'What are you doing?' cried Taora.

'So much for your canoe,' shrieked the Irishman.

Today, however, it's all changed. The cardinal rule now is: convert the chief before he converts you – into lunch. As for human flesh, you can get it delivered by post from various parts of West Africa not a million miles from a PO Box in Monrovia, Liberia.

The smart guys call it bush rat. The less than smart guys, who are usually found gathered around white sheets decorated with half-burned candles laid out on the banks of the Thames near Battersea power station at low tide, say, What the hell. It didn't do my family any harm. Why should it do me any harm? In any case, stomach linings can cause all kinds of problems to my enemies: fingernails and toenails can be made into various poisons; eyebrows, hair and noses can be used in curses; and as for the breasts and genitals, that's not something I've ever been able to get a grip on. Old habits, however, die hard. Even today when Cook Islanders finish their meals, they always count the children afterwards. Just in case.

Eating over, it was time for dancing. And what dancing. Mothers oiled, kneaded, stretched and even cracked the joints of their children from birth to make certain they would be the best dancers.

'Respecting the morality of their dances, the less said the better,' says one history book all prim and proper. 'The upaupa dance, introduced from Tahiti, is obscene indeed.'

What did they expect after gorging on a couple of missionaries? The Gay Gordons?

The men today, well, if they're the grandsons and great-grandsons of whalers, they've inherited all the characteristics: thick, stoic, blubbery, Yorkshire. Instead of eating their children, they go on and on about the mile-a-minute vine that blankets entire forests in an afternoon, the effects of the black rat and other invasive species. They don't even make jokes about passing missionaries in the street any more.

In one good enough shack one evening over a couple of cans of Tumu Nu, the local killer bush-beer, I met one islander called Bulwark, who impressed me more by his absence than his presence.

'Bulwark. Mister Bulwark,' he said shaking my hand up and down backwards and forwards like a Victorian traction engine. 'Third generation. Great-grandfather washed up here in a whaler. Stayed on. Two wives. Both sisters. First wife didn't give him any children. Married the other. All lived together. One big happy family. Seven children. All girls. One boy.'

If it weren't for his multicoloured shirt, the flowers round his neck, his baggy pants and his straw hat, he could have been your everyday Yorkshire mill owner.

The women, on the other hand, look as though they've inherited the blubber. They're not just fat. They are thick, solid fat. They are so thick, solid fat that they can't sway their hips, wriggle their toes or even – the mind shudders at the thought – twirl two tassels round in opposite directions. The only way they can even attempt to make whoopee at the fellas is by – this is true – twitching their knees. Go to an evening of traditional Cook Island dancing hoping for a bit of excitement and a touch of how's-your-father and, I promise you, you'll come away an expert on kneecaps.

If, however, you're not a fat, blubbery knee fetishist – and, believe me, half an hour in the Cook Islands and you'll never want to become one – there are other thrills and excitements.

There is that first delicious plate of parrotfish and chips.

There's watching the famous Cook Island chickens peck their way in and out of cafés, bars and restaurants. In one restaurant I went to there was more chicken pecking away under my table than there was on my plate. But the slightest word about campylobacter and other dangerous microorganisms carried by chickens and the Cook Islanders will be down from their perches and flapping their wings like mad. Because for some reason or other they treat chickens the way Hindus treat cattle. They're free to go and do whatever they like, wherever they like. They also have this chicken obsession. People are not people, they're chooks. Men are roosters. Women are hens. And a whole group of them are a coopful. They don't talk, they crow. They don't walk, they scratch. They don't get annoyed, they ruffle their feathers. And, as for a chickster, your guess is as good as mine.

The Cook Islands are also one of the few countries in the world where religion is religion. Until very recently the whole place used to close down on Sundays. Beaches included. It's not so strict now. They allow the tide to come in. Religious holidays, however, are still religious holidays. Take Gospel Day, for example, when they celebrate the arrival of Christianity in the islands on 26 October 1821, when the Revd John Williams landed on Aitutaki. Not only is it an official public holiday, not only does the whole country close down, everybody is up and off to Takamoa Theological College where from 8.30 in the morning they are watching strict twenty-five-minute *nukus* or playlets based on Abraham, the spiritual pilgrim; Gideon, the mighty man of valour; Samuel, the upright judge; Daniel, the statesman prophet; and so on through the Bible to Revelation 22:21 'The grace of our Lord Jesus Christ be with you all. Amen.' Still better than a day out with the wife and family.

There are also churches, churches and still more churches. There is even a Cook Island Christian Church, founded by our friends from the London Missionary Society. Go there on a Sunday morning – you might as well. There's nothing else to do – and you'll hear singing the like of which you'll hear nowhere else in the world. No, I don't mean the usual mumbling and murmuring and occasional grunting that passes for singing in most churches. In the church I go to the standard of singing is so bad they've insisted that the hymns are for the good singers and the plainchant is for the masses. Not so the Cook Islands. They believe in full-throated, give-it-all-you've-got, Shirley Bassey-was-my-auntie singing. The day I went, the singing was so loud it scared the chickens pecking away on the lawn outside the church. Even the cock crew three times. In tune.

As for cemeteries, they're on your doorstep. Literally. The good people of the Cook Islands believe in burying beloved Mummy and Daddy in the front lawn. Right in the centre where the rose bush should go. Under a pile of bricks and statuary the size of the Albert Hall. All plastered in white paint.

Now I don't know about you, but that, I would have thought, must take some getting used to. Burying mother-in-law, on the other hand, might not be so bad. Having to walk over her grave three times a day. Being continually reminded of her nagging that if you didn't stop eating and drinking so much she'd easily see you out. Resisting the chance to dance all over it because in spite of everything you did for her, the different houses you bought for her to live in – each one further and further away – the holidays you paid for, the weekend visits you suffered, she still left all her money to Mrs Tiggy Winks Home for Retired Cats. But it doesn't stop with the front garden. There are graves all over the place, even in hotel car parks.

It is such an idyllic, fun-filled sunspot that almost since the day the Cook Islanders first arrived on the Cook Islands they've been trying to escape. As far back as 1350 – and, I reckon, for thousands of years before then they were leaping into their canoes and heading off for the bright lights. Unfortunately for them they were the bright lights of New Zealand. Which just goes to prove that even for Cook Islanders the sea is not always bluer on the other side. But, slow, dull, plodding people that they are, they continue to head for New Zealand. Today there are over forty thousand of them there, more than twice the number there are at home. The poor French Polynesians, however, have to put up with Paris. Doesn't it make you weep.

All the books talk about the carefree abandon of the South Pacific; how the exhausted businessman, the public school drop-out and the would-be adventurer go there in search of serenity and to be far away from paternity summonses, unpaid alimony bills and the like. Don't you believe it. A couple of nights in Trader Jack's and you hear the same old moans and complaints. Why aren't they allowed to buy any land on the islands? They're allowed only to lease it and then for just sixty years. What's more, in the end not only does the land revert to the original owner but so too do any buildings on it. Any buildings, that is, that haven't been knocked down by a passing bulldozer in the middle of the night, what?

'I say, Jeremy. Another large gin, what? Good for the old sparkle, what?'

'And what about the tourists?'

'Those damn snorkellers. I don't know what's worse, the snorkellers or the birdies, what?'

'Hikers. They're the worst, what?'

'It's the whalers. I can't stand the whalers, what?'

'Now Cecil, it's my turn. How about a treble this time? The way you knock them back a double hardly touches the sides, what?'

In the mid-nineties, of course, they did have something to really crow about. The French nuclear tests were taking place on Mururoa Atoll. Just 500 miles away. The easterly trade winds came in their direction. The sea currents headed their way. What was going to happen to them, their children, the birds (the frigate birds, the black herons, the millions of mynahs), the fish (the warty frogshell, the mutable conche, the hailstorm, prickly winkle), their long, sandy beaches, the blue coral lagoons, the coconut palms rustling in the breeze not to mention their damn chickens and, finally, their wives.

Today nobody mentions it. Which means either that they've been bought off by the French, which is the usual French solution to any problem or that the French – and this is less likely – acted responsibly, they took the necessary safety precautions to stop the force of the explosions shattering the coral reefs and any radioactivity leaking into the open air. Or they'd just rather knock back the old treble gin and it and tell silly stories.

'Humphrey. Have you heard the one about the Cook Islander, the Tongan and the Samoan . . .?'

Not that life in the Cook Islands doesn't still have its dangers. First, there are the tourists who head there for the diving and snorkelling and windsurfing and generally playing about in boats. All I can say is that the more time they spend diving and snorkelling and windsurfing and playing about in boats, the better it is for all of us.

Second, and only marginally less dangerous, are the cyclones. And no I don't mean Jamie whizzing by on his motorbike to Sainsbury's to get some more haricots verts for his exciting French bean purée. I mean the real 100–200-mile-an-hour clockwise-spinning cyclones that destroy everything in their path.

So concerned is the government about protecting the people and property of the islands they have published their own how-to-survive-a-cyclone guidelines in the one book that everybody consults every day of their lives: the local Cook Islands Telephone and Business Directory. After Important Raratonga Numbers, Essential Telecom Numbers for Raratonga and details of Telecom Services for Raratonga, there, on page 18 – well, how important do you think protecting people and property *really* is? – is Hurricane Information.

Now I will admit that my practical experience of hurricanes is pretty limited – not only did I survive El Niño, which upset more than a few people I can tell you, I've survived any number of tropical storms too – but the advice they gave I found a touch confusing.

First, it announced grandly, 'A cyclone may hit us in the next 24 hours.' Which I thought was pretty reassuring seeing as nobody breathed a word about it until now. Not my round-the-world weather book. Not the weather news on television. Not even Michael Fish.

Then it calmly told me how to protect my home.

'Tie the roof to the base of nearby trees.'

Eh?

So what do I tie the rest of the house to? A passing chicken, campylobacter oozing out of every feather?

As if that wasn't enough to be getting on with, with a hurricane twenty-four hours away, it then went on calmly, 'Fill water bottles and containers.'

What with? Gin? Vodka? Scotch? Come on. Give us a clue. We could have only twenty-three hours left.

'Pack away loose objects.'

But what's the point if the roof is tied to the base of nearby trees? Any loose objects will be whirling anticlockwise round the northern hemisphere by the time you can say Loup de mer cru aux oeufs de hommard, let alone pronounce it correctly. Not that I need have worried, because the cyclone advice warning then says, 'Put loose objects inside.'

Inside? Inside a house with its roof tied to nearby trees?

Come on. Are you kidding me? Is this some Cook Island joke?

A boring island. A boring bar. Boring people. Nothing but chickens all over the place. A telephone directory that jokes about hurricanes. By now I was desperate for some hot, steamy action. Against all the odds I found it halfway up a deserted dirt track in Upper Tupapa. It was a 30-ton Polish steam engine. Its proud owner, Tim, even gave me a mug of real railway tea.

I tell you. You haven't got to be loco to go to the Cook Islands. But it helps.

Apia

Nomeneta Sopoaga's first kick is charged down. He knocks on. Referee Soanai Opapo misses it. Faiaai Metotisi is penalised for not releasing the ball. In the second minute of play Sopoaga kicks the penalty from 35 metres on the angle. Three point to Samoa Athletics.
Samoa Athletics 3 Samoa Wanderers 0

Samoa is rugby, open-plan living, rugby, more churches than they can handle, and still more rugby. It's as if they were born to play rugby and nothing else. The talk is rugby. Did you see Mataafa miss that kick the other night? The eating is rugby. How on earth did Ropati score off that offload? Fantastic. The drinking is rugby. Why Enelik wasn't penalised I do not understand.

In fact the whole country is a bit like a rugby pitch. If, that is, you're obsessed with rugby.

At one end is the island of Upolu and the capital Apia, population of one hundred and fifteen thousand and no end of rugby pitches.

At the other end is Savaii, the third-largest island in Polynesia behind New Zealand and Tahiti, home to forty-three thousand people, flying foxes and the rare Samoan tooth-billed pigeon, which is about as close as you can get to the dodo of happy memory.

In between, like two English hookers standing between Jonah Lomu, the legendary 20-stone Samoan rugby player labelled 'an unstoppable freak' by Will Carling, and the Colossus of Rhodes are the tiny islands of Manono and Apolima. They are so tiny that they have no hotels, no shops and no cars. And practically no tourists. But rugby players. Yes, they have rugby players.

Except all the islands are not so much islands as volcanoes. Experts got as far as 450 and gave up. Most of them, thankfully, out of action. Although some of them, like a caring, devoted wife, could erupt at any time. The last was Mount Matavanu, which rumbled and spurted and spat fire almost non-stop from 1905 to 1911. Which, in my experience, is a very short spat.

Where there are volcanoes there is lava. Samoa's lava, however, is not like the lava in any other place in the world. In some cases like around Mount Matavaru it's around 150 metres deep.

As if volcanoes were not enough to contend with, the poor Samoans also have to put up with one hurricane after another. The latest came in 1990 and again in 1991 when they were hit by 75-foot waves and 160-mile-an-hour winds. The place was flattened. Twelve people lost their lives. The cost of cleaning up and putting everything back together again: US$150 million.

> Hands in the ruck from Samoa Athletics. Palemia Reupena kicks penalty from similar distance to Sopoaga. Samoa Wanderers draw level with Samoa Athletics.
> Samoa Athletics 3 Samoa Wanderers 3

Samoa was also – not many people, as they say, know this – a far-flung outpost of the Imperial German empire. The shiny boots and pointed helmets arrived in 1900 and left on 30 August 1914. A squadron of the New Zealand navy accompanied by two Australian ships to make certain they knew what they were doing steamed into the harbour at Apia, the capital. The Germans, completely taken by surprise, offered no resistance and surrendered immediately. It was the shortest, quickest and safest battle of the war.

The following morning – why did it take so long? – a royal salute was fired, the Union Jack run up the flag post, and for the first time on Samoan soil a handful of troops no doubt mumbled their way through the National Anthem.

The Samoans were sorry to see the Germans go. In fact, they missed them so much that come the 1930s they formed their own Nazi Party, played Strauss waltzes whenever they got the chance and even started christening their children Hitlia. Probably one of the reasons they liked the Germans so much was because of the way they were treated by New Zealand, which at the end of the war stepped in as colonial administrator and took the Germans' place. Almost the first thing they did was to allow one of their ships, the *Tahuna*, to dock carrying passengers suffering from the global outbreak of influenza, knowing that the poor Samoans had little or no resistance to the disease. Within weeks 22 per cent of the population was dead. Not surprisingly the Samoans started to campaign slowly and quietly and peacefully for independence. In 1929 New Zealand shot dead nineteen of them. Still they persisted. Slowly and quietly. In 1962 they finally won. The first Pacific island nation to break free.

> Soanai Opapo plays a short Wanderers advantage from an Athletic knock-on. Wanderers lose the ball. Samuela Muagututia kicks downfield and beats a wrong-footed Wanderer to score the first try. It's his first point on the scoreboard. Sopoaga misses the sideline conversion.
> Samoa Athletics 8 Samoa Wanderers 3

Read the books, especially James Michener's *Tales of the South Pacific*, and Apia is nothing but 'Bali Hài', Bloody Mary and women washing men right out of their hair. In reality it's more of a B-movie. In black and white.

The setting is fantastic, especially the old part of town huddled around the waterfront. The sunsets are spectacular. Especially because they happen in Samoa later than anywhere else in the world. Not because the Samoans have any particular influence but because of the way the International Time Zone zigzags its way across the South Pacific. They're just 20 miles on the right side of it.

The waterfront apart, the town itself is a bit New Zealand meets Milton Keynes. Function triumphs over design. There are few exciting, let alone interesting buildings. That includes the bars, which are so good they could make a virtue of being virtuous. Aggie Grey's, the one decent hotel in town, is nothing like the legend or any other typical South Pacific hang-out like, say, the Gizo Hotel in the Solomon Islands with the toothless old croc behind the bar. I mean with the toothless old crocodile looking down at you from behind the bar. I didn't see one peg-leg in the place the whole time I was there.

The real Aggie Grey, daughter of a Lincolnshire chemist and a Samoan mother, who turned the place from an old hamburger joint into the hotel it is today, and who was the inspiration for Bloody Mary, the Tokinese madame in Mitchener's book, is still around. A tiny, fragile sparrow, instead of knocking the males for six, she seems more content on knocking out the e-mails for six. She did mine in no time at all. Thanks, Aggie.

Not that the hotel doesn't still have its characters. One evening I had dinner there. Sitting at the far corner by the open-air bar was a fully fledged auntikins who looked as though he walked Polari before he talked Polari. He was about 6' 6" tall and as thin as a rake. His face was as white as a sheet. He was wearing what looked like an all-over khaki jumpsuit, khaki jacket, thick heavy sunglasses, one of those old-fashioned ten-gallon hats and white gloves. Whenever he spoke, he spoke with that long deep American drawl.

As if that wasn't enough, he kept getting up throughout the meal and doing a Polari round and round his table with what looked like a circular green book of maps in his hands, mumbling and chanting to himself, then sitting down again and carrying on picking at his food as if for all the world he was the most sensible person in it.

Once he got up as if to walk across to the next table. The whole place froze. Even the traditional Samoan band on the stage suddenly came to a stop and missed a couple of men they seemed to be so determined to wash right out of their hair. Then he took another look at his book of maps and staggered back to his own table. The sigh of relief was so great it would have blown the walls out of the building. If, of course, the building had any walls. James Michener would have made an 800-page blockbuster out of it.

As for the rest of the island, it was Bali wonderful. No beach resorts. No Hard Rock Cafes. No never-ending streams of coaches. Only beaches, coves, waterfalls and, of course, rugby pitches.

> Touch judge Iasoni Rorotoga reports a potential yellow card offence against Samoa Athletics for rucking a Samoa Wanderers head but doesn't get the player's number. Samoa Athletics are off the hook. There's a lineout offence. Reupena misses a 43-metre penalty. After two try-saving Samoa Wanderers tackles from Faamanuia Mataafa on Koli Hopati and Metotisi on Alofa Wongsin, Samoa Athletics hooker Falesugi Musumusu scores a try from a lineout error. Sopoaga fails to cash in. He misses the kick.
> Samoa Athletics 13 Samoa Wanderers 3

Savaii is maybe twenty years behind Upolu. There's a tiny airport about the size of, well, a rugby pitch. The ferry to the capital, Salelologa, draws up not so much to a wharf but a slab of concrete. Around the slab of concrete is the occasional house, the occasional wooden hut that serves as a store, and trees. Millions of them. There is even a walkway that takes you from one tree to the top of another.

Not that I found the place boring. Now and then, I admit, I felt my heart beating like mad. Sometimes slowly. Sometimes all of a sudden. Then I felt this surge of energy building up and up and up. Then – whoosh – whether I wanted it to or not there was this enormous uncontrolled spurt sometimes, I was told by a woman who obviously has a firm grasp of the subject, 3 foot, sometimes 13 foot, sometimes even 30 foot high, which left me feeling, I admit, somewhat drained and exhausted. They were the famous blow holes at Taga, which are supposed to be the most powerful in the world. The most powerful, that is, when the wind and the sea are at their roughest. When I was there they were, how shall I say, discreet. Come hurricane time they can blow as high as 100–150 feet. Which, even I have to admit, is some blow.

After Taga, however, it was down to earth. With a bang. I went into the bar by the wharf. There I was confronted not with Savaii's answer to Bloody Mary, but with the very latest all singing and dancing, big-screen karaoke machine.

'Sing, "Do Waddy Do Wah Do Wah Wah."' The ditz of a barman, all suntan and an earring, thrust a microphone at me as soon as I went in.

'No.'

'Sing, "I've got these boots—"'

'No.'

'Well, sing anything on . . .'

It was the shortest time I've ever spent in a bar in my life. I didn't even stay for a drink.

Sopoaga's drop-kick at goal bounces back off the post. Samoa Wanderers lock Mika Ropati and his Samoa Athletics opposite Jimmy Yuki are sinbinned for a scuffle after some pretty vigorous rucking. Sopoaga's penalty hits the post. Samoa Athletics attack from a 5-metre scrum and Sopoaga powers through a blind-side gap to touch down. Sopaga nails the conversion.
Samoa Athletics 20 Samoa Wanderers 3

Open-plan living. There's no other word for it. Samoans live their life in the open. They never close their doors and windows, no matter what they're up to. Because their houses don't have any doors or windows. People, men, women, children, whole families wander in and out as they choose. They'll let down the bamboo shutters on their supporting poles only when it's time to sleep. Or whatever. They call it *fa'a Samoa*. I'd call it an edifice complex, although I suppose it means you're not faced with the usual dilemma. The wife is yelling her head off at the front door to be let in. The dog is barking its head off at the back door to be let in. Which one do you let in first? The dog, of course. Because at least when you let it in it will stop barking.

Every couple of houses with no walls seem to have their own village house with no walls where people gather together to sit, chat, debate, elect a leader, fall asleep.

Each village house with no walls then reports to another village house with no walls and so on up the ladder until they reach the national parliament house with no walls, where you can bet your life decisions are still taken in smoke-filled corridors.

'Does that mean Samoan society is based not on the family but on groups of families?' I asked an earnest research student from Hawaii I met while waiting for a plane out of Savaii. She had been studying what she called 'Samoan sociological phenomena' for about thirty years.

'The first thing to remember is that the Samoans have a very structured society,' she began.

'But are families families? Do they think like families? Do they act like families?'

'First you must remember—'

'Do they bring up their own children? Do mothers give their children to other people to bring up? Do—'

'Well, they have this—'

'Do they have any problems with society being so open?'

'It depends—'

I was beginning to wish one Hawaiian family had ditched one of their family members.

In the end, as is always the case, if you want something done it's best to do it yourself, especially if it would have meant involving the Americans.

The answers to my questions I discovered for myself were as follows: Samoan culture is what's known as *fa'a*. *Fa'a* is based on *fale*. Every *fale* has an *aiga*. Every *aiga* has a *matais*. There are eighteen thousand *matais* in the country. Every *matais* sits on a *fono*. Every *fono* elects not only their own *ali'I* but also their own *tulafale*. Who struts around with a *fue-sennit* or at least he does when he's on official duties. If he does it when he's not on official duties there's an acute danger people will think he's as queer as a *kiritiki* or a three-sided cricket bat who would like nothing better than to be a *fa'afafine*, which will mean mothers will stop other people's children from having anything to do with him. But whatever you do, whether there's a *fa'afafine* around or not, sit cross-legged on the floor and don't point your feet at anyone. And, yes, incest is a problem in Samoa.

Now, I hope that's clear. It might not be Margaret Mead. But it's a damn sight more accurate than her *once* classic, *Coming of Age in Samoa*, which later turned out to be nothing but a load of *ru'bbi'sh*.

> Tavita Luamamu makes two searing breaks in Samoa Wanderers' best attack of the game. Samoa Wanderers prop Joe Diwik makes a storming run. Samoa Athletics are penalised. Samoa Wanderers ignore the kick at goal. Centre Faaiu Kolopa scores a try, racing through the gap after a beautiful Mataafa pass. Reupena converts from in front. Fantastic.
> Samoa Athletics 20 Samoa Wanderers 10

Now that missionaries tend to be more off the menu than on, there's no need to despair. You can still eat well in Samoa. There's the foul-smelling nonu fruit. There's jellyfish wrapped in banana leaves. There's pigeon killed by Polynesian Airlines inter-island aircraft taking off from Apia airport and scattered all over the dirt road that runs alongside the airport.

And there are worms.

Samoa may not be the greatest Catholic gastronomic experience in the world – there are too many New Zealanders around for that – but it's certainly nonconformist.

Take the nonu fruit. Who in their right mind would want to eat something that smells a million times worse than the worst rancid, green stilton you discover at the back of the fridge when your wife goes away for the weekend? Or drink its juice even though it means you'll never get sick: never get high blood pressure; never get asthma; never get arthritis; never get diabetes. Never be able to taste anything ever again.

Jellyfish wrapped in banana leaves? Not bad. As long as you don't get stung. By the price that is. Walk along virtually any beach and you should be able to pick them up for free. The best ones are a bit gritty.

Then there's the rest of the menu: tapioca, bananas, breadfruit and potatoes washed down with either one of Aggie Grey's famous Bloody Marys, which to be honest are not worth making a film let alone a fuss about – I've tasted better in the North Pacific – or a large slug of neat kava made from ground yangona root, served in a coconut shell and knocked back in one go. The only good thing about it is that you don't have to stand in a bar with a karaoke machine in the background to drink it. You can drink it anywhere.

OK. Pass the clothes-peg.

> Samoa Wanderers forwards penalised for serious obstruction. Sopoaga misses 40-metre kick at goal by a mile. Mataafa's 22-metre drop-out goes out. Samoa Athletics botch their attack and Luamanu intercepts to send Samoa Wanderers charging upfield. Samoa Athletics penalised for hands in the ruck, Reupena kicks 40-metre goal. A beauty.
> Samoa Athletics 20 Samoa Wanderers 13

As for the worms, in spite of all the huff and puff the Samoans make about them being the caviar of the South Pacific, they are still worms. Huge, wriggling, fat, juicy worms. About 45 centimetres long. Reddish-brown, male. Bluish-green, female.

On the seventh morning after the October full moon in Savaii, you can find the Samoans sitting on the beach all night, gathered around bonfires, waiting for dawn. Then, just as the sun is breaking, they are leaping and wading and heading out into the sea in boats to grab as many of the worms – or *palolo*, as they call them – as they can as they break loose from deep inside the coral reefs, head for the surface and release their eggs or their sperm. A few hours later those that have not been grabbed and eaten head back deep into the coral reef for another twelve months of peace and quiet.

A month later the Samoans are at it again. This time in Upola. So, too, are the worms, breaking loose from the coral reefs, heading for the surface and being grabbed in great handfuls. For over a hundred years it's been going on, come rain, come shine, come hurricane or 120-mile-an-hour cyclone.

It's even headline news in all the local newspapers. 'Palolo fever has once again gripped our small population,' trumpeted the *Samoan Observer*.

Principle Fisheries Officer Mulipola Toni told *Newsline*, 'Scientific forecasts of how strong the rising will be, is information that is still far into the distant future.' With relatively limited data to go on, he was definitely not going to hazard any predictions. 'I cannot say . . .' he told an expectant nation. 'There are lots of unanswerable areas.'

The *Samoan Observer* then lamented the fact that *palolo* is no longer respected. In a dramatic story from the front line they reported that old granny Faleasiu Tiatia was in 'near tears' at the sight of the mad rush to grab all the worms they can.

'It is sad what has become of our people during the *palolo* season. They no longer respect the old traditions of welcoming the fish,' she told the newspaper.

As a child growing up in Avao, Faleasiu was well aware of the local tradition of waiting for the *palolo*.

'Back then we had respect for the catching and everyone wore good clean clothes, wore their traditional *mosooi ulas* or *ula maile* to welcome and attract the worm,' she said. 'Now people just go in with dirty clothes. There is no respect whatsoever.'

She said that the *palolo* catch was always an event to look forward to in her day because it was a celebration of a gift from God.

'*Palolo* is food and God gave it to us for free. To show our appreciation we dress up so that the gift would keep coming.'

That was no longer the case. But Faleasiu still sticks to her beliefs.

'You see, the reason why the *palolo* does not come strongly nowadays is because people have no respect for the worm any more,' she said. 'It hurts me to see that people are selling *palolo* for money. It is no longer treated as a gift from above. Now it has become a commercial product for our people whose ancestors valued it like gold.'

If you promise not to tell old granny Faleasiu, short of wading out into the sea in your *mosooi ulas* let alone your *ula maile*, the best place to sample the worms is at Stevensons at Manase in Savaii. There they've turned them into a delicacy. Cooked in lots of butter and onions. Served on toast. Close your eyes. Think of Russia. It *could* be caviar. Unless as you go to take that first hesitant swallow, you feel one of them still wriggling . . .

Reupena kicks another long-range penalty, cutting Samoa Athletics' lead to just four points.
Samoa Athletics 20 Samoa Wanderers 16

Oh. Ah. Ouch. Ooh. Aah. OUCH. Ooooh. Aaaah. JARRA-FAOUCH.

So it goes on. For hour. After hour. After hour. Sometimes for up to forty hours. No anaesthetic. No nothing. First, they pull the skin tight. Then tap, tap on the chisel: a boar's tusk polished and sharpened to a point as sharp as any surgeon's knife. The smallest, the *aumono*, is for the fine, intricate work. The *ausoni'aso* and the *laulau* are for short lines and curves. The real killer, the *autapula*, is like a rake with forty or fifty teeth. This is used for long, thin lines.

But whatever chisel they use, the work is incisive. The point punctures the skin. Blood oozes out all over the place. They wipe away the blood. In they rub some soot from a kerosene lamp. Just enough and you get a sharp image. Too much and it blurs.

So it goes on. Tap. Tap. YAARGH. Ooh. Ouch. Tap. Tap. YAARGH. Hour after hour after hour after hour. Welcome to the world of *pe'a*, traditional Samoan tattooing, the only art in the world guaranteed to truly move you. It is also, I suppose, the only art that you can also truly move.

A wristband. Certainly, Sir. That'll be two hours of torture: US$100.

A nice buttock job. Say, four hours of torture: US$250.

The full body, from the waist to the knees, including the flying fox: forty hours of agony – and I mean agony – around US$1500.

A Samoan head honcho once rang up a tattooist and tried to haggle over the price for the full body.

'So if you use old, blunt instruments will it be any cheaper?' he asked.

'Yes. I could do it for US$1000,' said the tattooist.

'If you do a rush job, just gouge away at the skin instead of taking your time, will it be any cheaper?'

'Yes. I could do it for US$500,' said the tattooist.

'If you don't bother to sterilise the instruments, forget the rubber gloves and use dirt instead of soot, will it be any cheaper?'

'Yes,' said the tattooist. 'I could do it for US$100.'

'Great,' said the head honcho. 'I'll send the wife in tomorrow.'

Agree to be tattooed and chicken out, and not only will everybody know that you chickened out, you'll be labelled a *peamutu*, a 'half-done', for the rest of your life. Your children's life. Your children's children's life. Samoa's tattooist extraordinaire, Sualuape Petelo, is a retired social sciences lecturer. Big, butch, fleshy, he is hailed as the Picasso of the ultimate in pointillism. Except his living, breathing works of art die with the owner not with the artist.

'A Sualuape you can recognise at a thousand paces,' a mini-Jonah Lomu told me. He had so many tattoos on him he looked like the living equivalent of interference on your television set.

Being of a somewhat nervous disposition, I didn't ask whether that meant the wristband or the full frontal.

I also didn't take up the offer to go and see the great tattooist at work. One word out of place, I thought, and I could end up looking like an advertisement for barbed wire. Another weekend when the mother-in-law 'just happens to drop in' and I might change my mind. Instead I promised to catch up with Sualape on one of his lecture tours in either Germany, Spain or the US, where in certain circles he is accorded godlike status.

However, I was tempted to visit a female tattooist – or rather a tattooist who specialised in females. An armband, four hours of torture: US$250. Fishnet stockings, eight hours of torture: US$500. The prices were higher than for men because of all the fuss and bother involved, although I was told that quite often thighs – ten days of yelping and squealing: US$1000 – were free. Depending on the thigh.

In the end, for all my research into the world of Samoan tattooing, I left with nothing to show for it.

Thank goodness.

> Samoa Wanderers fumble the kick-off but a fantastic tackle from Pepe Hissinaon on Iosua Tupuani forces Samoa Athletics onto the back foot. But it's too late. It's half-time.
>
> Samoa Athletics 20   Samoa Wanderers 16

The Samoans are cross. They have so many religions, believe in them so fervently – on Sundays some of the beaches are closed for business – that they've now decided to ban any new ones from opening up and trying to save them.

'*One* religion promotes religious unity, village unity and unity of all aspects of culture,' a Samoan lawmaker told me. 'But too many religions . . .'

In some ways you could say the country is more religious than the Vatican. They have more churches per head – or rather per soul – of population than anywhere else on earth. At the last count it was one church per eighty souls. The Vatican, of course, has only one church for all its inhabitants. Samoa's motto is 'The Country is Founded upon God'. The population is made up of Congregationalists, 47.2 per cent; Roman Catholics, 22.3 per cent; Methodists, 15.1 per cent; Mormons, 8.6 per cent; which leaves just 6.8 per cent for everything else. Every day around six o'clock in the evening at the sound of a conch shell or the ringing of a bell the whole country comes to a stop for fifteen to twenty minutes for *sa*, family prayers. Civil servants are even ordered to pray and fast during nation-wide weeks of prayers and fasting to protect the country against natural and man-made disasters.

Write a letter to the local daily newspaper. It's not like writing a letter to *The Times* let alone the *Guardian*. They invariably begin:

'I wish to make use this great opportunity to encourage on to my dear friend, Mr Prime Minster, to be strong in faith, as all other good leaders of God's flock had been. God the foundation of our Country had never had us out of HIS divine sight and encourage us all "*aua ete fefe o le ATUA lo ta faavae, o lo ta saolotoga*". As a matter of fact our Country is the one HE had chosen to RENEW his creation in this third millennium.'

Then comes the punchy bit:

> With regards to the Law of the Land which determines of what is constitutional and what's not. All what's supposed to be there is of God's Law, bearing in mind

> the fact that our land is founded on HIM. And God's law, I believe Mulitalo's recommendation of how we get to be very clear of it is logic. Such steps are; 1, Love Him first with all our hearts and minds. 2, Love our dear brothers and sisters or in broader terms 'our neighbours' like how we love ourselves. And 3, Respect our environment where God our Country's foundation had prepared for us all to live happily upon it. It is of the Holy Bible's direction as well wonder how you feel? While for our Culture, Samoa, I wish we would have no hesitation on the divine truth it carries. Mulitalo stated that it is similar to the cultural of the 'Holy Bible' our Country and most Christians of the world are adopting and I second the notion.

Finally, the sign-off, 'A friend of Christ.' You don't say.

In one village, Samamea in Leao's district of LeVaa o Fonoti, I discovered they had four religions for just two hundred people. One family decided to introduce a fifth, the Assembly of God.

The local Member of Parliament, Leao Dr Tuitama, was against it. Too many different beliefs would eventually create conflict in village affairs.

'If a population of two hundred is divided among four religions, each group would have only fifty members. A village of two hundred divided among five religious would alienate village life and lead to the creation of two separate villages not one,' he said.

The family who wanted to introduce the Assembly of God eventually dropped the idea and went back to being members of the mainstream Congregational Christian Church of Samoa.

In another village, Fagaloa, the MP told me the introduction of another religion created a split between the generations. Young people went one way. Their elders, the other.

'With one religion,' he said, 'we had harmony. With more religions, we lose that harmony.'

But isn't he trying to stop people from practising what they believe, whatever they believe?

'No,' he said. 'If a person strongly wants to practise one's religion, one doesn't have to go far. One can go to the next village.'

What do the Churches think? They want to set up a committee to do the government's dirty work for them and decide which Churches will be allowed in and which Churches will be locked out.

Which is crazy. Either you have religious freedom or you don't. To try to judge Churches that are all different is as absurd as trying to predict the past. Nobody ever gets it right. Especially churches.

Talalelei Duave's kick charged down and Samoa Athletics prop Savaii Punivalu is bundled out at the corner flag. Another poor throw from Samoa Wanderers hooker Ioune Samau goes to Samoa Athletics captain Sam Ropeti who steps his opposite Vini Molioo and drives over for the try. Sopoaga misses the simple kick.

Samoa Athletics 25 Samoa Wanderers 16

Poor Robert Louis Stevenson.

Fancy ending up in Samoa with not only his mother and his wife but also his wife's kids. If life wasn't difficult enough for him – he was dying of tuberculosis – they must have made it a million times worse. What he wanted was peace and quiet, a bit of loving, a bit of nursing, the odd Scotch, and to see out his days calmly and gently. What he got must have been bedlam.

His father, the lighthouse builder, has just died and left him the only real money he ever had in his life. He moves to Samoa for his health and also for the good postal service back to England so he can send off his manuscripts to his publisher. He decides to build a grand mansion, plantation style, set in 400 lush tropical acres in the hills behind Apia. It was the like of which Samoa had never seen and never saw again. He calls it Vailima (Five Streams), which was odd. You'd have thought that someone suffering from tuberculosis would want to call it something suggestive of clean, fresh air, warmth and comfort, and not suggestive of somewhere as damp as a Glasgow tenement in the middle of winter.

He brings his mother to live with him. Is she grateful? Is she hell. Like all mothers, she does nothing but moan. Moan about the builders. Moan about the noise of the building work. Moan about the house itself. She – not poor, sick, hard-working Robert Louis – is given a room of her own as far away from the building work as possible. Is she pleased? What do you think.

Then there is Mrs Stevenson, Mrs Fanny Matilda Van de Grift Osbourne Stevenson. Born in Indianapolis, she married her first husband when she was seventeen and Robert Louis was just six. Infinitely little. An extraordinary wig of grey curls. Insane black eyes. A non-stop smoker. She rolled her own. Continually wore a blue native dress, usually spotted with garden mould. Hellish energy, relieved by fortnights of complete hibernation. A violent friend. A brimstone enemy. The natives thought her uncanny and that devils served her. That's not my description. That is Robert Louis's. No wonder he called her his 'Folly'. He must have been out of his highly creative mind when he married her. Like most married men he learned to sleep more on his own after he got married than before. But for him it wasn't just the guest bedroom. It was the floor.

Not that they didn't have their time together. To amuse her beloved husband, Mrs Stevenson enjoyed nothing better than playfully bending back his fingers until he shrieked in pain. Even worse, as the marriage wore on, and especially during the time they spent in Samoa, he never wrote anything like he wrote before he met her. Probably not surprising when you bear in mind his fingers were causing him so much pain he could barely hold a pen. When he did manage to write anything any good, his loving wife would criticise it so much that he would invariably throw the lot in the fire.

As for her kids, Lloyd and Belle, instead of leaving them behind or locking, barring and bolting them out of sight, Robert Louis was forced to use up his precious energy telling them nonsense stories just to keep them quiet rather than getting on with the real stuff.

As the years went by, the poor man had hardly the strength to drag himself from his simple corner bed in his study, to his writing desk and back to his bed again. Sometimes not even that. Frail, fragile, close to death, he was forced to sleep on the bare boards. Finally – let this be a warning to you – in a huge house full of servants, all dressed in their Stuart tartan lava-lavas, his mother, his wife, goodness knows how many children, he died making his own mayonnaise for a salad. It was 3 December 1894. He was just forty-four. They say it was the mayonnaise that did it.

On his try line, Sopoaga attempts an overhead kick. It goes 15 metres straight to Molioo. From the ruck Samoa Athletics commit a professional foul. Reupena misses conversion from out wide. Sopoaga's 22-metre drop-out goes out on the full. Samoa Wanderers attack. Toni Betham drops the ball. Heikkila pounces, sprints 80 metres to score. Sopoaga converts from in front.

Samoa Athletics 32 Samoa Wanderers 16

The morning following poor Robert Louis's death, the local chiefs carried his coffin to the top of the mountain behind the house and buried him there. Carved on a stone by his grave is the epitaph he wanted;

Here he lies where he longed to be
Home is the sailor, home from the sea
And the hunter home from the hill.

'Here he lies where he longed to be'. See what I mean about Fanny? He'd rather be dead and buried at the top of a hill than stuck with her any longer. The Samoans mourned him as Tusitala. Some say it means 'Teller of Tales'. Others say it means 'A Poor Pathetic Character Whose Life Was So Unreal It Could Exist Only in a Tale'.

I know which one I believe.

Samoa Athletics penalised. Instead of kicking for goal, Samoa Wanderers work a fantastic line-out move with hooker Samau scoring from Duave's clever offload. Reupena misses sideline conversion.
Samoa Athletics 32 Samoa Wanderers 21

Did Mrs Stevenson stay on, turn the house into a shrine for her dead husband and dedicate the rest of her life to preserving his memory? Like hell, she did. Within a matter of weeks she was back in the States, whooping it up in San Francisco, having one affair after another, ending up with a pillar of the San Francisco establishment forty years younger than herself.

Vailima was next to go. Sold to a German businessman for a fifth of what it had cost, so eager was she to get her hands on Robert Louis's money. Not content with that she then fell out with Sidney Colvin, who had been commissioned to write Robert Louis's official biography.

Some grieving widow determined to preserve the legacy of her husband's genius . . .

> Kolopa breaks out. He is dazed by a high tackle from a jumping, prancing Panapa Eneliko. But there is no penalty. Opapo penalises Samoa Wanderers for pulling down a messy and static Samoa Athletic maul. Sopoaga scores a goal from in front, 35 metres out.
> Samoa Athletics 35 Samoa Wanderers 21

The house that Robert Louis built stands today, in near original condition, at the foot of Mount Vaea, surrounded by tropical plants and trees with the staff still wearing their Stuart tartan lava-lavas. It is also what it should have been from the moment he touched that deadly salad bowl: a memory to a great story-teller. In fact, it's more than a memory. It's a shrine. You have to take your shoes off before you go in.

The main hall/reception area is big enough to hold a hogmanay party with room to spare for a couple of pipe bands. Upstairs there are five more rooms, each with wide balconies, each capable of holding any number of couples eager to celebrate in their own way. Throughout the house there are books, mementoes of Robert Louis. Not as many as I expected. But enough to make it respectable.

I didn't read his books when I was young. They hadn't been translated into Latin and Greek. But I've read him again and again as I've got older, just as I've read Kipling more and more as I've got older. Maybe that's a reflection on Stevenson. Maybe it's a reflection on me. But I know one thing he's taught me: never go near a salad bowl.

> Reupena is lucky to escape the sinbin when, off the ball, he drags Muagututia back by the collar. From a scrum in front of the posts, Samoa Athletics rumble it up and

Apia

Hopati slips through Siaasi Roma's tackle and crawls over the line to score Samoa Athletics' sixth try. Sopoaga misses the conversion. It's all over.

Samoa Athletics 40 Samoa Wanderers 21

Suva

Whisper it not, but in spite of their being practically half a world away from each other, and the world and its grandmother claiming Fiji is a multiracial, multi-ethnic, multi-everything else society, it's as Indian as any Saturday-night takeaway. With or without poppadoms.

OK, the population is split 60–40 Fijian–Indian. Or maybe even 55–45. Or perhaps even 50–50. Who knows? Every survey is different.

OK, the Fijians walk the walk in their fancy leather kilts or *sulus*, from the old colonial English phrase: Even the slightest smirk and we'll feed you to the Zulus.

OK, they play rugby, wish everyone in sight a non-stop *bula* and dance around doing what looks like their traditional *meke* at the drop of a F$2 bill.

And march. My God, do they march. They're so hooked on marching you'd think they had been converted by Northern Ireland missionaries. As in Northern Ireland, most of their marches seem to end in violence. First it's the Methodist Church of Fiji marching in support of rights for indigenous Fijians. Then it's the National Federation Party marching against ballot-rigging. Soon others want to join in: the Sogusogo Duavata ni Lewenivanua Party, the Women's Crisis Centre, even the Ratepayers' Association.

But whatever they do, they do it with *yagona* or *kava* made from the ground-up roots of a pepper plant that they maintain is not to be sneezed at (although to me it always looks as if the whole village has sneezed into it). To the Fijians, it's six pints of lager, half a bottle of Scotch and a good smoke all rolled into one. It solves everything, they claim, from headaches to the menopause – well, the effects the menopause has on men. According to any one of hundreds of kava websites, it's the 'drug of choice. Just a few cupfuls and you'll find euphoria, tranquillity, friendliness.'

Don't you believe it. It's a bowlful of snot that, according to local doctors at the St Giles Hospital in Suva, the capital, who treat kava addicts every day, causes scaly skin, impotence, lethargy and no end of other problems.

But just as the French can't help but dominate whatever they get involved in, so too the Indians can't help but dominate the Fijians, yagona or no yagona. Try as they might to curry favour with the Fijians, they still control most of the action, most of the big businesses and definitely most of the small businesses. The Fijians might have their *sulus*. But the streets are full of *saris*. The newspapers are full of the latest goings-on in Bollywood. How Harry Baweja has just released his latest film, *Yeh Kya Ho Raha Hai*, how the four new boy stars, Aamir, Prashant, Yash and Vaibhav made a whirlwind tour of the Delhi cinema halls, and how Raveena Tandon, Anapam Kher, Akshaye Khanna, Manisha Koirala, Juhi Chawla, Om Puri and Sir Paul McCartney are launching a campaign in Hindi, Marathi, Gujarati, Tamil, Telugu, Kannada, Bengali, Malayalam and Urdu to campaign for animal rights. Not to mention – most important of all – who will be appearing in the Deewangee team's next great hit.

Fijian television is also non-stop Bollywood. Switch on and you're bound to see heads and necks and arms jerking all over the place. Three times I called the poor Fijian hotel maintenance man to check the set before I realised that was what they were supposed to be doing.

Similary the Fijian diet. It's going more and more Indian too. Just as chicken vindaloo is now Britain's national dish, so dhal is replacing vegetables in the Fijian diet. A government survey of 120 households in twelve different areas throughout the country revealed that while 100 per cent of Indian families tucked into their dhal so too did no less than 95 per cent of Fijian families. Chicken vindaloo, a couple of stuffed parathas and a six-pack every Friday are said not to be far behind.

Speaking of six-packs, the bars are full of young Indian men complaining that they don't know who their wives are until they marry them. Try as I might, I couldn't sympathise with them. They just don't seem to realise that it's the same wherever you are in the world.

As for Diwali, the Hindu Festival of Light, which some say is a Harvest Festival with a red spot in the middle of its forehead, the Fijians celebrate it as much as the next Hindu. Maybe more so. They certainly seem to let off more fireworks. Once when I was there they were letting off so many it was like World War II – or World War Eleven as George Bush calls it – all over again.

In many ways poor old George Speight was right when he tried to reclaim the island from the Indian community for home-grown Fijians. Trouble was, he got it all wrong. He wasn't quick enough. He didn't have enough back-up. He concentrated his efforts solely in the capital, Suva. And, of course, he wasn't ruthless enough. Coups are wrong. But if you're going to try to do it, you might as well do it properly. Fail and you'll end up like George: serving thirty years in jail for treason. You don't have to study Machiavelli let alone Freddie Forsyth for too long to realise that.

As always, it's the guys at the bottom, Fijians *and* Indians, who suffered most. Within hours of the coup taking place, there was hardly a tourist in sight. Hotels, tour companies and so on immediately started laying off staff. Children had to leave school, students had to leave university to try to support their parents. Schools and universities began to cut back. Parents who in spite of their children's efforts couldn't pay their bills had to sell up and move downmarket. Tenant farmers who couldn't pay their rent were evicted. And so the effects rippled on through the whole economy. Most survived. Many went under. But it will take time before they are all back to normal.

In the meantime, life goes on . . . as usual.

Refuse from international flights to and from Nausori Airport piles higher and higher because their incinerator is out of action.

The hospital in Matuka, Lau – and no doubt many others – have run out of drugs and doctors. Patients haven't seen one or the other for over six months.

Companies, especially, it seems, Chinese ones, make their workers slave away from 7.30 a.m. to 10.00 p.m. seven days a week, including public holidays, for F$1.26 an hour and F$10 a month for food, which is about half the price of nothing.

Small shopkeepers complain that soldiers are busy smuggling cigarettes and booze out of Lebanon, where they are serving with the United Nations forces, selling the contraband for next to nothing and ruining the market for them.

Cars are shipped in in two halves – probably by another regiment – to avoid tax and joined together again once in the country.

Senior accountants heading teams of auditors investigating million-dollar scams are suddenly asked to resign on medical grounds. Not that there was any cause for suspicion. It was not unusual, a senior official told me, for someone who had been working hard for a year to suddenly fall sick. No, of course not. Silly old me.

The police promise to investigate. But if they're anything like the police station I saw in Suva, nobody need worry. In one room there were forty detectives, eight desks, thirteen chairs, five of which were broken, a couple of old filing cabinets and a single thirty-year-old Imperial manual typewriter.

Not that progress isn't being made. Once when I was there the newspapers were full of headlines 'We Refused Bribes'. The upstanding National Federation Party councillors of Nadi refused to accept bribes from the low, scheming councillors of the Fiji Labour Party and vote for their man in the annual mayoral elections.

Stuck in the Pacific about two-thirds of the way from Los Angeles and one-third from Sydney, Fiji is not just Fiji – or rather Feejee, as we old South Pacific hands say – it's Melanesia rather than Polynesia. Melanesia is west of Polynesia, while Polynesia is east of Melanesia. Similarly Melanesians come from west of where Polynesians come from, while Polynesians come from east of where Melanesians come from. As for where they all came from, I haven't got a clue, although some people say they got as far as the Bering Strait, thought it was a bit too cold up there and headed south, stopping off in India on the way, something they've regretted ever since.

It's also not one island but three hundred – one hundred inhabited two hundred not – scattered horseshoe fashion across 80,000 square miles of ocean. The three largest, Viti Levu, Vanua Levu and Taveuni make up 90 per cent of the land mass and account for around 90 per cent of the population.

Viti Levu, 'Great Fiji', is like a very hot curry. Developed. Home to the capital, Suva, the largest, most cosmopolitan and many claim the filthiest and most disease-ridden city in the South Pacific.

Vanua Levu, 'Great Land', is actually more medium hot. Less developed. Fewer resorts. Mountainous. More traditional.

Taveuni, 'Great Leftover'. Did you put any curry powder in

this? It's more damp or rather diluted. Lush tropical rainforests. Green hills. Waterfalls.

As for the rest of the islands, they seem to be totally dedicated to swimming and snorkelling. In other words, the destruction of the planet. Although most people, I will admit, look better in their face masks and wetsuits than they do normally. After having been to Fiji I'm convinced swimming and snorkelling should be banned. Swimming and snorkelling destroy the soft, crystalline coral reefs with their purple and white blooms. With the coral destroyed, the pink anemone fish, blue ribbon eels, the black-white-and-orange polka-dotted clown fish and all the others don't bother coming around any more. We're on another downhill spiral. If that's not bad enough where do most environmentally conscious snorkellers dump their empty gas cylinders? In the coral. Who says so? Not me. *Les* crack *messieurs* at the Jean-Michel Cousteau Fiji Islands Resort on Vanua Levu say so, and being French they always speak the truth. What's more, they don't allow fishing or jet-skiing or sell anything in their Jean-Michel Cousteau Fiji Islands Resort shop made of shells or even serve reef fish in their restaurants. Which proves how serious they are. The French have given up eating fish to save the world.

The other big danger about swimming and snorkelling in Fiji is that you might come across the remains of Amelia Earhart, who disappeared with her navigator on a bid to fly round the world in 1937. From time to time, like the Loch Ness Monster, some bones are found. Half the experts say they're hers. Half say they're not. The Fijian government says it will investigate. But nothing happens: somebody else is using the police typewriter.

Not that health and environmental problems would end with the banning of swimming and snorkelling. Go to the main island Viti Levu and you're bound to catch a cold. Not for the usual reasons. But because you're forever going from one environment to another to air-conditioning and back again. The north is dry as dust. The east is nothing but rain. The south is cold. The west is dry. The biggest health problem – well, the second-biggest health problem – is not sunburn or even curry poisoning but flu. Because of the constant changes of temperature whoever touches down here for even a few days goes away with . . . with . . . with . . . YaaaaaCHOOOOOO.

One day I'm up in the north around Rakiraki. It's cowboy country. Over 17,000 acres of open ranch land. Over six thousand head of cattle. No end of cattle drives, branding and Indians, who, I was told, more often than not make better cowboys. It's broiling.

Another day I'm in Nadi (pronounced Nandy). At one end of town, a brightly painted Sri Siva Subramaniya Swami Hindu Temple. At the other, a rather plain-looking Catholic church. In between, a rock-solid mosque and a huge sprawling Jihad School of Muslim Studies. Not far from Nadi (pronounced Nandy) is the Garden of the Sleeping Giant, which they say was bought by old Ironside himself, Raymond Burr, to house his collection of orchids. But I don't believe a word of it. He'd never have got his wheelchair up and down all those steps. It's hot.

Another day. Another town. I'm in Lautoka, 'Sugar City', home of the biggest sugar mill the world has ever seen. Well, that's what they say. They're loading mountains of woodchip into one ship after another. I wander into a bar. The dishevelled-looking Indian behind the bar is frantically denying local newspaper reports that his shop has just been broken into and that thieves got away with gold bars worth over US$100,000 *and* the family jewels.

'Me. Poorman,' he kept pleading. 'Newspapers all wrong. Newspapers cause me lots of worries.'

Which, believe me, is Hindi for either 'The thieves got away with more than US$100,000 in gold and jewellery but I'm not telling anybody that,' or 'It was nowhere near that. But if I say it was and the police find anything I can always say it was all mine.'

Sitting at the far end of the bar was another dishevelled-looking old man, with a similar sing-song accent. He was Welsh.

'J. P. Morgan Morgan.'

He held out his hand.

'P. E. Biddlecombe Biddlecombe,' I said.

He'd made his money, he told me, in Newport. He'd sold out to the Americans. Now he was doing the islands. Fiji, however, was a class of its own. He'd been stuck in Lautoka for three days. Customs or Immigration or both wouldn't let him leave. They said he didn't have the necessary papers. They also wouldn't let him back aboard his boat. My Welsh not being up to it, I couldn't quite understand how he referred to them. A couple of drinks, however, a few words from me about the customs and traditions of Fiji, and he was out of the bar, off to the port for a few quiet words with his friends, the Customs and Immigration officials. In fact, he was so keen to see them, he left me to pay the bill. Typical Typical.

I'm now hot. Under the collar. It's humid. The poor Hindi behind the bar is still going on: it wasn't him.

. . . A few days later. I'm in the middle of the country, trying to cross the Namosi peaks which Rupert Brooke called the 'Gateway to Hell'. Gateway to Hell! They're nothing like it. He must have been having a bad hair day. Missed the honey in his tea. Or something. To me they're more the Gateway to Heaven, a bit like the Heavenly Mountains in Kyrgyzstan up towards the border with China. On a good day they're covered in mist. On a bad day, you can hardly see the bottle of whisky in front of your face.

Twice we tried to cross them. Twice we had to turn back. And I was in a 4×4. The road – rather tracks were practically non-existent. The gradient was impossible. There was also no room to manoeuvre. In places it was simply straight up or straight down and one wheel out of place and it's goodbye Fiji, hello . . . wherever.

Back down on solid soil again we came across the occasional traditional thatched-roof shack, cottage, house or even village where, whatever it was, we had to do the usual *sevu-sevu* routine: the so-called official presentation of a bottle of *yagona*, hooch, to the *turaga-ni-koro*, the head honcho or village chief with his perpetual hangover. We also did the name, rank and serial number routine. Who are you? Where do you come from? How many children have you got? How many cattle have you got? Oh, yes, and who's your wife? At which point, for some reason or other, they would all drink to my health. Routine it might have been. But I'm sure it'll stand me in good stead if I ever upset those champions of the four freedoms and end up on Guantánamo Bay with a hood over my face, my arms chained behind my back and grovelling around in the dirt. The air was cool, clean, almost crisp.

If it's rain you're looking for, go to Suva. I'm not saying it rains there all the time, it's just that the fish walk down the middle of the road. It's Manchester, Bergin and the South American rainforests all wrapped in one. It's also British, which may or may not account for all the rain. In fact, if you didn't believe the British ever set foot on Fiji, just two minutes in Suva and you'd realise how wrong you were. It's small-town British. Streets are named after famous British politicians: Gladstone, Disraeli and, of course, typical of all of them, Pratt. Buildings have to be no higher than a palm tree. There are Indian restaurants all over the place. Typical British Indian restaurants.

'Excuse me. Do you deliver?'

'No. We only do chicken curry.'

The Governor's Mansion, today the President's Palace, looks like any Home Counties golf club – big wall surrounding the whole place. Railings. A long driveway up to the nineteenth hole – with one exception. Standing on guard duty, unblinking, motionless, is a single red-bereted Fijian soldier which undermines all the government's warnings that Fiji is not immune to terrorist attack. Beware, the prime minister warned the day I was in Suva, terrorist elements could even now be planning to launch attacks on the country's scuba-diving facilities. Well, they made use of the flying schools in the States, why not the scuba-diving facilities in Fiji?

On the other hand, terrorist threats or not, Fiji has the most open, accessible, security-free parliament in the world. The Fiji Police Force have run out of money and can no longer afford to protect it.

I wandered all over the place, from the parliament, where for fifty-six days George Speight held the prime minister and at one time up to thirty government ministers and supporters hostage, to the High Court alongside it, to the various government offices all around it. In spite of the NO ENTRY signs, nobody stopped me.

Not that security is non-existent in Fiji. After all, in a matter of months at Nadi (pronounced Nandy) International Airport they allowed only one mentally unstable person to wander on to the runway; a Chinaman being deported to be put on a plane and then allowed to get off again and walk away without anybody saying a word; various items belonging to passengers in transit to be stolen from planes; and suitcases to be neatly slit open and the contents stolen between being taken off the plane and arriving at the carousel.

Best of all is the Fiji National Museum and its proudest display: the Revd Thomas Baker's boots. The Revd himself was given a warm welcome by the local people. They popped him in a huge warm bowl of soup and ate him. The boots survived. For three months they roasted them in an earth oven before finally giving in. His body may be gone but his sole lives on.

'Isn't it sad,' one museum guide, who looked as though he would kill for a slice of caterpillar fungus, said, 'to think that he was probably still alive when he was killed.'

Talking of cannibals . . . At enormous public expense the serious professors of Fiji University have come up with – would you believe it? – Cannibal Chutney, which is based on a real recipe for a vegetable relish traditionally eaten with human flesh during cannibal feasts. Hannibal Lecter eat your heart out. Or rather somebody else's.

When I went up to the university to talk to these serious professors and discuss with them the contribution they thought they were making to our modern society, I couldn't find them, for dirty washing. It was hanging out all over the place. Unless, of course, I made a mistake and ended up in the Department of Laundry. Between the sheets I came across some students – not for the first time I might add – who were complaining that they'd been given the wrong examination papers to sit. Did they wait until the problem was sorted out and they were given new papers? No they didn't.

'We make for the Fish Market to celebrate.'

'The Fish Market? To buy lobsters?'

'No. Marijuana. That's where the dealers hang out.'

Of course, silly me. And to think in the old days we were happy with half a pint of brown ale shandy during Happy Hour at the Purple Haze Nite Club.

The rest of the town, at least compared to the fish market, was somewhat earnest and subdued. Like a poor chicken tikka in Hull on a wet Wednesday evening. Fijians in their *sulus*, presumably government ministers, lounging back, laughing quietly with each other and playing pass the brown envelope in the restaurant of their number-one watering hole, The Holiday Inn, which tells you something about Fijian ministers. And about Suva.

The Indians seemed to be even more earnest and subdued.

Some say it's because that's the way they behaved with their colonial masters when they were shipped in by the British to work as labourers on the sugar plantations and they've never kicked the habit. Others say that it's just safer. Keep your head down. Don't look as though you've two rupees, let alone US$100,000 to rub together, and your so-called master might leave you alone.

In La Paz I was tear-gassed. In Omaha, Nebraska I was practically hijacked. In Suva I was lucky to escape with my life. The place is so filthy, there is so much rubbish dumped all over the place, that people are dying of leptospirosis caused by too many animals running wild and contaminating the soil and infecting the water supply. It's no wonder that the first thing that greets you when you come into town is a huge, apparently never-ending cemetery. There also seemed to be more kids living and working the streets than I've seen anywhere else in the South Pacific. Worse still, it's the kind of place where instead of experiencing all the usual thrills and excitements of a South Pacific port, you get stuck with New Zealanders who go on and on about having lobster thermidor for dinner.

'It was like they do in the films,' one serious-looking banking type giggled at me like a guilty schoolboy. 'I'd never had it before. I thought why not? Now's your chance.'

'What did you think of it?'

'I liked the cheese on top.'

Out of Suva and to the north I took a trunk road through Fiji's big mahogany plantations, the largest, purest and only mature mahogany plantations in the world, and which are now destined for the chop. The government has finally decided there's not much future in exporting smoke-cured bêche-de-mer sea slugs as there was in the 1820s and wants to turn the lot into fancy tables and chairs to be given as gifts to people who would prefer an IKEA garden table. But on a sustainable, environmentally friendly basis of course.

But not everybody agrees.

The villagers on whose land the trees are planted say, No. They're being ripped off. They want more money. The land was leased from the landowners by the British in the 1950s and 1960s when Fiji was still a colony. The leases gave landowners the right to share in the profits if the planting was successful. The planting *is* successful. They want their fair share. The government, however, has so far offered them only 10 per cent stumpage, and maybe a share with them of another 10 per cent. The villagers want 50 per cent of the sale price of the finished mahogany product. With the money they make they want to improve their living conditions – they don't have electricity or any other amenity – buy a truck to take their children to school and to take their yagona, cassava, dab, yams and other crops to market and generally catch up with the rest of the world.

The government, which owns the trees – 'green gold', they call them – says it's going ahead in any case. The trees were planted fifty years ago. They are ready for harvesting. They've made a fair offer to the villagers. Anyway, now is the time to move. The supply of mahogany from South America is drying up under pressure from environmentalists. What's more, the government argues that without the trees the villagers, especially those in and around the Vugalei district of Tailevu, will no longer have to drink from and wash in the dark, murky mahogany swamps.

So that's all right then. Chainsaws at the ready. Begin. Last time I was there, down came the first huge trees. Off they went to Malau Mill in Labasa. The government says they're going to test the market for two years: to see whether they should be aiming at the US, Europe or wherever and what price they can expect for it. Then the mahogany forests of Fiji will be alive with nothing but the sound of chainsaws.

What the environmentalists will say is another matter. So too is what George Speight is thinking, cooped up in his prison cell on Nukulau Island, across the way from Suva. For George was chairman of the state-owned Fiji Hardwood Corporation, not only the biggest mahogany company in the country but the only major industry in the Fijian east end of the island. He was just about to sign a multi-million-dollar deal with a giant American timber corporation when in came a new government determined to foil his plans.

That's why, the Fijians say, he decided to overthrow the government.

Talk to the Indians, however, and you get a different story.

The last night of my visit and I'm in an incense-filled room. Everybody is drinking whisky. Expensive whisky. I'm told the real story behind the coup attempt.

The official version is that George Speight, a leading local businessman, the son of an opposition MP and just a handful of soldiers from Fiji's elite counter-revolutionary warfare squadron stormed parliament, seized power and took the prime minister and all those cabinet ministers and government supporters hostage because they wanted to reclaim the island from the Indian community for Fijians.

The move took place on the first anniversary of Mahendra Chaudhry's appointment as the island's first ethnic Indian prime minister.

The talk in all the newspapers was of tensions between the two communities. Ethnic Indians made up 45 per cent, maybe more, of the population but controlled practically the whole economy: they were being victimised because of their hard work, their relative prosperity, their unexpected success in the previous general election and because they were now planning to take over the land they didn't already own. The Fijians had decided to get their retaliation in first.

As the coup wore on, as negotiations between the two sides dragged on, as tourists turned their backs and ran, Fiji's traditional chiefs stepped in and demanded that the prime minister should be replaced by a Fijian, and that the constitution should be changed to ensure the Fijians remained the dominant race, held all the big jobs and ran the show all by themselves. Ordinary Fijians took to the streets and smashed and looted Indian shops and homes.

The Indians complained, 'Unless we get help, we will die. If the West claims to advocate universal human rights, how can it just sit back?'

Outside experts claimed, 'We are now seeing the dismantling of Fiji as we know it.'

George Speight became a modern-day Fijian folk hero.

'The Indians', he regaled his supporters, 'look different. They act different. They even smell different.'

As the incense cleared and the whisky disappeared, I was told a completely different story.

First, the coup wasn't a Fiji coup, it was a Suva coup. What happened, happened in the capital. It didn't affect what happened in the rest of the country at all. Fijian and Indian kids still went to school together. Fijian and Indian businessmen continued to do business together, drink the same kava, eat the same curries and live the way they always lived, side by side.

Second, and most amazing of all, the coup was not inspired because Fijians feared they were being swamped and wanted to ensure their survival. It was inspired by the island's richest Indian businessmen, who were terrified that the new Indian prime minister was going to start collecting the millions and millions of back taxes they had forgotten to pay over the years and had instead reinvested in their own businesses. Obviously, they couldn't say so themselves. They needed a fall guy. They chose a Fijian, a businessman who once ran the country's huge mahogany business, who had been sacked by the prime minister, who bore a grudge, who could make the whole thing look Fijian rather than Indian, who could be rewarded in the traditional manner if the coup succeeded, who could be chopped up and hung out to dry if the coup failed.

Talk about Machiavellian.

'So how do I know your version of events is true?' I asked one Indian smoothie as another bottle arrived.

'I was there,' he said. 'I was at the meetings. We met two days before the coup. At Tokatoka. We all agreed there was no way we could buy off the Prime Minister. He was one of us. He knows the game. He knows how things operate. We needed to have a Fijian prime minister. He would know what to do. So would Fijian ministers. We pay them 10,000 dollars, 100,000 dollars, 200,000 dollars, maybe even 500,000 dollars. It is better than paying one million, two million, ten million dollars. It is good business. Yes?'

'Er.' Well, I could hardly agree could I? British. Justice. Sense of fair play and all that.

'So what would happen if George took over, suddenly became all righteous and refused to play?'

When Vijay Machiavelli had stopped laughing and dabbing his forehead with a huge brilliant white tablecloth of a handkerchief, he tried to compose himself again.

'If George suddenly became all righteous,' he giggled. 'You, funny man. You say funny things.'

'Yes. But say—'

'Plan B,' he carried on giggling. 'We Indians not like Fijians. We not stupid. We split the country in half, right down the middle, east and west. East has nothing but mahogany. East is the capital, Suva. East is run by Fijians. West has everything: tourism, trade, big international airport, big port, sugar cane, gold. West is run by Indians.'

'So how would you do that?'

'You, Sir, you ask silly questions.' He started giggling all over again and dabbing his eyes with his tablecloth. 'The chiefs. We use the Fijian chiefs. We get them to say they demand peace, stability, guaranteed future for their children. They don't want to be involved with illegal act by few people. They believe in democracy. They speak for their people. Their people are the majority. And so on.'

'How do you do that?'

This time he was howling his head off. Tears were streaming down his face.

'Money,' he sobbed. 'Money. You very funny man.'

Because of the noise he was making, we were joined by another Indian. He was wearing a suit, collar, tie, the real Savile Row. He was obviously a big poppadom.

I explained what we had been discussing. Instead of howling his head off, he merely smirked gently.

'Either way you look at it,' I said, 'you lost. George didn't end up as prime minister. The country wasn't split east–west.'

'Goodness gracious, no. We won. We have a new Fiji prime minister. Not George. Somebody else. We still have our money. How can that be losing?'

'But won't the new Fijian prime minister still want to collect all those back taxes?' Now he started laughing and howling as much as the other guy.

'And George,' I persisted, 'who is now behind bars, serving a thirty-year gaol sentence. What about him?'

They started laughing even more.

Which version do I believe?

Well, seeing as I would like to go back to Fiji again in the near future, I will say just this: It rains a lot in Suva. Best to take an umbrella.

Papeete

Lucky old Gauguin. He only lost an ear. Or was that Van Gogh? I always get confused. Either way when Gauguin first hit Hiva Oa, way up in the Marquises, he had to rough it. *La vie communale*. Everybody frolicking around with bare-breasted abandon beneath swaying palm trees without a care in the world. Women walking around stark naked, as if for all the world that was the way they had been born, sharing with everyone everything they had to share. A fourteen-year-old mistress. All the booze he could drink. His own thatched Maison du Jouir on stilts, which I would have thought – given the life he was leading – was pushing his luck. Virgin territory for as far as the eye could see. Not a taboo in sight. Which is amazing when you realise that 'taboo' was originally a Polynesian word.

Gauguin could have bought up the whole place, lock, stock and fourteen-year-old mistresses. But he didn't. Which is just as well. He would have lost not only an ear if he hadn't already lost one, but an arm and a leg as well. Because it's all gone downhill.

No *vie communale*. Today there's as much agony, heartache and violence in Hiva Oa as there is in the rest of the world. The *vahine*, the island women, are as good or as bad as *vahine* all over the world. Most of them wouldn't dream of wearing a grass skirt unless it had an Yves St Laurent, a Givenchy or, if there was nothing else, a Stella McCartney label. As for the naked bit, I've seen more naked flesh in American boardrooms. And that was the fellas. There are definitely no fourteen-year-old mistresses. What's more – poor Gauguin must be turning in his grave – there's only one bar in town. Not only is it pretty antiseptic, most people spend more time playing the Internet in the corner than collapsing on the floor smashed out of their minds. The police have also started putting an end to whatever chance anyone on Hiva Oa might have of going Gauguin and breaking out. Hardly a week goes by without some grande smooch from lui-même, Le Chef de la Sub-Division Administrative des Îles Marquises, swooping down in his little super Puma plane and spotting another poor farmer struggling to survive by growing a little *pakololo* – marijuana to you – on the side.

About the only excitement I had was, quite by chance, bumping into Monsieur Le Pen. Monsieur Le Pen, that is, of Hiva Oa. He collects pens. He has over six thousand of them. Big ones. Small ones. Metal ones. Gold ones. Once he worked a whole month just so that he could buy a Waterman and Please, can I have my biro back? *Merci beaucoup.*

What's more, and depending on whom you talk to, there is either a huge cloud of radioactive dust from French nuclear tests drifting slowly towards it or an ever increasing number of back-to-front-baseball-cap-wearing American tourists. Whichever is worse.

When I first cut my ear off on a Bali Hai and headed to the South Pacific I thought it was going to be like, say, the Caribbean: a *petit* bunch of *îles*, all close together, all desperately trying to outdo each other in not only money-laundering but also denying any knowledge of money-laundering. But it's not. It's over one hundred and twenty islands, 4100 kilometres from New Zealand; 6000 kilometres from Australia; 6000 kilometres from the US; 9500 kilometres from Japan; but closest of all to France, which is only 18,000 kilometres away. They are split into five groups: the Tuamotu Islands, the Gambier Islands, the Austral Islands, the Society Islands, and, my favourites, the Marquesas, which are almost on the Equator. The volcanoes that threw up the Tuamotu and Gambier are long since gone. They have sunk into the ocean and are now home for mile and mile of coral atolls. The Austral, the Society and the Marquesas have gone in the opposite direction and are now home to mountains up to 6500 feet high. Some of the islands, in fact, are nothing but mountains. They are also spread out over an area the size of Europe. The Australs are Madrid. The Gambiers is Albania. And Gauguin's Hiva Oa is practically in the Arctic Circle.

Neither are the people all *la même chose*. They are made up of Ma 'ohi, native Polynesians, 71 per cent; Afa Tahiti or Demis, 20 per cent; Europeans, mostly French, *naturellement*, 12 per cent; Chinese and Asians 5 per cent; and in Hiva Oa, 95 per cent descendants of Gauguin. The language they speak is straightforward Poly with French overtones: '*Maeva, bienvenue*' means 'How much money did you get out of the European Commission this time?' '*Nana, au revoir*': 'Please stay and tell us what to do.' '*Maururu, merci*': 'What's your cut?' '*Tama'a maitai, bon appétit*': 'How many do you want this time?'

They are ten hours behind GMT, two hours behind US Pacific Standard Time, twenty hours behind Australian Eastern Standard Time and a million years ahead of anything we do in this country. They even commemorate Armistice Day in 1918 with a public holiday.

Although to be fair, wherever you go, whatever time of day or night, they do keep rushing up to you, throwing garlands of flowers around your neck, wrestling you to the ground in what is virtually mouth-to-mouth combat and whispering, 'Lei. Lei. You want lei, yes.'

'Yes. Yes. Yes,' I kept whispering back.

I got so many flowers round my neck I couldn't see where I was going. Which makes a change. About the only flowers I get offered nowadays are wreaths.

A French *vieux de la vieille*, who got off the plane behind me, lit up his Gauloise before he even got to the bottom of the steps. By the time he got to Arrivals he was puffing away furiously and had so many flowers and paper garlands around his neck that they caught fire and practically burned down the terminal. Not that anyone took any notice. So it's another terminal. So what? The European Union will buy us another one. It's not as if he'd burnt the gigot d'agneau farci en croûte. Mon Dieu. That would have been a catastrophe.

'*La vraie Polynésie Française*.' Whatever they're on, I hope they stick with it. They're relaxed. They're charming. They're, well, French. Everything but everything is bedecked with flowers and herbs: the table in your hotel room, dining tables, bars, dashboards. The rest I leave to your imagination. The food is *fantastique*. There is no poule de luxe like a Polynesian poule de luxe. The drink is *fantastique*. The service everywhere is *fantastique*. The women – when they're not putting flowers around your neck and whispering sweet everythings in your ear – are the kind of women you could have a good time with even if you played all your cards wrong. As for Les Blokes, they seem to wander around all day with a sarong tied around their waists, a hibiscus behind their ears and, the more restrained, a large fossilised shark's tooth set in gold around their necks.

But beware the *mahus*: boys brought up as girls. Some say it's an old Polynesian trick dating back to the days of human sacrifice when mothers would do anything to stop their baby boys being killed. Others say, So what's the problem so long as he loves his mother?

A few old South Pacific hands I've come across in the past

have still not sufficiently recovered from coming across their first *mahus* to express any kind of opinion.

Not that the French Polys were always as peace-loving as they look today. Way back in 150 BC they were as aggressive and as cannibalistic as the next woman, though it is said that even in those days they were just as polite and accommodating. Man, woman or child, whatever was on the menu they always had it with déjà vu, the same mustard as they had the day before yesterday. They also never spoke with someone in their mouth. *Quelle politesse.*

Even though I hate myself for saying so, it's my favourite South Pacific island – or group of islands.

Tahiti – or Tahiti Nui to give it its full title – is not only the largest island and home to most of the population of French Polynesia, it is not strictly speaking an island at all. It's two islands, shaped like the figure eight and linked by the Taravoo isthmus or as the French would say, *cordon ombilical.* Known by *tout le monde* as the Pearl of the Pacific, it was discovered by Louis-Antoine de Bougainville in 1768 and found by Captain Cook in 1769.

De Bougainville's ship drifted lazily towards the coast. A girl wearing nothing but a sarong and an even bigger smile paddled alongside in a canoe. She clambered on board and standing in the centre of the deck immediately gave the crew, who had been six months at sea, the traditional Polynesian welcome. With a flourish, she cast aside what few inhibitions she had. Forgetting for a moment the joys of the breadfruit tree for no doubt other choice fruits to come, the captain found himself unable to make any kind of limp excuse for her behaviour. Using the flowery language you would expect of a Bougainville, he simply spluttered, 'I was transported into the Garden of Eden.'

From then on it was anything goes. Luxury hotels. Cruise ships. A million postcards. *Mutiny on the Bounty. South Pacific.*

Rupert Brooke. Somerset Maugham. James Michener. Swimming pools overflowing with penicillin.

De Bougainville became Tahiti's heroic founding father. His portrait is everywhere. In the French High Commission on rue du Général de Gaulle. In government offices. In hotels. His bust – like practically everybody else's – is exposed on the seafront at Papeete.

The friendly rivalry between the two powers continued, as it always has, until in 1881 the French made the islands a full colony the traditional French way. They bribed the King, Pomare V Signez, whose family had been installed, fairly and squarely, by the British. Sign this bit of *papier*, they said: 'We'll take your kingdom and in return we'll pay you FF5000 a month.' He signed. It was *au revoir* to *les rosbifs*. Until, of course, the French needed us in you know when. In 1977 the French then granted them, the last of their great colonial treasures, limited independence.

So today Tahiti is as French as today's copy of *Le Monde*, a freshly baked croissant and a café au lait.

Excusez-moi. It is not as French . . . It *is* France. It's a French *département*. No passports needed. No visas. No funny money. It's all euros. No funny food. It's all croissants dipped in huge cups of black coffee, a packet of Gauloises, three large Calvados for breakfast and so on until you finish the day with a *petite quelquechose*, if you're lucky. I've even been in restaurants along the rue du Général de Gaulle in which people bless themselves before they begin the meal. Many's the time I've done the same thing myself. But not for the same reason.

And it's been a good deal for both sides. The French have a foothold in the Pacific, somewhere they could use to test their bombs after they were thrown out of Algeria. Somewhere else they can keep the Americans out of. The Polynesians have the backing of the French, the security of being as much part of France as say Lyons, Marseille or, er, Vichy.

Being French, they also know how to handle the French. For thirty years the French carried out over one hundred and ninety nuclear tests, most of them underground, on the Mururoa Atoll in the Society Islands, 1000 kilometres away, which is a bit like exploding an atomic bomb in the Shetland Isles and saying London will be safe. When the tests were finally stopped by President Mitterrand in April 1992 there was uproar. The Polys went bananas. The tests meant jobs, income: 20 per cent of their income came from the tests. They demanded compensation. The French caved in. They agreed to pay them US$600 million over five years with even more to come in the next five.

Were the Polys worried about the fallout, radioactivity, all the other things that have driven other islanders in other parts of the Pacific apoplectic when nuclear tests have taken place in their backyard? Were they hell? They're French. They're Tahitians. A bit of sunbloc here. A dab of Factor 25 sun cream there. What can possibly affect them? Another glass of champagne please *ma chérie*.

But radioactivity is not the only reason you're guaranteed a warm welcome in Tahiti. The capital, Papeete, once known as the Las Vegas of the South Pacific, is not so much Gauguin as Damien Hirst on heat, although in some places it's more like Tracey Emin's unmade bed. It smells like it as well.

The town itself, which is huddled round the harbour in order to catch the tourists as soon as they set foot on dry land, is small and, in many ways, quite neat and tidy. There are some smart hotels. The main street, rue du Général de Gaulle has a way-out Polynesian Assembly at one end and a quaint old-fashioned French-style town hall at the other. In between there are a million cafés, restaurants, shops and bars. Go in any of them, *fermez la porte*, order a *coupe* and you could be in the middle of Paris. *Regardez les femmes* parading up and down in front of them practically all day and night with dogs that look like a cross between a golden retriever and a dachshund and you *are* in Paris.

The shops, not that I know anything about shops, seem to sell nothing but black pearls in rings, black pearls in bracelets, black pearls in practically everything you can think of. People go mad about them. To me they look like black ball-bearings. Every year they export around 10 tons of them, most of them to Japan, Australia, Hong Kong and anywhere women like to have a black grease mark around their neck.

As for the bars, Quinn's, once the most famous if not notorious bar in the whole of the South Pacific, closed down long ago. The others are still doing the business, taking the money and happily belting out Edith Piaf so they've obviously got no regrets about being there. Especially when the French fleet is in town.

I also noticed lots of Chinese, obviously a hangover of French times in Indo-China.

Faaa, the Tracey Emin part of town, has come a long way since the riots in 1995 when the French stopped their tests. Wandering around the place today you'd never imagine that just a few years ago it was practically a shanty town, a squalid hodgepodge of corrugated-iron huts, thatched lean-tos and filthy beer halls. It was the Marseille of the South Pacific. Today it's smart, clean, organised. Most people have decent brick-built homes. There is still the occasional corrugated-iron house. But it is more of a house than a shack. But whether you're looking at a corrugated-iron shack or a brick-built house they've all got satellite dishes on the walls and cars outside in the yard. Which is a fantastic tribute to the French who again and again around the world have shown that, fairly or unfairly, above board or below board, they can get things done. And done quickly. At the traditional Polynesian-style town hall, which is all separate thatched buildings, and in the bars by the beach, everybody I spoke to agreed.

One man, Robert, who told me he wasn't a Hinano, the name of the local beer, but a Dinano, Polynesian slang for a dirty old man, admitted, 'The French are good to us. They give us so much money. Of course, they keep a lot themselves. But that is the French. We cannot complain.'

So why are there still the corrugated-iron shacks?

'If you have corrugated-iron shack, the government thinks you are poor man. They don't ask for taxes. They give you money instead. That's why people keep metal houses.'

Makes you wonder whether there would still be the slums and shanty towns in South Africa and elsewhere if we let the French work their magic on them.

'So is French Polynesia French or Polynesian?' I asked a smooth, an ultra-smooth French *conseiller* of *quelquechose* or other at the Town Hall.

'It is autonomous,' he said.

'Does that mean it's independent?'

'*Oui.* It is independent.'

'But how can it be autonomous and independent?'

You have to be careful with these French.

'Ah,' he purred. 'It has an autonomous independence.'

See what I mean?

'But can they do whatever they want?' I had to persist.

'Why not?' He smoothed out an imaginary crease from the sleeve of his immaculate Yves St Laurent jacket. 'They are fully, totally, 100 per cent independent. They are a *département* of France. Their President sits in the French Parliament. He is a friend of M. Chirac. How independent can you get?'

See what I mean?

What he didn't say was the President was French, practically the whole of the government was French – well, if not French French, more French than Polynesian Polynesian. What he also didn't say was that, being a *département* of France, just as practically any other city in France is a *département*, means that probably half the money pouring in thanks to French largesse comes from the European Union. And whose taxes go to support the European Union? Yours and mine.

See what I mean about the French being, *et alors*, French.

On the way back to Les Trois Brasseurs – which is not what you think it is, it's worse – I thought I'd better call in at the Cimetière de l'Uranie. Remember the Brando family scandal? Dag Drollet, a young Tahitian, was killed by a single bullet through his left cheek in Los Angeles in 1990, fired by Brando's son, Christian. Thanks to some clever legal footwork by famous Hollywood celebrity lawyer Robert Shapiro, who later worked his magic for O. J. Simpson, Christian got only ten years for accidental manslaughter. Dag's body was brought back to Tahiti and buried in the Cimetière de l'Uranie. Buried alongside Dag is his girlfriend, Cheyenne Brando. Marlon's daughter. After the trial she hanged herself with a telephone cord. She was twenty-five.

And speaking of intrigue, suspicion and funny goings-on, there is Captain Bligh and the mutiny on the *Bounty*. Not that I'm an expert on Captain Bligh and the mutiny on the *Bounty* – or anything come to that – but wandering around Tahiti a number of things occur to me.

First, how come such a relatively trivial incident – mutinies happened all the time – was blown out of all proportion? After all, it wasn't the first time and I'm sure it won't be the last time a bunch of Brits go off on a foreign trip, taste the good life and decide not to go home. In any case, all the facts were there in the official account of the mutiny written by Sir John Barrow, Secretary of the Admiralty, and published in 1831. What more do you want?

Second, how come a not particularly good book written by an author whose name nobody can remember – Gotcha! It was actually written by two people – sold so many copies? It's not as if the mutineers had the time of their wives or anybody else's come to that. Some were hunted down in Tahiti and hanged. Five were murdered by Tahitians. One was killed in a fight. One died of asthma. One went mad and jumped off a cliff. Others escaped to the Pitcairn Island. Only one, John Adams, lived into old age.

Third, how come the film was more of a hit than the book when nobody could understand what anybody was mumbling and the white sand had to be imported? (Black sand was thought inappropriate for dusky maidens.) And those happy smiling faces? Forget it. They were all wearing false teeth. MGM imported over five thousand pairs of them to hide the authentic stained, rotting Polynesian teeth.

The answer, Mr Christian, is France.

Look at the facts. Who enjoys nothing better than embarrassing the British? The French. Who took two fiercely loyal pro-British American citizens, James Norman Hall and Charles Nordhoff, who wrote *Mutiny on the Bounty* and turned them against us? The French. Hall originally served with the British during the First World War. He landed in France in May 1915. He took part in the Battle of Loos. He joined the air section of the French Foreign Legion on 23 April 1917 where he met Nordhoff. After the war was over they were both commissioned to write the story of the air section's, naturally, glorious war. Then for no reason at all they end up in Tahiti where – surprise, surprise – they decide to write a book blowing out of all proportion a minor incident in British naval history.

Too much of a coincidence. That's what I say. After all, think about it. They both loved France, spoke French, fought for the country, travelled all over it. It would have been far more logical if they had written a book about a French military scandal – they've had more of them than we have. But no. They wrote an anti-British book. The French must have persuaded them how much bounty they could make out of the mutiny. And bounty they did make.

Go to Hall's home today in Arue, not far from the spot where the *Bounty* moored to take on supplies, and you can see all the trappings of a rich man: an elegant house, lavish furnishings, an old Royal typewriter and the kind of fast-talking, loud-mouthed yahoo of a grandson all great men seem to end up with. In fact, he's so fast-talking and loud-mouthed and such a yahoo that if he's not careful he'll end up with a mutiny among his own staff, which would serve him right.

But enough of Tahiti. The other islands in the same group are Moorea and Bora Bora.

Moorea, Hali Hai in the musical *South Pacific*, is so called because the place is now so overrun with tourists, who are interfering with their fishing rights, creating more and more pollution and ruining their peaceful way of life, that the locals keep saying, 'We don't want any Moorea.' In fact it's not just one man they want to wash out of their hair but the lot of them, wives included, if they come carrying suitcases.

Michener called Bora Bora 'the world's most beautiful island'. It might have been in his day. Today it's Bora Bora Boring. It's full of tourists who pay thousands of US dollars to live in reed huts on stilts, while the sensible locals live in modern bungalows complete with all the latest facilities. The tourists go on and on about the blues and greens of its lagoon, which it won't be much longer if they keep going there. If they keep going there much longer you won't even be able to see the sea for the reed huts they're building on top of it. Hardly an hour goes by without another cruise ship unloading yet more goggle-eyed tourists looking for anything to do with the filming of *Mutiny on the Bounty*; US bunkers left over from the Second World War; and the next traditional dancing show put on by any one of a thousand professional troupes composed of part-time bus drivers, out-of-work barmen and waitresses between lunch and dinner.

Head north-east from Tahiti, Moorea and Bora Bora Boring

(not to mention Raiatea and Tahaa, the birthplace of the Maoris; Huahine, the birthplace of watermelons – well, it could be, there are so many of them all over the place; and Tetiaroa, Marlon Brando's so-called secret hideaway) and you hit the Tuamotu Islands, which cover nearly 8000 square miles of ocean. The biggest, Rangiroa, is around 230 kilometres long and about 230 feet wide. Flying into it is like flying into the longest runway in the world. It's also where most of the black pearls come from. Staying on it is also boring. A bit like being Robinson Crusoe without having Man Friday around for the laughs.

The Austral Islands, way down in the south, are flat and fertile compared with the rest of them. Because they're so much further south, they don't have the coral the others have. The Gambier Islands are the pearl production islands. They turn out pearls, pearl jewellery and pearl everything under the sun. They're also big on mother of pearl. The cathedral, St Michel, is made out of nothing but blocks of coral. But, ladies be warned, it's difficult to get round your neck.

But my favourites, the Marquesas are not so much beach as mountains. Some of them are nothing but mountains. And mountains mean rain. Trouble is, when it rains everybody stops driving. I can remember being on Nuku Hiva once when we were racing to get to the tiny airport. Everybody leaves it to the last second to get to the airport on Nuku Hiva. It's that kind of place. We were about halfway there when suddenly the heavens opened. The driver stopped the car and refused to go any further. It was dangerous, he said. The road was slippery. In any case he'd never driven in the rain before. He was scared. In the end we had to draw straws to see who was going to walk back in the pouring rain to the house we'd been staying in to fetch another car and driver. Luckily for once, it wasn't me. As for the driver of the first car, I was later told he went on to excel in a completely new career: testing laxatives.

Herman Melville came here once on a whaling expedition and disappeared, it was said, into the jungle, went native and wrote one of his least successful novels, *Typee*. Or maybe he just had a driver who was scared of the rain.

Hiva Oa is, of course, Paul Gauguin island: a derivative of the olde Englishe phrase left behind by Captain Bligh and his merry men, something that Gauguin took to heart. '*Hiva*': 'Heave her'. '*Oa*': 'Over'. Roll her over, Let's do it again.

This is where he arrived in 1901 on board the steamer *Croix du Sud*, driven mad by his yelling, shouting, screaming bully of a wife, Matte Gad, who drove him out of his mind as well as out of his home – although feminist authors claim, in spite of all the evidence to the contrary, that she was 'a kind, clever woman who was victimised physically, verbally and emotionally by her husband'. Don't you believe it. What man – especially if he doesn't have Van Gogh's ear for non-stop yelling, shouting and screaming – is going to leave behind his wife and five children, travel halfway round the world and set up shop with a fourteen-year-old mistress, if his wife and children are the most beautiful, loving creatures under the sun?

In 1891 in a desperate attempt to find some peace and quiet he persuaded the cream of the Parisian literary and artistic world, admittedly at a huge banquet he paid for out of his own pocket, that they should come up with the necessary to enable him to visit Tahiti to produce the illustrations for the bestselling novel of the day, Pierre Loti's *The Marriage of Loti*. This they did largely because he told them that the natives there existed only to 'sing and make love', and that they'd be welcome to come stay and visit him at any time.

Two years later, mission accomplished, he returned to France. To nothing. To no big welcome. To no big smooch. Instead his paintings were immediately labelled 'dangerous'. None of them sold. He wrote the story of life in Tahiti, *Noa Noa*, words he probably never used the whole time he was there. That hardly sold either. He also discovered that *The Marriage of Loti* had been illustrated by three far more competent, far more original and far more important painters whose reputations have grown down through the years, Jacques Boullaire, Maurice de Becque and, er, Jean Galtie Domergue.

He returned to Hiva Oa a bitter and disappointed man. But not for long. His spirits soon started to rise. In Hiva Oa he was at home. He was known as Koke, or more often, especially among the female community, as Okay Koke. He drank huge amounts of wine, rum and absinthe. He lived off tins of anchovies and asparagus and in just a few months produced what some critics claim are among his finest works – not to mention any number of human works of art as well.

He died in 1903 at fifty-four.

Go to Hiva Oa today and, in spite of the Internet bar, you still get the feel of Hiva Oa in Gauguin's time.

The capital, Atuona, which looks as if it is being pushed into the sea by the surrounding, towering, cloud-topped Temetiu mountains, is not so much a capital as a collection of houses, shacks and whatever scattered around all over the place. But being French, it has its own Marie, Town Hall; its own Gendarmerie, which boasts a scruffy, dirty, sovereign independent French Polynesian flag flying limply alongside a proud, bright, brand-new French flag.

The Gauguin connection is there but you have to look for it.

His original Maison de Jouir, House of Pleasure, is not surprisingly long gone. After all there is only so much, er, activity a house can stand especially if it's made of bamboo, a couple of palm leaves and ten foot off the ground. The copy is like, well, any copy. Not so bright. Not so lively. Completely lacking that essential Gauguin spirit. It's small. It's tatty. It's like any old Polynesian barn on its last legs. In fact, if it weren't for the fancy wooden panel at the front grandly proclaiming, '*Soyez amoureuses et vous serez heureuse*', which roughly translated means 'Get married and you'll be miserable as sin for the rest of your life', you wouldn't think it had anything to do with Gauguin.

Downstairs, however, I discovered the remains of what must have been the tourist company Gauguin ran on the side. Stuck on the wall was a scruffy hand-painted map of the island, '*Situation Site Historique Tehueto. Temps: 45 minutes du Point Zéro*'. When I got back to London I had it valued at Sotheby's. They said it was probably worth around US$10 million. That, of course, was when they were still playing games with Christie's. Scratching around in the dirt, chewing away at the foundations and begging everyone in sight for a free meal were no end of dogs which I assumed must have been art critics. All around were empty cans of Heineken which I can only assume means Van Gogh dropped by from time to time. Not that he would have brought them with him. He was after all Dutch. Poor old Gauguin probably had to buy them himself.

I asked an ancient combatant, who looked as though he could have been one of Gauguin's drinking partners, what Maison du Jouir meant.

'Wet bed hotel,' he grinned.

Facing it, raised up on stilts, is for some reason an old fighter plane. At first I thought it belonged to the local bishop who was around at the time of Gauguin's stay on the island.

It turned out to belong to some poet and singer called Jacques Brel who came to the island to die in the 1970s. But as he wasn't French he's not important. He was Belgian, which makes him less important still.

To the left is the Paul Gauguin Museum, which is so important to French cultural history that it is permanently closed. Or, at least, it was the whole time I was there. Stuck on the windows were signs saying, '*Pour la visite de Musée s'adresser à Jo*' which is a bit like turning up at the Louvre and finding a sign on the door saying, 'To visit the museum see Jacques in the café opposite. He's the one with the moustache and the Gauloise.'

In front of everything – the Maison du Jouir, the Museum, the plane – there is, as you would expect of the French, a wide-open space. But it is dedicated not to Gauguin but to their other major cultural activity: football. Trouble is, it looks prehistoric. The whole thing, terraces included, is made of huge rocks and boulders. Either that or it was built the last time France won the World Cup with a team of nothing but Frenchmen.

Heading for the nearest bar to celebrate in the manner that Gauguin would have thought appropriate, I bumped into Ezechial Randy Tuat and his wife, Fleur. Actually I couldn't avoid them. They were taking up practically the whole road.

'Gauguin?' they said.

'*Oui*,' I said.

You should go and visit Maison Gauguin, they said. Very interesting, they said. We go there every day.

Maison Gauguin turned out to be the local store, which makes you wonder what kind of paintings Monsieur Tesco turns out. My time was not wasted, however. Everyone in the store took one look at me and suggested I got myself across to the cemetery as quickly as possible. There at the front, just under the big white crucifix, was where the man himself was buried.

Never having been able to resist the satisfaction of looking at a dead Frenchman, I took their advice. Out of the store. Turn left. Past what will be the Paul Gauguin Cultural Centre, although Le Dieu only knows how they can justify spending their money promoting as an example someone whose life, not to mention lifestyle, they totally disagreed with. At the time of Gauguin's death the local bishop denounced him as 'a contemptible individual . . . a reputed artist . . . an enemy of God and everything that is decent'. But the French, being the

French, will I suppose find a suitably logical Cartesian reason for doing so. They'll also, I guess, have problems filling it. The whole place has been stripped clean of all his paintings. Even the Gauguin Museum in Tahiti has only a couple of not particularly interesting early daubings. More like practice shots before the booze kicked in. It's not like the early 1910s and 1920s when the likes of Somerset Maugham could mince by, pick up three Gauguin-painted glass doors for FF200 each, ship them back home and sell them later one at a time for FF130,000 a shot, which is probably more than he made writing *The Moon and Sixpence,* a novel about a French stockbroker who leaves wife, work and family to go to the South Seas to become a painter, which he maintained had nothing to do with Gauguin.

Just outside the Gendarmerie is a war memorial. It is dedicated to just two men: Soldat Naopua a Puufafian, who died in the 1914–18 war, and Soldat Tchaamoana-Tohiau, who died during the 1939–45 war. OK, leaving aside the question of whether the French were fighting anyone in 1939, if so whom, and if they were, what the hell was a poor Polynesian doing 18,000 kilometres from home helping them when they weren't all exactly helping themselves, you've got to admire them. If the French are still loved, honoured and respected in so many of their old colonies they deserve it. The British still haven't put up a memorial to their own soldiers – let alone anybody else's – who died during the Charge of the Light Brigade, and how many years ago was that?

Up the hill I trudged, panting and dripping with sweat – halfway up, I thought I was going to have an art attack – and there right at the front of the cemetery overlooking the perhaps appropriately named Bay of Traitors is the grave of the great man. All the graves around him are flat, inconspicuous, the occasional border, maybe a cross. Gauguin's is piled high with volcanic rock as if they want to make certain he stays there.

On the left is, as he wished, a bronze statue of the pagan god Oviri, crushing its young to death. Close by, leaning precariously to one side no doubt as a result of the amount of booze they had to absorb from the soil, are some flowering gardenias and hibiscus trees.

Further up are much larger, much grander, much more impressive graves, surrounded by white metal railings, with little roofs and twiddly bits. These are obviously the graves of local art dealers who sold more of his paintings than he ever produced.

But the real surprise is that though everybody on Hiva Oa looks like Gauguin and suffers the same physical defects – every time I spoke to one of them they didn't quite seem to hear what I was saying, so I had to repeat myself, something that usually happens only when I'm at home – none of them claim to be related to him. Except Jason. For years Jason was the Anastasia of the art world. He claimed he was the great man's son but nobody believed him. He ended up in Tahiti, a broken-down might-have-been.

Nobody believes Jason's son Alfred, either. Instead of having apartments in Paris, London and Rome, homes in St Trop, Marbella and San Fran, he is holed up in a tiny pale blue shack about 100 metres up a concrete track by the Magasin Tehaamoana in a tiny village on the north side of the island called Puamau.

Today he is sixty years old, as thin as a rake, married with thirteen children, seven sons, six daughters. Like everybody else in the village, he works like the rest of us, by the sweat of the brow.

How am I convinced he is the grandson of Gauguin? Easy. When I drove all the way across the island from Atuona, through never-ending forests, along dirt tracks on the side of mountains, skidding down muddy slopes to see him to help him demand his rights and receive his just entitlements, he treated me as if he were the grandson of a great painter.

He gave me the brush-off.

But he was probably sore because his great-grandfather didn't make all those investments years ago that would have made him today a multi-multimillionaire.

Unfortunately for Alfred, Gauguin was not only a failed painter but a failed stockbroker as well.